polymer clay

clay

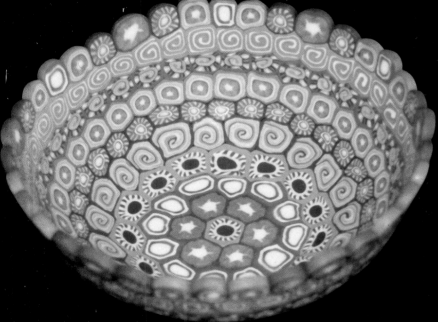

Creating
Functional
and
Decorative
Objects

jacqueline gikow

Published by

krause
publications
700 East State Street • Iola, WI 54990-0001

Please call or write for our free catalog of publications. Our toll-free number to place an order or obtain a free catalog is 800-258-0929 or please use our regular business telephone, 715-445-2214.

Library of Congress Catalog Number 00-111284
ISBN 0-87341-952-9

Some products in this book are registered trademarks of their respective companies:
Armor All® protectant (The Clorox Company); Dockyard™ wood carving tools (Dockyard Model Co.); E-6000® silicate glue (Eclectic Products, Inc.); Feel Good™ Bone Folder (SDK Distributors); Fimo® polymer clays, Fimo® pulver (Eberhard Faber, GmbH); Fiskars® scissors; Gold Leaf™ Metallic Powders (Neuberg-Ebel); Handi chopper™ (Black and Decker); Jacquard™ Pearlescence powders (Rupert, Gibbons, Spider); Kemper® pattern cutters, Kemper® clay gun (Kemper Enterprises, Inc.); Liquitex® Artists colors (Binney & Smith); Magic Leaf™ (Blattmetall GmbH & Co. KG); Marxit™, NuFlex™, and NuBlade™, Kato, Fimo® modeling materials, Fimo® SOFT, Fimo® Puppen, WireForm®, Genesis™ oil paints, Friendly Cutters™ (Amaco); National Artcraft Company; Prismacolor®, Sharpie® (Sanford® Corporation); Rainbow Wrap® (Hallcraft, Inc.); Sculpey III® Translucent Liquid Sculpey®, Prémo!®, Sculpey®, Super Flex™, Sculpey™ Diluent, Super Sculpey® (Polyform Products, USA); Speedball® linoleum cutters, brayers; SureHold® Plastic Surgery, Super Glue, Super Gel; Thomas™ surgical tissue blades (Thomas Medical Supply); Wild Wire™ jewelry tools (National Science Industries, Ltd.); WireForm® mesh (Paragonam); X-Acto®; Zap-A-Gap® (PacerTechnology); Ott-Lites®; Coca-Cola®.

The projects within and at the end of each chapter relate to chapter techniques and topics. Contributors to this book generously provided some of the end projects. I created all other projects. They are all copyrighted with all rights reserved. Please be observant of copyright laws. You may reproduce any of the projects for personal, but not for commercial use.

-Jacqueline Gikow

Table of Contents

Introduction   4

Part I: Chapters 1—3: All about Polymer Clay 8
Chapter 1 Polymer Clay Basics 9
Chapter 2 Tools and Equipment 17
Chapter 3 Preparing and Using Polymer Clay 24

Part II: Chapters 4—7: Techniques of Constructing Vessels 32
Chapter 4 Free-form Vessels 33
Chapter 5 Covering Existing Containers 47
Chapter 6 Boxes and Other Constructed Vessels 59
Chapter 7 Mold Making for Polymer Clay Vessels 73

Part III: Chapters 8—10: Technique Applications 91
Chapter 8 Polymer Clay and the Literary Life 91
Chapter 9 Diversions, Entertainment and Pastimes 108
Chapter 10 Home Décor 121

Appendices 136
Bibliography 136
Glossary 137
Resources 139
Safety 139
Artists Listing 143
Index 144
Footnotes 144

$ 400
wolf
3/19

Introduction

These three tube vases were made and decorated with Premo polymer clay. The construction method used molds made from cardboard tubes wrapped with aluminum foil. The diameters are all about 2-1/2" and the heights vary from 6" to 10". Artist: Jacqueline Gikow.

Introduction

Polymer clay is frequently viewed as a new artistic medium, but history indicates that polymer clay was actually first developed in the early 1940s, both in Germany and the United States. Primarily used at first as a doll maker's medium for parts, such as heads, hands, and feet, it was first used by jewelers in the 1960s. Since the 1980s, the popularity of this flexible, colorful, bakable, plastic medium has grown by leaps and bounds. As usual with new materials, artists experimented with and tested the limitations in the qualities of polymer clay. What they found was a medium that adapted to small and large objects and could be worked using similar construction and decorated methods of other craft materials, such as ceramic, metal, glass, and wood.

My Path to Polymer Clay

I discovered polymer clay after many years as a craftsperson and designer. Although I started out as a sculptor, I felt most creatively challenged when form and decoration intertwined with function. Nature led me quickly to pottery, a sculptural, but also functional, form. When I finished graduate school, I established and ran a production pottery studio, selling my work to wholesale markets. After ten years in that business, I moved to a city where finding the sizeable space a clay studio requires that I could afford was impossible.

"Nothing Gold Can Stay," by Robyn Priestly, is an accordion-bound book, made of polymer clay, molded, carved and painted, incorporating a variety of techniques including marbling, mokume gane, and faux stone effects, and mixed media. The text is from a poem by the same title, by Robert Frost. 4" x 24", open.

I continued to be drawn to three-dimensional expression, however, and in the early 1990s, when I discovered polymer clay, I was pleased to discover a medium with many of the same qualities of clay, but didn't require the expense of setting up a pottery studio. I wasn't part of the vanguard of polymer clay artists, but they were generous in sharing their experiences and methodologies.

Most of the information available about working with polymer clay at the time I began working with it was about jewelry. Like many people, I discovered Nan Roche's book, *The New Clay*, which is like a bible of basic techniques, but I had to extrapolate what I could from the collective information available. I also adapted whatever techniques I could from ceramic clay methodology. Towards the end of my involvement with pottery, I was experimenting with colored clay. Discovering the color range of polymer clay in already available colors was intriguing. I also revisited other media I'd experimented with over the years, including wood, metal, and fiber, and devised ways to use those techniques in my work. At the same time, I noticed a small, but growing number of artists working in polymer clay sharing and looking for information about vessel making.

Polymer Clay: Creating Functional and Decorative Objects is the result of wanting to share with others the information I discovered and collected about creating three-dimensional polymer clay objects. The books about polymer clay I found in the beginning were not too helpful in my search for information about construction techniques for boxes, bowls, and other containers. I owe a lot to those who came before me, who developed working methods that parallel mine, and who have graciously shared with me their discoveries. Creativity involves translating our unique gifts, talents and vision into a new and useful reality for all. The methods artists use to work with polymer clay are not necessarily new inventions, but they do demonstrate how creative minds take existing ideas and processes and combine them in different ways for new purposes. When we share our discoveries, a craft can grow and develop, and all artists benefit.

(Photo: Jodi Jones)

"Ancient Bowl" by Rhea Scheafer *is from a mold. The many layered decoration techniques include mosaic canes, cut polymer pieces (tiles) and acrylic paint, with baking in between stages. After baking, very soft clay was used as grout and "squished" between the white tiles. 5" x 2-1/2".*

There is more to polymer clay than jewelry and beads. In this book I introduce to both new and experienced clay users the techniques for working in three-dimensions by providing in-depth information, step-by-step demonstrations, and hands-on projects.

I hope it will also serve as a source of inspiration by showing how contemporary polymer artists working with vessel-objects develop their ideas. Some of those artists have been generous enough to provide projects for readers to try.

Drawing on Tradition

Older, more established crafts provide a rich and varied supply of methods and tools for making and decorating vessels in polymer clay. Although clay is a natural product and polymer clay is manufactured, the parallels between polymer and ceramic clay are numerous. Pottery and books on pottery are splendid sources of inspiration for polymer vessels. Slabs can be assembled into boxes, free-form pots, and many other shapes.

(Photo: Krause)

"Leafy Vase" by Jacqueline Gikow. *This vessel, also seen on the cover, is made from individually-shaped leaf forms of three layers. The outside layer is a light champagne, the middle layer is black, and the inside layer is jellyroll canes combining the other two colors. The vase was formed over a chicken-wire and aluminum foil support. 13" x 15".*

(Photo: Will Truchon)

This wheel-thrown bowl by Will Truchon *is made with polymer clay mixed to a natural clay-like color. Making polymer clay vessels on a potter's wheel is similar to working with regular clay. 6" x 3".*

Thin, flat sheets can be draped and wrapped around a form. Coiling rolls of clay, or starting with a ball of clay and "pinching" it into a pot can make a vessel. Even forming objects from molds is possible.

Most of the methods I began using in working with polymer clay I derived from my experience as a potter and clay artist. Even today I tend to refer to traditional pottery methods to solve many of the technical questions that arise.

Other traditional crafts that provide inspiration and techniques include fiber arts (weaving and surface design), glass forming, leather, metalsmithing, mosaics, stone carving, and woodworking. Wood techniques include carving, assembling, and lathe forming. Leather

(Photo: Dotty McMillan)

"Inro Purses" by Dotty McMillan. *Inro/Inru is a small container originally intended to hold a Japanese man's seal and ink, or to store a supply of medicines. It was so popular that it soon became an object of high fashion. Created with carving, sculpting, as well as stamped and textured impressions. The lid slides up the neck cord. 4-1/2" x 3".*

tooling is possible in polymer clay, and it can even be woven and crocheted. Glass techniques include decorating methods, such as millefiori, and lampworking. Decorative techniques also exist that result in the effect of semi-precious stones, wood, leather and metal. And there are certainly many more.

Content Review

Polymer Clay: Creating Functional and Decorative Objects is divided into three sections. Part I examines the qualities of polymer clay, the tools, equipment and supplies needed. Part II provides in-depth instructions to making three-dimensional objects and vessels from polymer clay, and how to work with larger forms. Methods included are coiling, pinch pots, covering existing vessels, making and using molds and supports, creating freeform vessels from sheets of clay, and the use of armatures. Part III uses many techniques introduced in Part II of the book by showing how you can create vessels for use in and outside of the home. Making books, lighting, clocks, knobs, musical instruments and games are only a few of the topics introduced.

Measurements in this Book

Most of the measurements in this book are in inches or pasta machine settings. Here is a chart with measurement translations of slab thicknesses for everyone:

Inches	Millimeters (mm)	Centimeters (cm)	Pasta Machine (Atlas)*
1/32	.75	.075	#5
1/16	1.5	.15	#3
1/8	3	.3	#1
1/4	6	.6	2 x #1
1	25.4	2.54	

*The actual thickness of a slab of clay from any setting of a pasta machine may vary according to brand and from machine to machine. Also, a firm piece of clay will result in a slightly thicker slab than a softer piece because the firm piece resists being compressed.

Creative Vessels From Polymer Clay

Let your imagination run free and observe it in action as you think about vessels you might create: hollow utensils, containers, canisters, boxes, cans, receptacles, crock pots, bottles, jugs, decanters, carafes, flagons, pitchers, bowls, mugs, beakers, cups, tumblers, goblets, chalices, vases, urns, lachrymatories[1], pails, buckets, cauldrons, etc.

A vessel is anything that contains liquids, solids, space, light, time. Dare yourself to discover new shapes and concepts: Must a box be a cube? Challenge yourself to think differently of hatboxes, egg cartons, toolboxes, puzzle boxes, jack-in-the-boxes, sculpture as boxes, modular boxes, etc. Transform boxes so they are not what they seem: jewelry boxes or boxes as jewelry, sewing boxes or boxes that are sewn, sculpture as a box or a box as sculpture.

So, enough philosophy. Let's get to work.

These three slab vases incorporate a variety of decorative techniques. Simply designed using differently designed layers of clay on the inside and out, they take advantage of the fluid qualities of polymer clay and its ability to be constructed without forming supports. The hanging vase has a Wireform core and the other two are constructed totally of polymer clay. Sizes range from 3" to 5" in diameter and 8" to 12" high. Artist: Jacqueline Gikow

These three petal-shaped boxes, by Wanda Shum, *are slab-constructed with a polymer clay veneer in a variety of techniques with transparent layers.*
2-1/4" x 2".

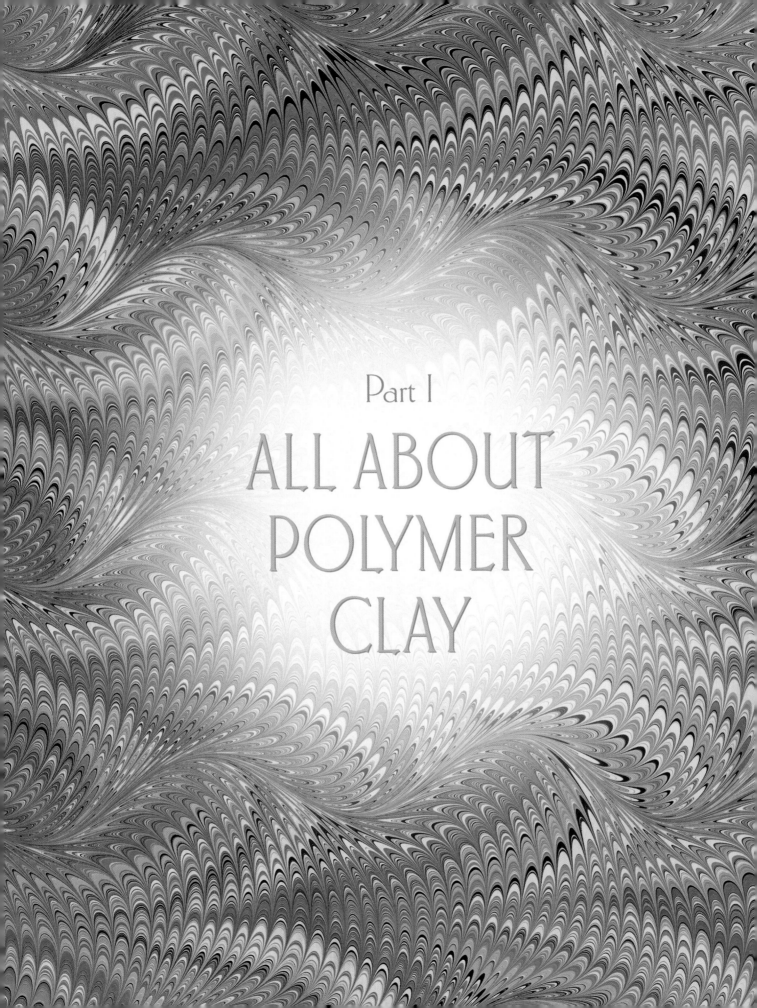

Part I

ALL ABOUT POLYMER CLAY

Chapter 1

Polymer Clay Basics

Polymer clay is a man-made, oil-based alternative to natural clay. It's not true-earth clay that is made up of fine particles of silicate suspended in water; polymer clay is fine particles of polyvinyl chloride (PVC) suspended in plasticizer. A plasticizer is an organic compound used in modifying plastics, to incorporate flexibility and toughness.

(Photo: George Post)

"Stone and Shell" by Kathleen Dustin. *This evening bag is constructed around an interior mold made of scrap clay with a cornstarch mold release. The surface is stone, made by mixing embossing powders into translucent clay. The shell is also metallic Premo with imitation and 22k gold leaf layered into translucent clay, then sliced at an angle, pressed on, baked, sanded, and polished. 7" x 5" x 3-1/2"*

Because of its make-up, polymer clay can be used much like clay. A high-temperature kiln is not needed, though, because the temperatures needed are easy to manage in a home oven (265°F to 275°F).

There are several different manufacturers of polymer clay. Some clay is manufactured in the United States, and some comes from companies worldwide. Which brands are available depends largely upon what part of the world you're in. Each of the brands has somewhat different properties, but they are all fundamentally the same sort of substance, and for the most part can be substituted for each other.

What makes polymer clay special, and well suited as a craft material, is its versatility. The clay's pliability lets you use techniques from glasswork, textile arts, sculp-

ture, and more. Additionally, polymer clay doesn't dry out, so you can sculpt and form it without worrying about a time limit. The process that fuses the particles of polymer clay together is done at a low temperature, low enough to use a home oven as your kiln. When fired, the clay gets hard enough to make durable objects that can be finished in various ways to obtain textures ranging from glassy to stone-like.

History Of Fimo

In 1912, a German scientist discovered how to synthesize PVC (polyvinyl chloride) from petroleum products, and patented the manufacturing process. In the 1930s, other German scientists discovered how to adapt PVC for practical applications such as plumbing supplies, by adding material that made it somewhat flexible. This new material attracted the attention of Fifi Rehbinder, a doll maker. She observed that the substance softened slightly if heated, but didn't melt (the technical name for this is "thermosetting" plastic). She experimented with some of the residual products of PVC, and developed a moldable, clay-like material that could be baked at a medium temperature. Her discovery of this plastic clay allowed her to create the first polymer clay dolls. Eventually she began to sell the product to other artists, and called the clay "Fifi Mosaik." Fifi Mosaik was eventually taken over by the German company, Eberhard Faber, that changed the product name to "Fi Mo." Later, the name was shortened to just "Fimo," and was the only polymer clay available in Europe until the 1960s. At the same time as the German discovery of this pliable, easily baked, plastic material, a similar product was developed in the United States.

Polyform History

In the early 1940s, Zenith Products, a company that manufactured coatings for the fastener industry, tem-

(Photo: Jacqueline Gikow)

Two "Dragonskin" bowls. *These bowls, by Margaret Reid, are formed over an existing bowl mold, with intricately patterned cane slices applied to give a scale-like effect. The right hand bowl stands on miniature dragon's feet. The versatility of polymer clay allows you to emulate materials from many areas, including mystical ones such as dragons. Approximately 5" x 3".*

porarily shelved a product unsuccessfully formulated for potential use as a thermal transfer compound. In the mid 1960s, a visitor to the plant was toying with a lump of this clay-like substance, and created a small figure. In a test, it was baked in a lab-testing oven, and discovered to be a workable sculpture medium. By 1967, white Polyform Sculpey was being manufactured and sold on a small scale in the United States. Mike Solos, the company founder, was marketing his product at craft shows and demonstrating its use to small retail shops by 1976.

Another person interested in polymer clay, Marie Segal, and her husband, inadvertently became the developers and promoters of a brand new polymer clay product, Premo. In 1994, the Segals approached the Sculpey/Polyform company with a question: Why not make a high-quality, American-made clay? The result was a reformulation of Premo for professional use in creating jewelry, wearable art and surface decoration, and large sculpture or vessels. The new version of Premo also included intense colors that mixed in a similar fashion to artists' paints. Premo debuted in 1998.

Selecting Polymer Clay

(Photo: Jodi Jones)

"Goldstone Boxes." *These two boxes are made from a combination of Fimo Stone Jade, Premo gold polymer clay, and a small amount of Premo black. It's hard to appreciate the effect in a photograph because the tactile quality is missing. Blending the two clays caused the smooth gold to be pulled through the rough stone texture. The result is a stonelike gold tone with subtle jade color throughout. Left: 3" x 5", Right 4" x 6".* Artist: Jacqueline Gikow.

Many new users ask what the best brand is, but there's no simple answer to this question. Every clay brand has its good and bad aspects for any particular application including softness or firmness, translucency or opacity, color choice, and so forth. The best brand will depend on what you want to use the clay for, your personal preferences, and how you like to work with it. You can also mix different brands of clay to get the qualities you want.

Each brand is made with similar, but varying combinations of raw materials. Therefore, all brands will mix, but the resulting qualities will depend on what charac-

teristics are needed. Brands are optimized for different uses. The type of plasticizer and fillers, and the ratio of one to the other, determines the feel of the clay when raw and the strength of the clay when baked. You may end up choosing one brand for one type of vessel and another brand for another. Of the many brands of polymer clay available, Fimo and Polyform's Premo are probably the most appropriate for use in creating larger objects such as bowls, vases, or covered containers, because of their strength and flexibility after firing.

The softer polymer clays, such as Sculpey III, SuperElasticlay, and SuperFlex are good for projects that don't involve extensive manipulations. They are easy to work with for simple shapes and color combinations, but colors and shapes can start to blend more than you might want.

Brand Differences and Characteristics

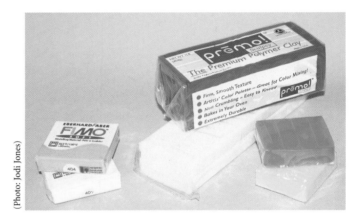

(Photo: Jodi Jones)

Fimo, manufactured by Eberhard Faber in Germany, is a widely available polymer clay, and very popular among clay artists. It comes in two formulations; the original is very stiff clay, difficult to condition, but results in an extremely strong finished object. The other, newly developed clay, called Fimo Soft, is an easier-to-work clay, and retains many of the characteristics of the original.

Premo, developed by Polyform Products, in collaboration with polymer clay artist Maureen Carlson, is an easy-to-work-with clay that, when fresh, needs minimum preconditioning and retains after-baking flexibility and durability. The colors are similar to a "painter's palette," and those with a background in color theory will find it easy to mix custom colors to their specifications.

Other Polyform Products

Sculpey III is an extremely popular clay that is soft, easy to work with, and comes in strong, vibrant colors. It accepts decorating by carving and painting after baking, and goes easily through extruder guns. Sculpey III, because of the fillers added to make it pliable, is some-

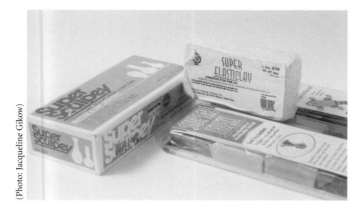

(Photo: Jacqueline Gikow)

what fragile, and vessels created from it should be kept small.

Sculpey SuperElasticlay is an intriguing polymer clay product. Easy to work with, it is manufactured only in a cream color, and after firing, it retains a rubbery or elastic feel. It is quite useful in making vessel molds because of its stretchy quality. That quality allows castings to be released from the mold easily. Super Elasticlay also can be mixed with stiffer clays to increase their flexibility.

Translucent Clay

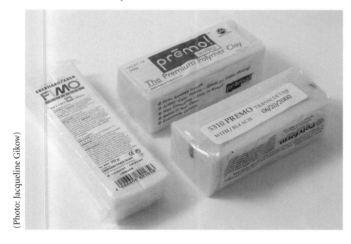

(Photo: Jacqueline Gikow)

Translucent clay, manufactured by all brands, is polymer clay with no pigment (coloring element) and no opacifier. Polyform and CFC (a private label related to Premo clays), and Fimo each offer one or more translucent clays. There are no truly transparent polymer clays, due to the limitations of polymer chemistry, but you can obtain a near-transparent effect by putting a very thin layer of translucent clay over an object, firing it, and then wet sanding and buffing it.

Some transparent clay has very smooth finishes and some develop round, flat, almost colorless patches (sometimes called "plaquing") within the sheet. Fimo art translucent #00 in particular tends to plaque. Some artists seek out this effect, because it can be used in faux stones to make the pieces look more like natural stone. You can reduce the plaquing by using a different translucent clay: for example, Fimo transparent/opaque #01 or

(Photo: Diane Dunville)

"A Little Night Music." *This art lamp was made from translucent polymer clay overlaid with thin layers of tinted translucent clay applied to create a subtle, underlying wave effect. 7" x 12".* Artist: Diane Dunville.

CFC #06 Transparent, or by placing your pieces in a cold oven, turning it on for firing, then letting the pieces cool down in the oven after firing.

Polyform Products offers Sculpey translucent #510, one of the most transparent of the clays. It is very soft, and tends to pick up a yellowish tinge when fired longer than the minimum time, but it is also brittle when cured, and easily breakable. Premo transparent #01 is an easy-to-work-with clay with a milky, porcelain finish.

Fimo offers two translucent clays. Fimo Art Translucent #00 is preferred for making faux stones because of the plaquing effects that enhance the clay's resemblance to natural stone. This clay tends to darken at high temperatures, so watch the oven carefully. Fimo transparent/opaque #01 is one of the least transparent of the translucent clays, but unlike Art Translucent, it does not readily change color at normal firing temperatures of 250°F to 275°F and does not plaque as much.

Similar to Premo translucent, CFC 06 Transparent/Bleach is the clearest and most transparent of all the transparent clays.

Stone Clay

(Photo: Archie Miles)

"Stone Gecko Paperweight," by Hen Scott. *Hen covered a small stone with Cernit stone clay (Cernit is another brand of polymer clay, not as widely available as Fimo or Premo). The lizard was then sculpted onto the baked surface. 2-1/4".*

Imitative techniques, or those that make polymer clay appear to be another material, are favorites among clay artists. Clay is cheaper and easier to work with than the actual materials such as ivory, quartz, or turquoise. With polymer clay, you can do many things which would be difficult or impossible using the natural substance, such as embossing, working with larger pieces than occur in nature, or experimenting with color.

The stone clays (Polyform's Granitex and stone Fimo) give clay artists new ways of imitating rocks and semiprecious stones such as granite, jasper, and quartz. Stone clay is one of the newer innovations in polymer clay. Stone clays consist of clay in a base color plus tiny fibers, in one or more contrasting colors, mixed through the clay. These fibers provide granular appearances that, unlike marbled clay, don't get blended away as you use the clay. Stone Fimo comes in six colors: lapis lazuli (dark blue), granite (gray), china jade (pale green), rose quartz (pink), jasper (brown), and turquoise (light blue). Granitex comes in eight colors: pink, light blue, dark blue, purple, gray, brown, orange, and green.

Granitex is softer and easier to work with than stone Fimo, which has the stiffness characteristic of Fimo. Some of the stone Fimo colors (in particular lapis lazuli and granite) are more realistic if you are planning to use the clay by itself. Both clays also mix well with the other clays and bring interesting, previously unavailable textures to pieces.

Liquid Sculpey

Liquid Sculpey is a pourable form of polymer clay that was developed for commercial use about twenty years ago. Originally meant to be poured into metal vacuum molds and baked, most polyclay artists use it as glue to join two baked pieces of clay together, and as a surface treatment (painting, washing, or stippling).

(Photo: Jodi Jones)

Liquid Sculpey can be used as a "glue" to join two baked pieces of clay together, and as a surface treatment (painting, washing, or stippling).

Brushes are cleaned in the same manner you would an oil-based paintbrush, using turpentine or mineral spirits. Liquid Sculpey, now manufactured by Polyform Products, comes in two versions, opaque and transparent. In its raw state, Liquid Sculpey looks like white glue and has the consistency of honey. Transparent Liquid Sculpey, in its raw state, is a milky, ivory color. When it is baked, it is semi-translucent, flexible and strong.

Storing Polymer Clay

(Photo: Jodi Jones)

Although exposure to air will not hurt it, it's best to keep polymer clay wrapped for protection from dust and lint.

Unlike earth clay, polymer clay does not contain water, so nothing evaporates as it ages, and it can be stored for months, even if left uncovered. When wrapped, the shelf life is at least two years, but polymer clay will last longer if you keep it away from sunlight or ultraviolet light, and excessive heat—these can partially cure the clay, making it unusable. It's also better to store your clay in a cool, dry place and wrap it so the colors don't stick together. Without being wrapped up, the plasticizer that keeps the clay soft will eventually leach out, leaving hard, crumbly clay.

You don't need to store polymer clay in airtight containers since it has no water to evaporate, but be careful about which plastic containers or wrap you use. Some types of plastic can be used with polymer clay, but others react with the plasticizer in the clay, and the clay eventually will begin to bond with the container. In particular, avoid storing polymer clay in polystyrene (recycling #6). Polyethylene (#2 or #4) and polystyrene (#5), however, seem to be compatible with polymer clay for storage.

You can wrap polymer clay in waxed paper before putting the clay into a storage box. The plasticizer does not react at all with wax, although some plasticizer may leach into the paper over time. You can also store finished, unfired pieces this way. Separate different colors of clay from each other with a leach-poof barrier; otherwise, they'll eventually bond together. As an alternative, you can keep your unconditioned clays fresh by storing them in the freezer.

Hard plastic containers and plastic zip lock bags that are clear plastic (microwave safe/dishwasher safe/ and freezable) are excellent for storing clay. Raw clay can be directly exposed to this plastic, which will not eat into or stick to it. Storing clay in these bags lets you see exactly what you have. They come in different sizes and will accommodate large sheets of clay, stacked and separated by wax paper, and you can see them all at a glance.

Color In Polymer Clay

Polymer clay comes in dozens of colors, and while sometimes the color of the clay right out of the package is perfect for your needs, often you won't find just the right color in the clay brand you want to use. One of the most exciting characteristics of this clay is that you can blend clays together like paints to make your own colors. After all, why buy almost the green you want, when you can easily mix exactly the one you need?

Mixing your own color palette is one of the most pleasurable aspects of this medium. Because many clay colors are highly saturated, you have plenty of options for making full range of hues. All brands offer a variety of tints, but you can make any color you choose, from the palest pastel to the deepest jewel tone, by combining various amounts of the primary colors—red, yellow, and blue—and adding black, white, and translucent. Most artists are drawn to certain color families and combinations; even if two artists have colorful palettes, it's more than likely their choices of colors will be different.

For practical purposes, there are two color mixing processes: additive and subtractive. Each has a set of primary colors traditionally defined as colors that cannot be mixed from another.

Additive Color Mixing

Additive color mixing employs light as the medium. Most people are familiar, even if they don't know it, with additive color mixing through the medium of television

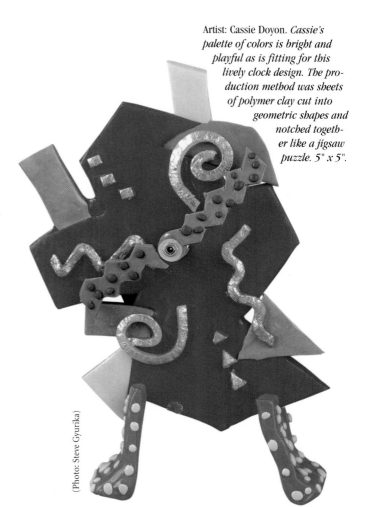

Artist: Cassie Doyon. *Cassie's palette of colors is bright and playful as is fitting for this lively clock design. The production method was sheets of polymer clay cut into geometric shapes and notched together like a jigsaw puzzle. 5" x 5".*

(Photo: Steve Gyurika)

(Photo: Trudy Burrill)

"Geisha," by Trudy Schwartz-Burrill. *Trudy also works with bright colors, but in this modern Inro evening bag, she has used them subtly. Here, her choices reflect the rich colors of Japanese culture. 7" x 4".*

COLOR THEORY

Color theory is so complicated that volumes have been written about it, so I'm not going to cover much of it here. In simple terms, colors are defined using three indexes:

Hue: the term for pure spectrum colors commonly referred to by the "color names" —red, orange, yellow, blue, green, violet

Saturation: the amount of a single hue in a color mix

Value: relative lightness or darkness (shade or tint) of a color

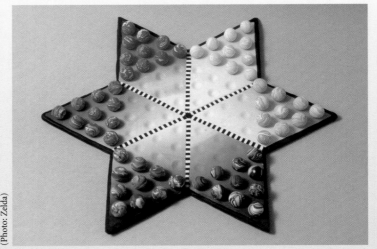

(Photo: Zelda)

"Chinese Checkers." **This six-pointed star-shaped game was designed using the three primary colors (red, yellow, and blue) and three secondary colors (orange, green, purple) that make up a basic color wheel. 12".** ©2000, Jacqueline Gikow

and computer monitors. The primaries of light—red, green, and blue—combine to form white when they are mixed. They are known as "additive" primaries because light is added when they mix; for example, red and green create yellow. This is because yellow is lighter than the other two colors.

Subtractive Color Mixing

Subtractive color mixing employs pigment as the mixing medium. Red, yellow, and blue are traditional artists' colors of paint, ink and dye. They are called "subtractive" primaries because light is removed as the colors are mixed together. The more intense the colors are, the darker the mixture. Mixing the primaries produces black.

Recent research in color theory shows that the traditional artists' primary/secondary color wheel is inaccurate. There is no universal red, yellow or blue. You can create a variety of color palettes by mixing different hues of red, yellow and blue. To begin, experiment with color mixing what might be considered a "cool set" and a "warm set" of color combinations in polymer clay:

❖ Cool Blue (Fimo Blue #37)
❖ Cool Yellow (Fimo #1)
❖ Cool Red (Fimo #23)

❖ Warm Blue (Premo Ultramarine)
❖ Warm Yellow (Premo Cadmium)
❖ Warm Red (Premo Cadmium)

(Photo: Zelda)

It's important to learn to distinguish hues from one another.
(A) Premo Cadmium Red has an orange cast to it, while Fimo Soft Cherry Red has a blue cast.
(B) Premo Cadmium Yellow leans toward orange, while Fimo Soft Lemon Yellow is green-tinged.
(C) Premo Ultramarine Blue has a purple tone, while Fimo Pacific Blue leans slightly toward green.
©2000, Jacqueline Gikow

Mixing Polymer Clay

The colors above are only guidelines, and there is at least one way to break any "rule" you can think of and still get excellent results. You may find other colors that meet your criteria within the brand of your choice, or you can mix among brands of clay. After some practice, you'll be able to exploit the differing qualities of the brands and colors.

To make intermediate (secondary) colors, add together two primaries that lean toward the color you

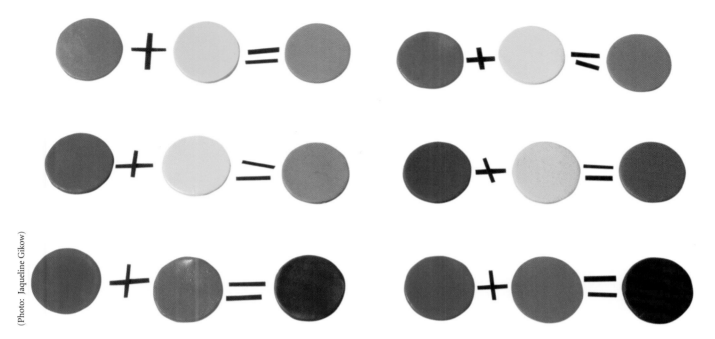

(Photo: Jacqueline Gikow)

To make the purest intermediate (secondary) colors, add together two primaries that lean toward the color you want. Using the colors above, here are the effects that will be achieved. (Left to right, top to bottom)
TL. Premo Cadmium red + Premo Cadmium Yellow = bright orange
TR. Fimo Soft Cherry Red + Fimo Soft Lemon Yellow = dull orange
ML. Fimo Pacific Blue + Fimo Soft Lemon Yellow = bright green

MR. Premo Ultramarine Blue + Premo admium yellow = dull green
LL. Premo Ultramarine Blue + Fimo Soft Cherry Red = bright purple
LR. Fimo Pacific Blue + Fimo Soft Cherry Red = dull purple
©2000, Jacqueline Gikow

want. This will take some practice to understand because you have to train your eye to see the subtleties in a color. Reds, even if called "true red," tend either towards orange or purple. For example, Premo's Cadmium Red has an orange cast to it, while Fimo's Cherry Red has a blue cast.

It isn't "wrong" to add a warm yellow to a cool (slightly purple) blue, but the result will be a dull green. On the other hand, adding a greenish-yellow to greenish-blue will make a bright green; it just depends on what effect you desire.

To avoid disasters, start with the lighter, lower value clay (usually yellow), and add the brighter, darker, or more saturated color (red or blue) in small amounts until you get the effect you want. It's easy to darken a color, but much more difficult to lighten it. Adding white to a color lightens it by making it pastel. To desaturate a color, add black. If you want to retain the true color but lessen its impact, you can "thin" it by using translucent clay. Start with the translucent and add small amounts of color until you have the effect you want.

Translucent Clay as Color

Translucent clay, although not truly a color, can be used for a variety of special effects. Since there is no significant pigment (coloring element) or opacifier, it looks something like alabaster. You can use translucent clays for anything you use colored clays for: conditioning,

mixing and marbling, molding, pinching, and constructing objects—but there are a few differences. Conditioned translucent clay is often softer and stickier than the same brand of colored clay. Additionally, by adding translucent clay to colored clays, or colored clay to translucent, you can alter the saturation of a clay color without changing its value too much. As an example, an undiluted watercolor is equivalent to a highly saturated color, while the same hue, when diluted with water, looks lighter, but without the same characteristic of the addition of white.

"Egyptian Dragonfly." This lamp, by Barbara McGuire, illustrates how a variety of effects can be achieved using transparent clay. The triangular dragonfly canes are made of translucent clay tinted with small amounts of opaque color. 5" x 4".

(Photo: Barbara McGuire)

Creating a Personal Color Palette

Of course, there is no reason you have to limit yourself to primary colors, but they're useful in learning how colors interact with one another. Most artists eventually develop a personal palette of colors made up of the colors, tints, and values they are attracted to. If you seem to have trouble assembling a personal color palette, look in your closet, at your interests, or the colors in your home. Mix a range of the colors to which you are attracted. As an example, some people surround themselves with bright colors, others with neutrals, and yet others with colors of nature. Use these as a base palette, and add a few accents to balance these choices. Even a black and white palette can be very "colorful" if you know how to mix colors and add the accents that are part of your personality.

(Photo: Larry Sanders)

"Tall Teapot." By Rebecca Zimmerman. *Highly colored and textured clay is Rebecca's signature style. She developed her personal color palette from her interests in floral gardens and ocean life including foliage and coral. This teapot uses a pre-formed armature of junk clay that is removed after the first baking. Design is done with cover overlays of clay carved so that the earlier layers show through. 18" x 11", handle to spout.*

"Napkin Rings." By Christl Pelikan. *Christl designed many black and white polymer clay cane patterns to cover the metal bases of these napkin rings. Her personal palette is comprised of black and white. If you ever meet Christl you will see what influences her color palette derives from. She dresses from head to toe in black and white, and her personal accessories using the black and white polymer clay canes are striking with her outfits. 2-3/4" x 1-1/8".*

(Photo: Gerard Barnier)

Chapter 2

Tools and Equipment

Tools

There aren't many tools necessary for creating polymer clay vessels, and all are easy to obtain. Your basic tool kit should include a work surface, something to cut with, and something to roll with. Depending on your approach, you may eventually accumulate dozens of tools, or you may find you repeatedly use only three or four.

A Work Surface

(Photo: Jodi Jones)

Possible work surface materials illustrated here include laminated particle board, Plexiglas, illustration board, and graphic self-sealing cutting board.

Your work surface can be any nonporous material that is smooth, flat, hard, resistant to polymer clay chemical reaction, and stain resistant. The surface should also be heavy enough that it doesn't slide around when working on it. Possible materials for work surfaces include glass, marble, Formica, Corian, Masonite, Plexiglas, graphic self-sealing cutting boards, and mat and Bristol board. If your work surface must be portable, select one of the lighter weight materials.

All surfaces have advantages and disadvantages. Plastic laminates and paperboards have fine textures that easily release the clay as you work with it; however, they tend to get dirty with time and use. Slick surfaces such as glass and acrylics are difficult to handle because polymer clay tends to adhere to them. In many cases, taping sheets of wax paper or tracing vellum to your work surface will provide the qualities you need, and you can replace them when they get soiled.

Something to Cut With

There are many choices for cutting polymer clay. One essential tool is a sharp, flat blade to make precise cuts. An X-Acto knife works well for many applications, but you will also need longer cutting edges for many of your projects. You can use anything from a wallpaper

(Photo: Jodi Jones)

There are many choices for cutting polymer clay including (left to right) an 8" wallpaper scraping blade, an X-Acto knife with a #11 blade, a ribbed cutter for making zigzag shaped cuts, and a flexible tissue-slicing blade. The last is a Kato blade, which is similar to the tissue-slicing blade, but longer and less bendable than the tissue blade.

scraping blade to a tissue-slicing blade, which is one of the sharpest and most versatile for cutting clay.

Freehand cutting, important in vessel-making, can also be done with a needle tool for ceramics, dental picks, a medium-sized needle or straight pin that you make a handle for, and any of a dozen sharp items you may be able to find, construct, or buy.

Cutters can also be appropriated from their intended uses, such as aspic or canapé cutters, cookie cutters, vegetable cutters from Japanese markets, alphabet cutters, scissors, metal ceramic ribs, wire, saws, utility knives, rotary-type cutters, non-serrated paring knives, dental tools, razor blades, ripple blades, wallpaper blades, and other flexible and non-flexible blades. I've been getting great use from an eight-inch plaster spreader that I sharpened with a whetstone—it's rigid and works for cutting wide sheets of clay, as well as making even slices from a block of clay when I start conditioning.

Something to Roll With

You can use your hands when flattening clay into sheets, but it is a lot easier to use a roller of some sort—an old rolling pin, an acrylic tube, a long cylindrical drinking glass or bottle, or a brayer.

Note: I don't recommend using glass for rolling out larger quantities of clay. It may work for jewelry, where the amount of clay rolled out is small, but too much pressure, especially on a drinking glass, can cause it to shatter, and result in injury.

Polymer clay tends to stick to wood more readily than to acrylic plastic, but you can alleviate this by paint-

❖ Don't get distracted from what you are doing when using cutting tools or you might get hurt.

❖ Don't use sharp cutters when you are tired. It's easy to slash yourself without noticing until it's too late.

❖ Do not use dull tools. Dull cutting tools are more dangerous than sharp ones. Keep replacement blades available, and invest in a whetstone so you can easily re-sharpen your cutting tools.

❖ Keep your fingers out of the blade's path. Use a straight edge when you cut sheets of clay. Keep your fingers out of the way when you are doing freehand cuts.

❖ Stop round, sharp tools from rolling off the table into your lap or leg by pushing the cutting edge or bladed end into a lump of clay, handle up.

❖ Do not put cutting blades in your mouth, or clean off clay with your fingers.

❖ Finally, do not throw out dull blades without wrapping them in something before putting them into the trash. I wrap mine up in masking tape as I retire them, and then put them in a paper bag inside the plastic trash liner.

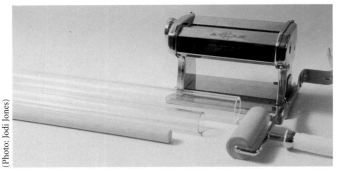

(Photo: Jodi Jones)

These are a few rolling tools I use with my polymer clay. Depending on the task, I might also use a tube-shaped pen, chopsticks, or even a round wood bead for concave shapes.

(Photo: Jodi Jones)

You probably recognize some of these tools from crafts, but others come from the kitchen or I have made them to satisfy some need that has come up. In the upper left corner is a set of round pastry cutters that range in size from 7/8" to 4". Next to the circle cutters is a kitchen drain spout because, well, you never know. The wood thing with the bulb at the end is a sock darner. The black and white-handled tool is a carving blade baked in a polymer clay handle. It's good for close work, when I need more control than a full-sized handle allows, and the little tool at the front with the striped handle is a bead on a wire. It's great for applying a rolling band of pattern.

ing your rolling pin with a coat of polyurethane. If your projects call for using many sheets of clay of consistent thickness, consider buying a pasta machine. Not only is it useful for conditioning and blending clay, but it can also produce miles of clay sheets in a variety of thicknesses, some much thinner than you can easily make by hand.

When working with clay sheets thicker than 1/8 inch (6 mm), combining the results of a pasta machine with those of hand rolling will be necessary. Chapter 6 discusses making clay slabs.

Miscellaneous Tools

Although you can get along with a minimal tool kit, you'll probably find that the right tool can make all the difference in the world, and end up on the lookout for the perfect cutting, piercing, carving or modeling tool. Tools for working with polymer clay can be found everywhere, whether they are manufactured, hand-made, discovered, or "jerry-rigged." Raw polymer clay is so malleable that you can incise, model, or texture it with just about anything.

Extruders

A clay extruder is a tool that allows you to push clay through a tube with a die at the end. A die (usually metal) is a piece with a shape cut out of the center that fits into the end of the extruder. When clay is pushed through the extruder the result is a long piece of shaped clay.

Similar to an extruder, a small clay gun originally created for ceramic slip decorating is available inexpensively at art and hobby stores, and it works well with polymer clay. It comes with dies that extrude lengths of clay in configurations such as triangles, petals, squares, as well as a variety of round dimensions.

Some artists keep several extruders—one for each color group, so they don't have to be cleaned out often.

To clean small clay extruders, put them into the oven with your next group of polymer pieces; the clay stuck to the inside of the metal will cure. When the extruder cools, the baked clay is easily knocked out.

Clay Pushers

Because this small craft clay extruder was made for use with soft wet clay, it's not that easy to get polymer clay to pass through it with "normal" hand strength. Artists, sensing the value of this little tool, have been creative in devising methods of easing the effort needed to push the clay through.

Caulking Gun Clay Pusher

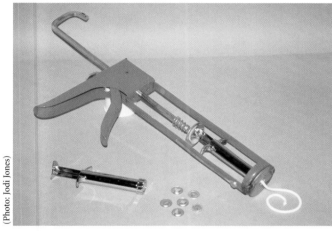

I made this caulking gun clay pusher with some hardware I had around. I had help from a couple of welders working on a building next door to my apartment building one day. The small tool in the foreground is the clay gun.

One tool developed using a caulking gun makes it easier to push polymer clay through the clay gun. Don't get the cheapest one because you don't want it to bend or collapse. Most people make their own caulking gun clay pushers, although you may find individual polymer clay artists or commercial suppliers who offer them already assembled. Converted caulking guns still require squeezing effort, but the handle gives more leverage than using the clay gun by itself. For a good description of how to make a caulking gun clay pusher, see the June 2000 issue of *Bead & Button* magazine.[3]

Bellows-Type Clay Gun Pusher

Diane Black, a polymer artist who generously shared the instructions with me, devised another pusher that functions by mimicking the shape and action of an air bellows. It is constructed of two hinged pieces of wood, with a hole in one piece and a stopper on the other, which provide leverage to move the clay pusher handle

through the tube that holds the clay.

To construct this clay pusher, you'll need two 12" to 18" lengths of 1" x 4" wood hinged together at one end. The longer the boards, the more torque you will generate. More torque makes it easier to push the two boards together and moves the clay through the clay gun faster. Use a sturdy, 3" hinge with at least a 1" flange. You'll also need a 7/8" (22 mm) drill bit or hole cutter.

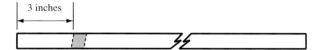

Drill a hole with the 7/8" drill bit, at one end of one board, and about three inches from the edge. This will be large enough to accommodate the barrel and screw-on cap of the clay gun, but too small for the finger holders. If you want to lessen the stress on the clay gun barrel when you push the clay through the die, drill the hole using a hole-cutter instead of a drill bit, at approximately a 10° angle.

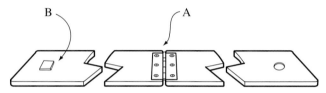

Position the two boards lengthwise and screw the hinge to both boards on what will be the inside of the pusher. If you are compulsive, you can inlay the hinges by gouging out a 1/8" depth. Make sure the board with the hole in it is the top board and at the end opposite the hinge. Attach a small block of wood to the bottom board, as a "stop" for the base of the plunger. It's not necessary, but again, it may prevent stress when the plunger goes through the extruder. Sand the corners and edges of the board to finish and prevent splinters.

This is an optional step, but when I made my clay pusher, the clay gun immediately started to dent the wood. Diane suggested putting a large washer on the inside of the top hole to keep stress off the wood, and covering the washer with a rubber O-ring so the extruder handles don't slide around.

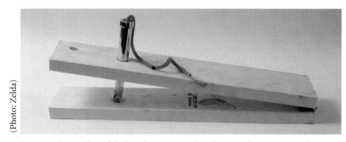

To use the pusher, fill the clay gun with polymer clay, insert it from the underside of the top board as shown, and press the top board down with the palm of your hand (or stand on the top board).

To use the pusher, fill the clay gun with polymer clay, insert it from the underside of the top board as shown, and press the top board down with the palm of your hand.

If you will be working with larger polymer clay shapes, wall-mounted clay extruders are available from ceramic suppliers. Most are expensive and are too big for working with polymer clay, but there are a few available with 2" or 3" diameters. Clay extruders also come with dies that allow you to extrude hollow shapes. If you are handy and resourceful, you can also make your own.

Equipment For Polymer Clay Vessels

An oven is the only piece of equipment necessary to work with polymer clay, but you may find others convenient and useful. Additional equipment that artists find invaluable for vessel making include a pasta machine for rolling, a food processor for pre-conditioning the clay, and a buffer for finishing. These pieces of equipment process larger amounts of clay more easily and faster.

Curing Clay

Polymer clay needs to be heated in order to attain a finished state. You must have an oven because it is essential to cure the clay. You can use your home oven, or a portable convection or toaster oven. Gas ovens are preferable to electric because the heat tends to remain more stable from top to bottom.

Although the following heat sources are not customary, depending on your circumstances they can work in a pinch: crock pots, covered electric frying skillets (place clay on a grid inside), a metal cookie tin, propped over a camp fire, the sun—hot climates are great for this!

Heat Guns

(Photo: Jodi Jones)

Heat guns do a good job of partially or fully curing liquid Sculpey or thin pieces of polymer clay.

A heat gun is similar to a hair dryer but much hotter; in fact, don't ever try to dry your hair with one. Heat guns do a good job of partially or fully curing Liquid Sculpey or thin pieces of polymer clay, including those you may attach to already baked clay. Cynthia Tinapple, a polymer artist, uses a heat gun to cure her inlayed clay in the wood bowls and on-site installations she and her husband collaborate on. She says, "The trick is to keep heating until the entire thickness is thoroughly baked. Generally, I go back for repeated firings just to be safe. It's a boring process and takes quite a while ... heating, turning, heating, turning."

Grant Diffendaffer, whose work appears in this book, concurs, "The heat gun ... took a long time. The vase ... was well suited for it because I could aim the gun right down inside the vase and it acted as a kind of furnace—the heat collected inside and soaked through." Heat guns can also provide support to free-form constructions by curing the lower form to lend support as you build your vessel up.

There are different kinds of heat guns on the market. When you are shopping, look around and read the packages of the different guns. Heat guns used in construction by sculptors can be very dangerous, because their temperature can exceed 1200° F. Since polymer clay cures at temperatures of 265° F to 275° F, this is not only unnecessary, but dangerous as well. Most craft stores sell heat guns meant for crafts, usually in the rubber-stamping department. They range in price from $15 to $35, depending on the store and the extra gadgets that come with it.

A heat gun needs only about ten seconds to warm up. Don't touch the metal parts at the tip of the gun because they get very hot. Position the gun about 6" to 7" away from the area you are heat-setting. Keep the gun moving from side to side so the heat doesn't settle in one area and scorch your work. Depending on its thickness, your piece should be heat-set in about one to two minutes. When you want to test the firmness of the set, turn off the heat gun, and let the clay cool for a minute.

Pasta Machines

Many clay artists use pasta machines as aids in conditioning fresh clay, to give a crackled finish to metal leaf on clay, to roll thin sheets of clay, and to make a continuous blend of two or more colors.

A hand-cranked type of machine, one with metal

Heat Gun Safety and Warnings

❖ Read the safety literature provided by the manufacturer and heed any warnings given to you about your individual heat gun.

❖ Do not get the gun too close to your piece. Most guns do not have a temperature gauge, and you may melt or burn your work before you realize it.

❖ Do not hold your clay in your hand as you use the heat gun. Prop it up on a surface and keep all body parts, including hair, away from it.

❖ Do not use a heat gun on glass and be very careful if you are drying clay-covered papier-maché.

Polymer Clay: Creating Functional and Decorative Objects

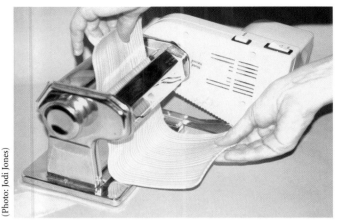

(Photo: Jodi Jones)

Clay artists, to make conditioning fresh clay easier and to blend two or more colors in an even gradation, mostly use pasta machines.

rollers, is the best model for the purpose. The extruder-type machines aren't strong enough to work with polymer clay. One widely available brand is Atlas, and another is the Pasta Queen. Artists have reported that these, as well as other machines made in Italy, seem to be sturdier than most. I haven't tested them all, so you're best off trying them yourself. Standard size pasta machines yield approximately 5-1/2" wide sheets, but there are some available that produce sheets up to 9" wide.

Pasta machines can be pesky pieces of equipment. They're not, as the name indicates, equipment made specifically for polymer clay, and therefore are not accurate in creating slab thicknesses. Also, because they are intended for pasta dough, the oily polymer clay material is apt to get caught on the guards that protect the rollers. You may notice that streaks or chunks appear on the sheet as the clay runs through the machine. Make it a general habit to clean the rollers with a degreaser and to turn the machine over to scrape off clay that has become stuck on the chrome guards. Pasta machines can be taken apart for a thorough cleaning. If you do decide to take the machine apart, pay close attention to how each piece is connected so you can easily put it back together again.

Treat Yourself to a Motor

Once I got a motor for my pasta machine, I wondered how on earth I ever got by without it. They are incredibly sturdy, and they certainly relieve the ache from hand cranking. I can also condition more clay faster, and I can make blends as long as my arm since I have both hands free. I don't find it too noisy, either. I live in an apartment building, and have been able to use it at night without anyone complaining.

Food Processor

A food processor is not a necessity for working with most polymer clays, but many clay artists find it a helpful time-saver for conditioning and mixing Fimo Classic. Look for a unit with a strong motor because chopping clay is tougher than most of the food tasks for which the processor was intended.

Food processors are good for conditioning small quantities of clay, especially Fimo Classic clay. Slice the clay into small chunks to avoid jamming the motor, and chop for approximately 60 seconds. The clay will divide into small pieces and then clump together when it begins to warm through heat and friction. Empty it out onto a work surface or piece of waxed paper. Press or roll it into sheets, send the sheets of clay through a pasta machine to eliminate air pockets, blend color, and prepare the clay into even sheets of the desired thickness.

Buffing Wheels

(Photo: Zelda)

You can finish a polymer piece by sanding and buffing by hand, but like a motorized pasta machine, power buffing makes the process much faster.

Of course, you can finish a polymer piece by sanding and buffing by hand, but like a motorized pasta machine, a power buffer makes the process so much faster. Dremel tools can buff small areas, but if you want to polish a bowl, or other large surface, you need a buffing surface that won't leave uneven marks or gouge the clay. You can get a buffing wheel that fits onto your home drill for $5.00, or you can spend hundreds of dollars for high-end jewelry polishers. Realistically, you can expect to spend from about $35 to $100 for a dependable bench grinder that can accommodate a buffing wheel; keep in mind that variable speed control is important.

I purchased an inexpensive holder (under $5.00) that lets me attach my hand drill to my worktable. Because my vessels can be intricately shaped, having a large buffing surface is useful. I use a sheepskin pad on my drill and set it at a medium speed. Using this configuration can be dangerous, however, because of the tremendous torque of the spinning buffer. If you try this method, start with smaller items that you can keep a firm grasp on. Always wear safety goggles! Speaking from experience, you'll need to be extra careful if you are left-handed: the normal direction of a drill is counter-clockwise, forcing you to work with your non-dominant hand. If your drill (or buffing machine) has a reverse motor direction, experiment with it.

Scrolling/Jigsaws

Scrolling or jigsaws are great pieces of equipment for polymer clay artists, especially for any work with flat, already cured, sheets of clay. Both MicroLux and Dremel make bench-mounted scroll saws. A smaller model, the MicroLux palm-size hand saw, is ideal for working with baked clay. It's small, dependable and powerful, and will cut intricate patterns. The saw can be used freehand or converted to a tabletop scroll saw using an inexpensive stationary table accessory.

Supplies

The number of art supplies and craft materials that can be adapted for use with polymer clay is vast. There are many books available already that detail many decorative materials. Some will be introduced in this book within the context of a project demonstration; others you may find in some of the books and Web sites listed in the Bibliography. Two categories that bear discussing here are glues and mold supplies. These supplies are central to the structural needs of polymer clay vessels.

Adhesives and Glues

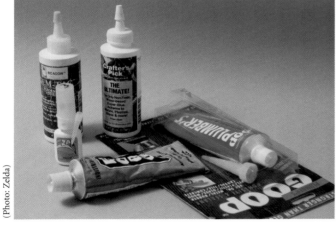

(Photo: Zelda)

Various adhesives and glues used in attaching polymer clay together or adding embellishments.

There is no such thing as the "perfect" all-purpose glue for bonding polymer clay. Each glue has pluses and minuses. The secret to successful bonding is to keep in mind the following glue basics:
1. All glues work best when aided with a physical attachment. Whenever possible the combination of glue and a screw, nail or staple, glue and a joint, glue and stitching or binding, will guarantee a successful bond.
2. There is no point in using glue stronger than the materials you are bonding. Any glue is only as strong as the weakest material in the bonding union.
3. A successful bond depends on the amount of surface area it has to adhere to. The more surface area you can incorporate, the stronger the bond.
4. Always use the least toxic material that meets your bonding requirements.

Types of Adhesives and Glues

Understanding how glue works will help you choose the right one for the job. Manufacturers know their glues better than the cashier at the hardware store does. Reading the label thoroughly will help you to decide if a specific glue is appropriate for your needs. For more information, many manufacturers have a help line or a Web site. Some glues that work with polymer clay for small objects will be inadequate for supporting large vessels and containers.

PVA

PVA (polyvinyl acetate) glues, like Sobo, and Gem-Tac, can be used to glue raw polymer clay to porous and nonporous surfaces. PVA glues are similar in chemical make-up to polymer clay (PVC: polyvinyl chloride), and are heat resistant. When the glues are heated, the clay and glue fuse together and then to porous materials such as papier-mâché, fabric and wood. These glues also stick polymer clay to nonporous surfaces, such as metal and glass, that are to be covered with clay. For polymer clay use, the heat resistance of PVA means it will remain a flexible bond with the clay. Sobo seems to work best with porous surfaces, while Gem-Tac, being more viscous (thicker), is better for non-porous surfaces like glass or metal.

Cyanoacrylates

Cyanoacrylates (the "superglues") bond to polymer clay in seconds. Be judicious in applying the glue to the clay. Applying too much will cause joints to fail.

It is a known fact that heat degrades cyanoacrylate adhesive, so it's best to apply it after the clay has cured. A NASA reject that first came on the market in the late 1960s, extensive tests proved that heat weakened the bond between the space capsule and the shields when using a cyanoacrylate adhesive, and the shields fell off as a result! A bond created with Zap-a-Gap, for example, will separate if you apply heat at 300° F for about 15 minutes.

The surfaces to be bonded must fit exactly when attaching clay to already baked clay or to other non-porous surfaces because most cyanoacrylate glues travel the gap by surface tension. There are also viscous cyanoacrylate glues available that can fill gaps up to 2 mm. Surehold "Plastic Surgery" Super Gel, for example, is one brand that is a real winner. It is gap-filling and thick, and works very well with polymer.

Another big disadvantage of cyanoacrylate glue is that it will bond skin. It also degrades with time even in the tube or bottle. Refrigerating cyanoacrylate glue helps check the speed of the deterioration.

Silicon-type Glues

E6000 and GOOP, which maintain a flexible quality when cured, can be used for gluing baked clay to non-porous surfaces like baked clay, metal, glass, etc. Use enough glue to avoid a "starved bond."

The instructions for bonding with silicon glues are similar to those for contact cement. Read the instructions carefully. These glues degrade slightly when heated, and the thicker the glue, the more likely it will pull apart later. The worst by far for health hazards is E6000 glue because of inhalation health risks and symptoms of exposure, and possible central nervous system damage from overexposure.

Polymer Clay-Related Bonding Materials

Although they are not adhesives, polymer clay-based products, such as Liquid Sculpey and Sculpey Diluent can be used to bond either raw or baked clay during baking. These have no strength to support while firing, but when cured they will create a bond. You simply need to use other glues to hold the pieces in place while firing. I've found Gem-Tac and Adhesive Crafter's Pick work best for this application because they dry quickly and prevent clay pieces from sliding apart.

Mold Materials

Many materials can be used as molds for polymer clay. They can be divided into two categories: found and created. Found molds include such things as household bowls or woks, and work as drape or slump molds. You can also make your own molds from materials such as polymer clay, including Elasticlay, silicone rubber, and plaster of Paris. In this case, you would work from a model shaped like the finished piece you want. These and others will be discussed and illustrated in detail in Chapter 7.

Mold Releases

A mold release is material that makes the object being molded easily come away from the mold when it is removed. Mold releases are used when a mold is made, to make sure the object you are making a mold of (a button, or a textured surface, for example) can be removed from the mold when it is finished. Mold releases are also used when you want to make a reproduction of whatever you made a mold of. A number of materials exist that will act as a barrier to having either a model or object stick to the mold.

Talc or cornstarch applied with a soft brush, to one or both surfaces of a mold, works well. Talc isn't great for the lungs and leaves a residue that won't wash off after baking. The cornstarch does wash off with cool water, even after baking. Using water as a release on polymer molds usually allows for 2 or 3 impressions from one damp mold.

Potato starch is a multi-purpose additive for dyes; when mixed with water, it forms a stable medium that works as a resist or thickener. Potato starch can be used as a mold release for polymer clay, and leaves no residue like that associated with talc. Corn or rice flour also work well—they have smaller particles and are semi-transparent to begin with.

Talc, cornstarch or any other powdery mold release can be applied using a pounce ball. A pounce ball can easily be made with a section of old nylon stocking. Using a layer or two of nylon, dump the powder inside and tie it up in a tight little ball. You can then tap the pounce ball gently on the mold to use it, evenly releasing a small amount of powder onto the mold.

ArmorAll, a non-toxic spray, (usually used for rejuvenating car surfaces) contains no alcohol or solvents, and is a great mold release. Artists have reported some problems with ArmorAll when trying to paint or stick the clay together because of a residue. Try wiping or rinsing the piece well with alcohol, a non-oily soap, and/or using superglue under the new pieces. If an inadequate amount of release agent is used and clay sticks to the mold, these solvents will resolve that problem, too.

For simple round, square, or cylindrical molds, aluminum foil makes a good release; clay doesn't stick to it. Cotton rag paper can also be used as a release for simple shapes.

(Photo: Zelda)

Mold releases are used to make sure the object you are making a mold of, or from, can be removed from the mold when it is finished.

Finally, materials used for decorative effects, such as Pearl-Ex powders and pigments, and even metallic foils, can be used as mold releases because they form a barrier between the mold and the artwork.

Chapter 3

Preparing and Using Polymer Clay

Conditioning Polymer Clay

Conditioning does not make polymer clay stronger; flexibility is affected somewhat, but polymer clay becomes stronger in the baking process, not through conditioning. All polymer clays must be conditioned before use, but only to make the clay pliable. This means doing a lot of conditioning for some brands and less for others. Polyform Products, for example, found the polymer clays they manufacture do not need conditioning beyond getting them soft enough to work with.

It is not true that clays that are easier to condition are necessarily weaker. As with wedging pottery clay, conditioning prepares the clay by eliminating air bubbles. Conditioning also warms and aligns the clay molecules so the clay becomes pliable.

Conditioning Polymer Clay by Hand

(Photo: John Polak)

You've got one tool to condition clay with you at all times - your hands.

You've got the tools to condition clay with you at all times—your hands. Start by warming the clay. Even a little heat from your body or the room temperature will make the clay softer. If the clay is hard, like the Fimo Classic brand, you may want to start with a small amount. Many people like to warm the clay before kneading by using something that gets warm but not too hot. You can put the clay next to your body, sit on it, use a heating pad set on low, immerse it in warm water, or expose it to a light bulb for a few minutes before conditioning.

Additives to Soften Clay

Most clay will stiffen after sitting awhile, even if it has been previously conditioned. If the clay is too firm to work easily by hand, various things can be mixed in to soften it. Mineral oil, glycerin, or any petroleum product will work. Other materials that can be added are products developed by the polymer clay manufacturers:

Sculpey Diluent and Fimo MixQuick, even Liquid Sculpey. Another way to soften hard clay is to leave it touching soft clay or a diluent for a day or more—some of the plasticizer will leach into the harder clay.

Leaching

(Photo: Zelda)

Left: slabs of clay between layers of typing paper. Right: slabs of clay layered between sheets of brown paper bags, rolled up, and held loosely with a rubber band.

If the clay is too soft, possibly because it's very fresh, you can make it firmer by "leaching" it. Leaching removes some of the plasticizer. To do this, roll the clay out and place it between several clean sheets of typing paper (not clay coated desk jet papers). It's best to then weight this with something heavy; leave for an hour or more or even overnight. The paper will absorb some of the plasticizer, and the clay will stiffen.

Brown paper bags, cut into strips, can also be used for leaching clay. Put the clay through the pasta machine on a number one setting, lay it on the brown paper, place another piece on top and roll the whole thing up like a jellyroll. Put a bunch of rubber bands around the whole tube, to give it extra pressure. In about 24 hours, the paper will be saturated with oil and the clay will be stiffer.

Meat Grinders

Chunks of hard clay, about 1" sizes, can be put in a meat grinder and cranked through with a few drops of mineral oil added. It all comes out like new, soft clay in one or two passes. Once out of the meat grinder, flatten and run the clay through the pasta machine a few times. The meat grinder is great for conditioning large quantities of clay in larger chunks, with the peace and quiet of a hand-crank tool.

Pasta Machine Conditioning

One of the best ways to condition polymer clay is with a pasta machine. Whether you use a hand-cranked

(Photo: Zelda)

Clockwise from lower left. A block of Sculpey III; Fimo Lapis stone, one pass through pasta machine; partially conditioned slab of clay; fully conditioned slab of Premo.

or motorized one, it can make conditioning easier and faster, as well as leave you with a workable sheet of clay when you are done. Working from an unused block of clay, cut the clay slightly thicker than the number one (thickest) setting, and start by running it through the machine at that setting. Fold the sheet in half and feed it through again, fold-first, eventually using thinner settings until you get to #5 or #6. Don't jump to a thin setting too quickly or the clay will ripple and tear. Finally, fold the thin sheet so that it will pass through the machine at the thickest setting. You might want to let the sheets of clay cool a bit before rolling them through the thinnest settings. By this time, the clay will be conditioned and ready to use.

If you are reconditioning clay, start by pounding a mass of clay into a thick, roughly square, chunk of clay. Cut it into slices slightly larger than the thickest setting, and feed it through the pasta machine at the widest setting. Continue conditioning by following the instructions for working with a new block of clay.

If the clay isn't soft enough prior to running it through the pasta machine, it will shred instead of making a smooth, flat sheet. If this happens, condition your clay a little more. Stiffer clays may not run through the roller at the thinner settings. If you have trouble getting a sheet as thin as you want, roll it through at a thicker setting several times, and then try again at the thinner setting. If the clay seems to be sticking to the rollers, try laying it between sheets of waxed paper and running this "sandwich" through the machine. Or brush the surface of the clay very lightly with talc or cornstarch, then run it through the machine.

Conditioning White Clay

White polymer clay is like any polymer clay color in a specific brand, but it gets dirty incredibly easily. The simple solution is to make sure your work area is super clean, work on parchment or scrub a glass work surface thoroughly, cover everything around with lint-free white cloth, don't wear clothes that are dark and fuzzy while working, keep animals away. Anticipate the ways the clay could get dirty and head them off.

Clean your hands often while you are using white clay. Rather than washing your hands every five minutes, squish a piece of white scrap clay around in your hands until any lint or dirt is gone. Wash your hands with cleaner and water after working with other colors because the residue from other colors is difficult to get rid of.

Firing or Baking Your Work

The terms "firing" and "baking" are used interchangeably in this book. In ceramics, you put a raw piece of clay in an oven called a "kiln." The kiln is heated, or fired, to the correct temperature that changes the raw clay to stone. With polymer clay, you do the same thing using a household oven. The raw clay goes through a chemical change that makes it hard. Just as pottery can never be clay again, once baked or fired, polymer clay will never be raw plastic again.

You can put your clay pieces into either a cold or a hot oven, although putting them into a preheated oven may make it easier to gauge the firing time. If you're covering a surface (such as glass or metal) with clay, it may be better to put the piece into a cold oven, heat it to the firing temperature then let the piece cool down in the oven after firing. This gives the underlying material more time to expand and contract with the changes in temperature; the clay is less likely to crack off the item it's attached to.

Aids to Baking

An inexpensive oven thermometer will work for tracking the oven temperature. I recommend one with large numbers. Radio Shack has a probe thermometer with both a stand and magnet so you can put it wherever it is convenient. You can set the desired temperature and time, and an alarm sounds when it is reached. The probe

(Photo: Jacqueline Gikow)

A kitchen timer can prevent over-baking clay. Additionally, an oven thermometer is a necessity to make sure you are firing at the right temperature. Even 10 degrees can be the difference between whether your piece is over- or under-fired during curing.

How Much Clay Do You Need?

It's actually possible to figure out how much clay you need for a project. You can measure the area of the object to be covered and compare that to how much area at what thickness a block of clay will cover. So, how much area does a 2 oz. block of polymer clay cover?

Fimo—A small block of Fimo weighs about 2 oz. (58 cm) is 2-1/8" (5.5 cm) wide, 2-1/8" (5.5 cm) long, and 5/8" (1.75 cm) thick. A block of Fimo can cover a square area of 9" x 9" (23 cm) at 1/16" (1.5 mm) thickness.

Premo or Sculpey III—Blocks of Premo and Sculpey III also weigh about 2 oz. (56 cm), but their measurements are slightly different; 3/4" (1.9 cm) thick, 2-1/4" (6 cm) long, and 1-3/4" (4.5 cm) wide. Regardless, they will also yield a 1/16" (1.5 mm) layer of clay, 9" x 9" (23 cm).

As you can see, as you increase the thickness of the clay slab, the slab size decreases. The templates will help you determine how much clay to estimate for a project.

For example, if you are covering a box, measure the square inches of all the sides together (a calculator

You can measure the area of the object to be covered and compare that to how much area at what thickness a block of clay will cover.

will help you). Find the square root and enlarge as many squares as you need. A box has six sides. If each is 2" square, the result is 24"² (42 x 6 = 242). The square root of the total is almost 5. If you are building a box with 1/8" sides, you will need almost 1-1/2 squares of clay from the 1/8" thick clay template.

It sounds harder than it is. With a little practice, you'll find these templates quite helpful.

**2 oz. block yields a 5-1/4" square x 1/8" thick slab of clay.
(Enlarge 200%)**

2 oz. block yields a 9" square x 1/16" thick slab of clay. (Enlarge 300%)

**2 oz. block yields a 3-5/8" square x 1/4" thick slab of clay.
(Enlarge 200%)**

Enlarge these templates as indicated and you will have a guide for measuring the yield of a 2 ounce block of clay at 1/4", 1/8", 1/16" thick. To measure more clay, simply enlarge additional templates.

fits inside the oven with a 3' insulated wire coming out of the oven. You can also get fancier, and buy a digital thermometer that has the readout outside the oven.

An oven timer is another accessory you'll use enough to offset its cost. How many times have you looked at the clock when putting a piece into the oven, only to find when you look again, that it's an hour later?

Avoid Disasters During Baking and Firing

(Photo: Zelda)

Make sure your work is fired successfully. Use an oven thermometer and provide supports to prevent the clay from slumping. Otherwise you may end up with these delightful results.

How many times have you opened your oven to find your work has slumped during the baking time? Here's how you can avoid this disaster: Make sure your project is solidly balanced when it's in the oven. This means, if needed, prop your project up with a coffee mug, tin foil, oven parchment, or other ovenproof things, and of course, use a flat, stiff surface. The goal is to avoid any unusual movement when the clay gets hot. Slumping or bending will change (and ruin) the whole look of your artwork. Don't jump or stomp heavily near the oven when you are firing a piece.

Do pay attention to manufacturers' baking temperatures. Fimo cures at 265° F in about 20 minutes per 1/4" thickness. Premo and Sculpey cure at 275° F in about 15 minutes per 1/4" thickness. The more saturated colors and translucents of all brands burn at higher temperatures. Firing Premo or Sculpey at a lower temperature for a longer time may still result in underfiring, resulting in a lack of strength. Firing Fimo at a higher temperature than recommended may result in burning. In many cases, careful firing for longer periods of time at the correct temperatures has resulted in stronger, more flexible finished artwork.

Supporting Pieces in the Oven

Firing surfaces often are selected on the basis of requirements of the piece being fired. Baking surfaces must be oven-safe, evenly distribute heat, and be durable enough to last through several (numerous) firings. A variety of firing surfaces can be used depending on need.

Some possibilities include: Bristol board, parchment, printer paper, glass, ceramic tile, non-stick baking sheet, cornstarch bed, a polyester fiberfill bed, and polymer clay armatures for holding needles. An ideal firing surface should not alter the surface finish or change shape of the piece being fired.

I don't recommend that you bake directly on a smooth glass surface because the clay will become shiny or smooth where it touches the glass. Even if you find this a desirable quality you will more than likely find the results uneven because it's difficult to control.

Ordinary paper or parchment has about the same texture as baked polymer, so placing items on them is usually safe. The surface underneath the paper must be flat, so place the paper on a baking pan, tile, piece of glass, etc. Beware of using cardboard, which will sometimes warp, especially if there is a coating on one side. Additionally, cardboard gives off fumes when heated above 250° F and it may burn as well.

If the item is shaped like a bowl or vase, it can be placed on a cloud of polyester stuffing or batting, on top of a baking sheet. Vessels can also be baked standing on their feet, but any long or heavy protruding items should be propped with something like batting or aluminum foil, to keep them from drooping during the baking process. Sometimes baking the object on its rim might provide more support for an object that's wider on the top than the bottom (and has an even, sturdy edge).

Clay is hot, soft, and flexible when removed from the oven, and an object won't reach its normal hardness and

(Photo: Jacqueline Gikow)

Pieces can be supported to help them retain their shapes. Left to right: a vase supported by a paper cone, holding another vase with gauze protecting it from the rim of a glass, a pot nestled in cotton-wrapped fabric.

stiffness until it cools. If you have an object that might droop when cooling, don't remove the props until the item is completely cooled. Clays also differ in their finished "hardness," and this will be more noticeable in thin items. Sculpey items are harder, but break easily. Premo and Fimo feel rubbery, but are strong and flexible when cool.

Firing Large Vessels

(Photo: Jodi Jones)

This vase was formed over a triangular bottle and removed after baking. In the oven, the bottle was placed on a riser because the flared top was longer than the bottle. The clay and bottle were left in the oven to cool so they could be removed without distorting the vase. 15" x 6". By Jacqueline Gikow.

With large polymer clay artworks, such as vessels or flat panels, baking with an even temperature is even more important than for small pieces. Because they take up more space in the oven, they are more apt to be exposed to uneven temperatures than small pieces. Use a good oven thermometer, and make sure your oven does not have hot spots, or spike temperatures too high during the baking process.

Here are a number of tips for reliable results:

1. Pre-heat your oven before placing your piece in it.
2. Put your item in the center of the oven. Raise racks higher if you find the bottom of your oven is hotter than the top.
3. If you are baking a tall piece that calls for placing it at the lowest rack setting, watch the temperature carefully, perhaps using two thermometers.

4. If your piece can stand on both foot and rim, it might be a good idea to fire it in two stages, half the time upright and half upside down.
5. Shield or enclose your item to even out the temperature around it. A piece of foil (not touching the item), a paper bag, or an aluminum roasting pan, for example, will create an air buffer.
6. Don't bake longer than is recommended for the thickness of your piece.
7. If an object is mostly or completely translucent, or white, lower the baking temperature and bake it a little longer.
8. Set the item on a piece of unglazed tile, or fill a cookie pan with plaster to provide a buffer from the heat source and protect the bottom from burning.

Finishing

(Photo: Jodi Jones)

This bowl was formed using a shallow soup bowl as the mold. The patterning is black and white faux marble. The bowl was made with Premo clay that was sanded to result in a smooth, matte finish. 9" x 1-1/2". Artist: Jacqueline Gikow

You can leave fired polymer clay without any special finishing treatment. For many pieces, the clay's natural finish enhances the effect you want. For other pieces, you may prefer a shinier or glossier finish requiring various finishing techniques, such as wet sanding, buffing, and glazing. Sanding polymer clay is the most time consuming, resulting in a slight luster to the clay. Buffing produces a deeper, subtler sheen; glazing produces a harder shine and takes considerably less time. The finish each brand of polymer clay exhibits right after firing varies. Fimo has a slight gloss, Sculpey and Premo have a matte finish.

Sanding

Wet/dry sandpaper, the best material for finishing polymer clay, comes in numbered grits, with lower numbers being coarser than higher numbers. The numbers correspond with number and size of grit per square inch. Sanding sponges and sanding films with plastic backings are also available.

Work with a bucket of water close to your piece so you can wet the sand-paper often. Start with the coarsest grit, and progressively switch to finer ones, as the piece becomes smoother. When you are finished, rinse your work under a faucet and let it dry.

The following grits each result in a different finish:

150 grit—very coarse, cuts through and removes a lot of clay very quickly (good for reshaping a lumpy piece)

220 grit—removes a lot of clay

320 grit—removes clay reasonably quickly

400 grit (approximately the same grit as polymer clay)—removes some clay; plain, brown paper bags also have the same grit

600 grit—polishes clay surface

1000-2000 grit—found in auto supply stores, polishes clay to a very smooth surface

The Sanding Process

Keep your piece and your sandpaper wet, and rinse them frequently. Even better, sand the clay under water, either under the tap or in a basin. Sand each surface a few strokes with each grit of paper, starting with the coarsest. Each successively higher sandpaper grit removes scratches from the previous coarser grit. When done, wipe off the piece and let it dry.

Sand in a circular motion, and not always in the same direction. Most of the time, 600 grit is high enough unless you want a silky finish.

I usually tear the 8-1/2" x 11" sheets into eighths and quarters, and label them with the grit number. After you sand with a sandpaper grade for a while, you will feel less resistance. This tells you have reached the smoothness limit of the grit you are using.

Faster sanding is possible by partially baking your piece at 210° F to 220° F for 15 minutes, then sanding. Support your piece very carefully since partially baked clay is soft and fragile. 400 grit sandpaper results in the same finish on partially baked clay as 320 grit used on fully cured clay. Sand up to 600 grit, and before you finish the curing process, remove any sanding dust from crevices. Finish firing your work for the normal time and temperature. Baking will remove any sanding marks. A light sanding at 600 grit or above can be done after baking.

Removing Fingerprints

It's easy to sand away small flaws in your finished pieces with 320 or 400 grit sandpaper. Don't press too hard. You can restore the sheen of the sanded area by sanding it gently with a finer grit paper, then lightly buffing the piece all over. You can buff polymer clay without sanding first, but you will not obtain as great a shine.

Buffing Your Artwork

Buffing is a process that is done to give a piece a sleek sheen, or smooth, shiny surface. To get a good shine you must sand your work first. You can buff polymer clay without sanding it smooth first, but the shine you obtain will not be as high.

Buffing by Hand

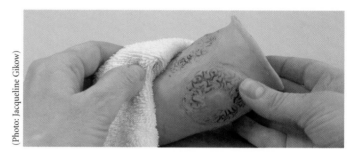

Buffing by hand will result in a soft sheen.

Buffing by hand will result in a soft sheen. Simply rub the piece for several minutes with a clean, soft cloth such as terrycloth, a T-shirt, or the pique knit used for polo shirts. A piece of worn denim from old blue jeans also works well. An alternative is to use fine steel wool made for wood finishing. Steel wool is available up to 0000 grit. Lightly rub the smooth, sanded clay with the steel wool, and then use a cloth, briefly, as above, to bring up a subtle shine.

Using a Buffing Wheel

To begin, bolt your bench grinder to a stable surface. Put an open box behind the wheel to catch buffing residue. Tie your hair back and remove any loose dangling jewelry. Tuck in your clothes. Wear protective eye gear. A buffing wheel can snatch things out of your hands and fling them away at a high speed.

Using a bench grinder can be dangerous. Follow the safety instructions for the machine carefully. Keep the clay moving and hold it lightly against the wheel. You can gouge the clay if you use too much pressure. Use a clean, dry, unstitched flannel or muslin wheel, with no

A buffing wheel can produce a high shine, but you have to be careful using the machinery.

buffing compound. If you drop something, turn the machine off, and wait till the wheel stops completely before bending over to pick it up.

Use your wheel at medium speed (bench grinders without variable speed are too fast for polymer clay). The buffing wheel rotates counter clockwise. Grip the piece firmly with both hands, and place it lightly against the lower front quadrant of the wheel. Use a gentle circular motion, keeping the piece moving, making sure the entire surface is buffed evenly. If you press too hard into the wheel, it may cut grooves into the clay and friction heat can begin to melt the surface.

Glazing

"Carousel Bowl." This bowl was formed in an asymmetrical bowl. A multicolored striped cane was cut into thin slices and used as the interior decoration, further offsetting the non-symmetrical nature of the form. The bowl was glazed with a soft urethane finish. 8" x 3 1/2". By Jacqueline Gikow.

If you are dissatisfied with the natural finish either sanding alone or sanding and buffing produce, there are several finishes you can apply to the clay that will produce a harder shine and take considerably less time than sanding or buffing. Avoid water-based glazes because they have a tendency to peel over time.

Future floor polish can be used as a glaze because it is actually an acrylic coating. It is very thin, however, and to get the best shine you should sand and buff your pieces before using it. I don't like Future as a finish because it's too glossy and doesn't result in a hard enough finish. It also tends to yellow after a while. Another product that works for glazing is a urethane finish. Urethane, a lacquer available in hardware stores, doesn't react chemically with polymer clay. A piece with urethane on it can be re-fired to attain a stronger glaze. Flecto Varathane Elite Diamond Finish (satin-matte, semi-gloss, and gloss) is a urethane finish recommended by many polymer artists, who report that Flecto will bend and flex, without peeling—an important consideration if you're using the clay in thin, flexible sheets. Both Polyform and Fimo make gloss and matte brush-on finishes that dry in about an hour.

Use care when selecting glazing products. Many lacquers, including most nail polishes, will react with the clay over time, causing it to turn sticky. Some glazes, especially spray-ons, never dry properly when used on polymer clay. Acrylic matte or gloss mediums are water-based and should be avoided as well because they, too, will leave the clay surface tacky. Once this has happened to a piece, not much can be done to salvage it. You can try placing the piece in a low oven (200°-250° F) for an hour or so, and this sometimes sets a gummy glaze.

Gradient Blended Clay Instructions

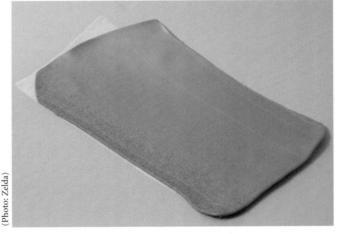

Use your blend for whatever project you are working on. You can use it for anything from slab pots to beads, and everything in-between.

This technique, which I didn't invent but use a lot, produces smooth transitions between two or more clay colors. Imagine the setting sun, deep blue above flaming red at the horizon, and the purples of dusk in between. It's possible to replicate these kinds of color blends in one sheet of polymer clay from two clay colors. You can blend as many colors as you like, even a rainbow.

1. Select two colors of clay. Be aware of the colors you use, however. Even if you love purple and yellow, a blend will give you a muddy gray in the middle.

Polymer Clay: Creating Functional and Decorative Objects

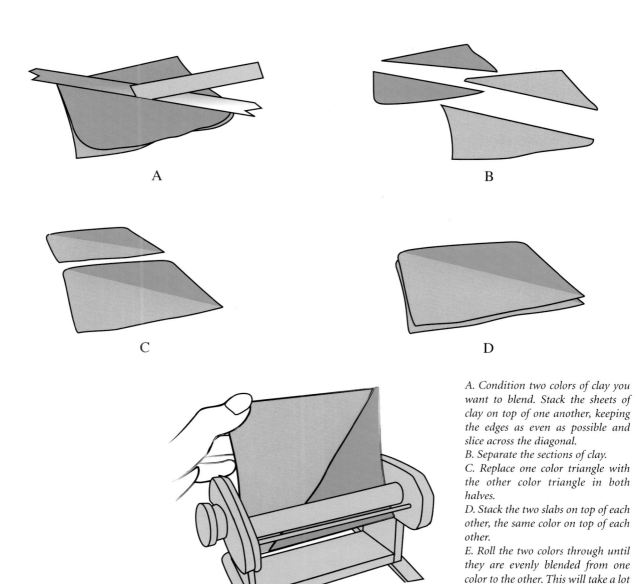

A

B

C

D

E

A. Condition two colors of clay you want to blend. Stack the sheets of clay on top of one another, keeping the edges as even as possible and slice across the diagonal.

B. Separate the sections of clay.

C. Replace one color triangle with the other color triangle in both halves.

D. Stack the two slabs on top of each other, the same color on top of each other.

E. Roll the two colors through until they are evenly blended from one color to the other. This will take a lot of passes through the pasta machine, so be patient.

2. Condition and roll out the clay at the largest setting of your pasta machine. Lay one sheet on top of the other and trim to make a rectangle.

3. Cut through the rectangle at an angle as indicated. The reason for this configuration is that if you cut the diagonal from corner to corner, the blend will go from edge to edge, leaving no pure color.

4. Separate the two sheets and re-assemble, diagonal edge to diagonal edge. At this point, the rectangle will have two solid color edges and two edges composed of both colors.

5. Roll the blend through your pasta machine. I recommend using the slow speed on the pasta machine for the first few times so you get a feel for keeping the slab even.

6. Fold again, matching up two-color edge to two-color edge and roll through.

7. Repeat until you have a perfect blend of the two colors with no streaks.

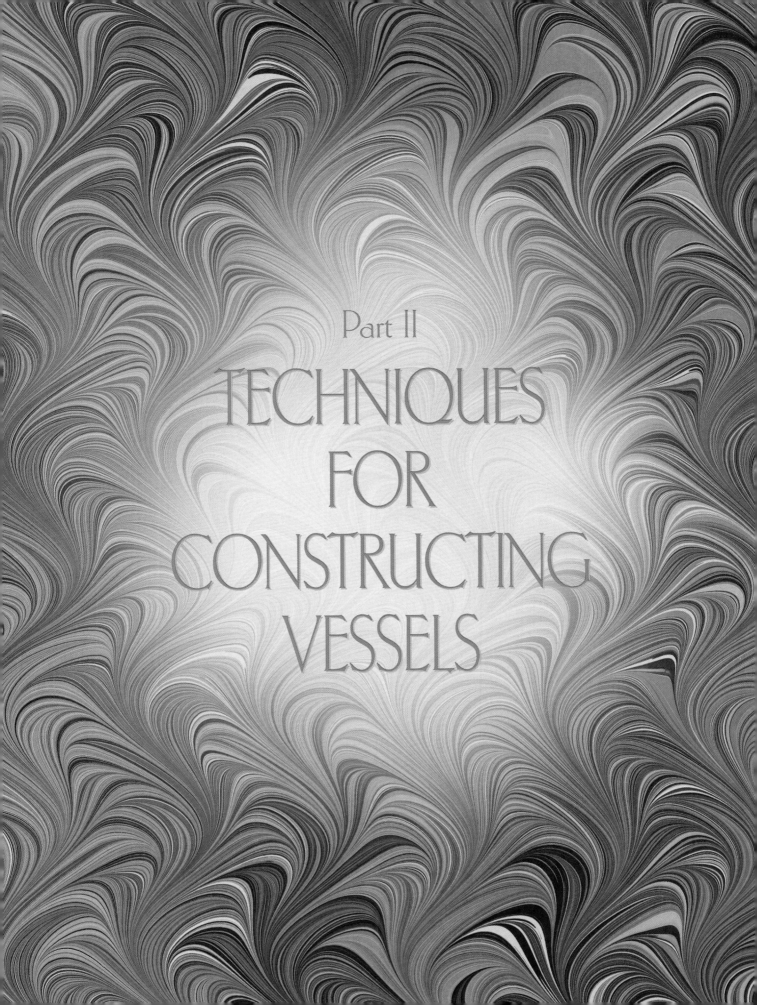

Part II

TECHNIQUES FOR CONSTRUCTING VESSELS

Chapter 4

Free-form Vessels

Two techniques in this chapter, pinch pots and coiling, are ancient methods for making vessels from clay. Making pots these ways doesn't require anything but your hands and clay, which can be very satisfying in this hands-off, technological world of ours. Weaving polymer clay, a technique derived from basketry and textile crafts, also produces unique results.

pinched together, the coils may be flat rather than round, and the base may be molded or slab-like.

Pinched Vessels

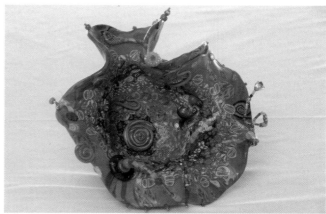

(Photo: D'Mont Reese)

"Party Bowl." *This vessel started out as a waste clay pinch pot and took on a life of its own. After creating and baking the free-form vessel framework, Lori overlaid it with marbled clay and cane slices. Larger slabs of clay were collaged onto the bowl as well. The piece was then baked again and wet sanded. Finishing touches include beaded wire, more glass and polymer beads and small, baked polymer shapes. The bowl was finished with Sculpey gloss medium. The piece was created with Sculpey III. 4" x 6-1/2" wide. By Lori Glessner.*

(Photo: Tracy Van Buskirk)

"Grapes and Leaves." *This mural, by Tracy Van Buskirk, was made for a kitchen wall area. Tracy sculpted the grapevine design in Premo clay and applied Pearl-Ex powders as highlights. The work was created directly on the tiles before installation, cut carefully at each tile edge, and baked. When cool, the clay was glued to the tiles with E6000 and finished with Flecto Varathane for protection. The tiles were professionally installed. 12" x 32".*

A malleable, soft material such as polymer clay generates two immediate reactions. One is to grab a lump and pat, squeeze, and pull it to model a form like a bird, head or figure. The other is to roll it into a ball and stick a hole into it, pinching it or mushing it around—to make a crude pot. These methods are the direct skills used in hand-forming pots from one piece of clay.

Coiling, the process of adding clay to a vessel in stages, lets you control the speed and intricacy of building a form. While pinching a vessel is an easily definable process, coiling is harder to contain because it may include other methods in construction. The clay may be

Of all hand forming pottery techniques, making pinch pots is usually one of the least favorite of potters. Suggestions to make pinch pots remind people of the third grade, and usually bring about loud groans. On the other hand, there is no better way to see and experience the texture of clay, or to feel all its characteristics. I started to pinch clay pots as more than a beginner's exercise after reading Paulus Berensohn's book, *Finding One's Way with Clay*. He discusses how pinching pots can connect you to what you do and feel, as well as help you find your artist's voice. I've discovered many structural forms

"Shmoo Pinch Bottles." These tiny pinch pots were inspired by the Li'l Abner comic strip in the 1950s. The Shmoos were bulbous shaped things with bottle-neck-like heads. Unlike the Shmoos, these pots don't satisfy all the world's wants, but their amusing shapes are meant to bring happiness to those who view them. Decorative effects were achieved by using different colored clay in the clay ball and then adding colored powders over the black clay. About 1-1/2" to 2". By Jacqueline Gikow.

and decorative finishes unique to pinch pot structures by experimenting repetitively. I also found this repetitiveness both deepened and expanded my skills and helped me find my artistic voice.

The same potential for creativity can be found by making pinch pots using polymer clay. Polymer clay isn't earth clay, and it has unique characteristics that call for a different working method. For one thing, polymer clay doesn't have the same structural strength as ceramic clay, and cannot be shaped quickly into unique forms. However, as my understanding of polymer clay increased, I began seeing that if I was patient and worked more loosely, I could make strong statements with my work. Polymer clay is a lot of fun to play with. Don't be too demanding with it, simply experiment and let it happen. If you don't like the shape of your pinch pot or the walls get too thin and collapse, fold up the clay and start over again. With a little practice you will gain more and more control over the process.

Shaping Pinch Pots

Left to right: the steps of forming a pinch pot from the original ball to the final vessel. The finished vessel has a foot that was pinched separately. The foot, also pinched, was attached and joined in a second firing, creating a goblet.

Although it's easy to make a lumpy pinch pot, with a little practice you can create some beautiful and interesting forms that are almost impossible to make with any other process.

Small free-form vessels. Left to right: amphora in a wire stand, flat flask with handles, and tiny ancient mosaic vessel. Sizes: from 1" to 2". By Rhea Scheafer.

1. Forming the Floor and Walls

Left to right: The starting ball of clay, opened ball with floor and walls formed, opened vessel cut in half to see profile.

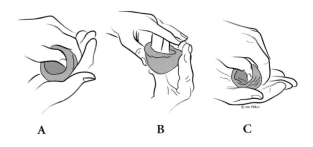

A   **B**   **C**

A. Start with a ball of clay and pinch outward with your thumb while rotating the clay in your hand.
B. As you form the pot, support it with your other hand or fingers.
C. Guide the shape of your vessel from the base upwards.

Use your thumb on the inside of the pot and the two middle fingers of the same hand on the outside of the pot to slowly spread the bottom wider. Press/pinch with your thumb, and then rotate the clay about 1/4" with your free hand. Repeat this all the way around, at least once, using the same pressure and the same degree of rotation for each pinch you make. After spreading the bottom, move up the wall and repeat this technique of press pinching until you get to the rim.

Leave a little extra clay at the rim. This will provide strength once you begin shaping the piece.

If you want your vessel to be symmetrical, you have to repeat the same technique all the way around the ball of clay. The idea is to make small changes, repetitively.

To check for symmetry, it helps to hold the bottle against a plain background and look for any uneven bulges, side to side. Additionally, set it upside down on the plain background and see if it "lists" to one side, or if the bottom isn't centered on the body. It's not too late to change the shape until you've baked it.

2. Working the Inside

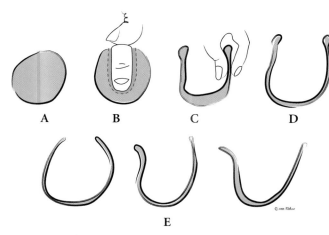

A. Start with a flatter ball.
B. Keep your thumb flat.
C. Stoke out using strong pressure with the thumb.
D. Pinch and press the bottom out.
E. Three possible shapes.

The front of your thumb is an excellent tool for hand forming vessels. If you bend your thumb as far back as it can go, it resembles the curved wood, metal or rubber ribs that some potters use for shaping bowl forms on the wheel.

Place your bent thumb as near to the center of the bottom of the pot as you can reach. Use the two middle fingers of one hand to support the form and your other hand to rotate the pot slowly, stretching the clay to the rim. Slowly spiral your thumb from the inside, to round out the inside. This evens out the walls and thins them slightly. This is an especially important step for pots with a bowled-out feeling.

If the clay becomes too soft, let the pot sit or place it in the refrigerator before going on to steps 3 and 4. Always place a small piece of paper between the pot and the table or turntable work surface, so the pot doesn't stick. A small piece of paper, or cardboard paper toweling lets you rotate the pot freely with a slight movement of your fingers.

3. Reinforcing the Rim

The rim of your vessel can become too thin to be attractive when finished. Even if it doesn't, it's still helpful to reinforce the rim. Press down and smooth the top of the rim after each pull up of the clay, while supporting both sides with your other hand.

4. Shaping Your Vessel

(Photo: Zelda)

Left to right: pinch pot with bowed walls, straight-sided pinch pot, pinched vessel with flared sides. All vessels started with 4 ounces of clay.

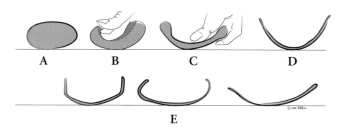

A. Hold a roughly spherical, small ball of clay in your palm.
B. Thumb starts flat and ends straight.
C. Stoke up with even pressure.
D. Reinforced rim + bottom pinched and pressed out.
E. Three possible shapes.

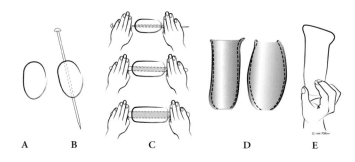

A. Start with an oval ball.
B. Insert needle or dowel.
C. Roll to make hole wider.
D. Pinch to shape (two possible shapes).
E. Pinch the bottom closed (or use a clay disk).

As you've seen, the procedure for shaping lifted pinch pots and open ones is similar except for direction. For a lifted pot, your thumb movement is out and up; for open pots your thumb movement is out only.

For a cylindrical pot, the shaping movement is primarily up. No matter which you are aiming at, start in the center of the pot's base, or as far down as you are able to reach. Press and stretch the pot wall smoothly with your thumb against your outside fingers.

Tip: When working with water-based clay you can reduce the friction of the clay against your hands by wetting your hands with water. I discovered a similar solution if your polymer clay is a bit stiff or resists easy shaping. If you apply a thin coating of petroleum jelly to the inside of the pot, the clay won't resist the thumb's pressure, making bowing out or pulling up easier. Adding the lubricant results in a smoother clay surface. Additionally, the petroleum jelly works its way into the clay and leaves no greasy residue.

As you shape the pot, you can bow out the form so it becomes wider at the middle than at the bottom or at the rim. If you want the form to be open or straight at the rim, press and rotate with your thumb on the outside of the pot.

The amount you can open the top of your vessel will depend on how much clay there is at the rim. If the rim is thin, pinching the walls to an even thickness will result in a shape that closes in. For a straight-sided wall, you need enough extra clay at the rim so it can be pinched out to make a straight profile. For a form that opens out at the top, even more clay must be left at the rim, so the form will flare out.

5. Finishing up

If you want to thin the walls further, repeat step 1 and/or step 4, or use any pinching technique that feels comfortable, as long as you repeat it all the way around the pot to maintain the symmetry and keep the walls even.

There is no special virtue in extremely thin-walled pinch pots; a better goal is to learn to make even walls. As a learning exercise, however, try pinching the clay as thin as you can; to 1/8" thick wall, 1/16", 1/32" and even paper-thin. How far can you push before the clay disappears? If you can pinch a form thinly and evenly, then you have control and can stop, by choice, at any thickness that feels right for the forms you pinch in the future. The great thing about polymer clay is you can't ruin the material! If your pot falls apart, just recondition it and start again!

Coloring Pinch Pots

The colors available for polymer clay make it easy to move intuitively into integrating color as part of the form. Although there are many ways of coloring pinch pots, one of the ways I often use is to wedge colored clays together to make multicolored pinch pots. The process for this includes conditioning two or three col-

Left: Example of colored clay ready to be joined.
Right: Restraint is needed or you will end up with a marbled look. If you cut the ball in half you'll see how the clay is mixing.

(Photo: Zelda)

ored clays and joining them together in a manner that will result in different patterns when the pot is completed. The quantities of clay and the way you place the clays together before you start to pinch determine what the result will be.

You can place three balls (or rectangles, for that matter) of clay next to each other, or you can push a hole in one ball and insert a smaller ball into the indentation. You can also start with a ball of clay wrapped in a slab of a second color and then a third or even fourth. The variations are endless.

(Photo: Zelda)

A lifted bowl and a bottle were made with the clay joined as shown in photo above. 3" x 2-3/4".

This process yields better results the more you practice. You don't even have to discard the clay if the design doesn't work out. Simply blend it together, add one or two new contrasting colors, and start again.

Another approach involves onlaying shapes to the ball of clay to add color, texture, and design. These can be seen as symbols of your connection to the clay. Using color from the very beginning, pinch forming of a pot brings new liveliness and dimension to a polymer clay work.

(Photo: Jacqueline Gikow)

(Photo: Jacqueline Gikow)

Previous page: starting a pinch pot with onlay decoration. Above: the finished vessel.

Making Closed Forms

Closed pinch pots are a variation of the lifted pinch method. Most important is to leave enough clay at the rim to pull the top inward, and in the case of a necked form, enough to pull upward.

A Necked Vessel

Start a necked form the same way you make a lifted pinch bowl. Work from the inside of the bowl so your thumb will swell out the form. Leave a generous roll of extra clay at the rim. The amount of clay you have at the rim will determine how tall you can make the neck and/or how small you can make the pot opening. When you are satisfied with the pot's walls, place your thumb inside under the rim and stroke the clay inward with your two middle fingers of the same or other hand on the outside. Try to stroke in, not up. Because you have to keep your finger inside the pot while you work, it's next to impossible to completely close a pot this way unless there is enough extra clay left so you can pinch it closed from the outside. One other way is to work in a little disk of clay to cover the opening. That will allow you to punch a tiny hole and blow air into the sphere.

For the neck, pinch in the clay as far as you want it and then pinch up the remaining clay to form a collar. If you leave enough clay, it's possible to put a pencil in the pot's hole and squeeze the extra clay up the pencil (or dowel, or toothpick) to make a neck and rim at the top. You can leave the shaping aid in while baking, or remove the form before baking. In either case, use a mold release to help. These might include dusting it with talc, wrapping it with aluminum foil or paper, or spraying it with ArmorAll.

Experiment with your clay to see what happens if you alter your approach:

Change—
❖ The shape of the ball you start with
❖ The way you hold and move your thumb in opening
❖ The direction and pressure of your thumb and fingers in the initial pinching

And vary—
❖ The amount of clay you leave at the bottom of the ball of clay when opening
❖ The amount of clay you leave at the rim in the early steps of pinching out the pot

If you lack inspiration one day, here are some ideas:
❖ Pinch a plate
❖ Pinch a postcard or letter to a friend
❖ Pinch a napkin ring
❖ Pinch a box and lid
❖ Pinch a lunch box

"Snake." By Hen Scott. *This pinched bottle color comes from a mixture of Fimo granite and lavender. The snake is a stopper sculpted in a similar manner to the "Mouse" how-to project at the end of the chapter. 3-1/2".*

(Photo: Archie Miles)

Three pinched vessels with narrow necks. The length of the bottle's neck depends on how much clay you leave at the top of the pinched form. 3" to 4-1/2". Jacqueline Gikow.

A Balloon or Bubble Vessel

These balloon/bubble vessels started out as hollow closed shapes constructed from a single ball of clay or two pinched bowls. They were manipulated to change the original shape, embellished, or cut in two to make covered vessels.

A balloon or bubble form is a hollow, closed sphere. It can be made with a single ball of clay or from two pinched, lifted pots attached together. If you create a balloon form in two pieces, the pot walls should be even and the same circumference at the rim.

After pinching two bowls for a bubble vessel, join them with a coil of clay.

When you finish the two halves, let them sit or cool until the clay is not too soft. Join the two halves rim to rim. Add a coil of clay around the joint and work the excess clay into the walls above and below it. Because air is now trapped in this sphere, it is possible to alter the

shape by rocking or rolling the form on your table. Additionally, with polymer clay, unlike with pottery, you can fire a completely closed form.

If it doesn't feel like there is enough air trapped inside the closed form, firmly attach a small bead of clay at the top. Puncture the bead so a small hole forms and blow gently into the sphere. When form feels full, press your lips together to seal the hole in the bead (wash your lips when you have finished). Left: the bead attached to the vessel and a needle tool used to puncture it. Right: the inflated form with the bead closed.

If, when you put the two pots together, it doesn't feel like there is enough air trapped inside the sphere, firmly attach a small bead of clay at the top. Puncture the bead so a small hole forms and blow gently into the sphere. When the form feels full, press your lips together to seal the hole in the bead (wash your lips when you have finished). The air swells the inside of the sphere, and acts as a support for further work—the pot will not collapse. Don't press the sphere too hard, as you may burst the balloon.

You can use a printer's brayer on the form's surface, or use your fingers in a light, quick motion to smooth it. The more fingerprints you eliminate now, the fewer you'll have to deal with later—and ultimately less sanding.

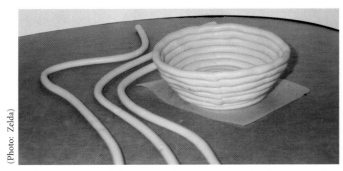

Roll out the coils of clay you need so you can work without stopping. Notice that the coils are cut to create a seam at each layer.

Coiled Vessels

Many of the most beautiful pots, from all parts of the world and from many historical periods, have been made by the coil method. Coiled vessels can be made either from a long, round rope or flat strips of clay and can be open or closed. Often, it isn't easy to identify

Polymer Clay: Creating Functional and Decorative Objects

whether coiling, pinching, or slabs form a pot. The more careful and skillful you are with this technique, the more difficult it will be to identify the process, unless you desire it. Whether you smooth the clay, texture or embellish it, there are a variety of ways to approach the coiled vessel as a blank canvas. Coiled vessels may include other methods of hand building, such as adding pinched bits, round coils, flattened strips, or little pellets of clay.

Forming the Base

Left to right: coiled base, hand-formed clay disk, disk of clay laid into a mold.

The base of a coiled vessel can be formed in different ways.

1. The base, of course, may be coiled. A snake of clay is coiled into a spiral, starting from the center and continuing until the desired diameter is achieved. Pressing the clay together and dragging your fingers across them to close any gaps bonds the coils.
2. The vessel may be started with a disk of clay formed from a ball and flattened between your palms or on a flat surface, or even rolled out with a rolling pin or pasta machine.
3. A flat sheet/disk of clay can be laid into a mold such as a deep or shallow bowl, a plaster mold, or a basket, depending on your desired shape. You can even create the entire coiled vessel in the mold, laying the coils of clay on top of the base and flattening them against the mold's walls. An alternative to this is to form the base on the mold outside and form the coiled pot upside down.

Adding to the Base

Sometimes a hand-built pot declares its construction method by its scale, shape, or texture. It may have a round bottom, a bulging profile, or mottled look. Often, however, it's not easy to identify construction from appearance.

Roll out clay coils and smooth them together until the pot is as tall as you want. As you build the sides of the vessel, adjust the length of your clay log to shape it. Polymer clay doesn't require scoring or the use of slip to ensure bonding between layers, but you should pinch each coil ring together slightly to obtain full contact.

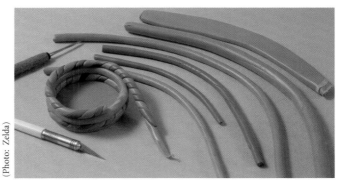

As you build the sides of the vessel, adjust the length of your clay log to shape it. You can leave the coils as they are, pinch them together to produce a texture, or press them together and smooth them.

The coils of clay used to create this bottle combine form and decoration. After baking, blue interference acrylic paint was added to the black clay surface, while the green base was "antiqued" with brown acrylic paint that is wiped off before drying completely. 3-1/2" x 5-1/2".

Don't coil the coils continuously around in a circle. Instead, cut each layer to the length needed, attach and smooth the coil to the previous layer, before starting the next layer. If you spiral the coils, the vessel's top edge will end up uneven.

The higher the walls, the thicker the coils need to be to keep their shape. The larger the pot, the thicker the starting coils should be. If the pot gets flimsy, try these techniques:

Fill it with strips of wadded up sheeting or muslin to hold the shape. The filling can be left in while baking if you don't attach your pot bottom until the form has baked or if the top has a wide enough opening to pull them out.

Bake the lower section for about 15 minutes.

Use a heat gun to partially cure the lower part of the vessel to provide support.

Polymer clay doesn't require scoring or gluing to bond between layers, but do press the rows together to assure full contact; pinching the coils together can create interesting textures.

You can also use flat strips of clay to "coil" a vessel. Layered canes work well as strips. Try making a striped cane by layering clay slabs of contrasting colors and cutting them in strips vertically.

Weaving Polymer Pots

Unusual baskets and other woven forms can be constructed from coils or strips of polymer clay. The base can be coiled as above, woven like a piece of cloth, or a sheet of clay can be used.

A traditional woven vessel can be woven using fired coils or strips of clay for the "warp" (vertical supports).

(Photo: Zelda)

"Stoppered Bottle." *This bottle was built from slices of a striped cane, 1-1/4". The slices were coiled layer by layer to create the shape you see. I made the strips quite thin and when the bottle was 3" high, I cured it in the oven for 15 minutes. 3" x 6-1/2". Artist: Jacqueline Gikow*

(Photo: Steve Pack)

"Woven Cylinder Box." *The texture of this vessel, made by Cindy Pack, comes from weaving thin strips of clay, in a manner similar to textiles, to create a flexible fabric that is made into a cylinder.*

They will provide the support for weaving soft clay coils or strips into a basket. Using this method, coils of clay for the "weft" are rolled out by hand or extruded from a clay gun. You can weave the vessel with raw clay, or with baked Sculpey SuperFlex. Sculpey SuperFlex is a polymer clay that remains flexible after baking and has the strength to withstand the stress of the weaving action.

You can weave a polymer "cloth" in a manner similar to using fiber. Using a variety of styles, weave flexible surfaces in different textures that can be formed into cylindrical containers and draped baskets.

If your vessel walls are thin, periodically bake the partially completed piece for about 10 or 15 minutes. Partial baking will lend support when adding clay as you build the vessel taller. After baking, let the piece cool and continue coiling on the baked foundation. Take care to smooth the seam between the baked and unbaked clay. For maximum control, you may want to bake the pot every few layers. You can also use a heat gun to partially cure the clay as you work upward. When you've finished the vessel, bake it according to the clay manufacturer's instructions.

Wet-sand the vessel, starting with the coarsest paper (320 grit) and progressing to a fine (600 grit). To finish the vessel, polish it with fine steel wool, a soft cloth, or a buffing wheel.

(Photo: Steve Pack)

Cindy Pack, a polymer artist, demonstrates how you can weave unbaked polymer clay into a "cloth" in a manner similar to using fiber.

Polymer Clay: Creating Functional and Decorative Objects

PROJECT 1. JADE MOUSE BOTTLE

By Hen Scott
Beginner/Intermediate

Materials and Supplies

Fimo Clay:

    2 oz. translucent
    Pea-sized ball of green
    Pea-sized ball of turquoise
    Trace of violet
    Trace of orange
    Small piece of Black

Tissue blade
Short metal tube or dowel, approximately 3/8"
diameter and 1" long, covered with tin foil
Glue stick
Various needles for sculpting
Cornstarch

(Photo: Archie Miles)

Instructions

Making the Jade Mix

1. Mix the two pieces of green in with the translucent. The exact quantities are not important as there is considerable variation in the color of real jade, but the mixture should look much paler than the desired effect in the finished piece, as it will darken when baked.
2. Divide the mixture into thirds, adding a trace of violet to one of the thirds, and a trace of orange to another. Leave the remaining third as it is. The resulting three parts are all green, but with very slight variations among them.
3. Roll out a very thin sheet of the black, bake it in the oven, and then chop it very finely to form tiny black dots. (The reason for pre-baking the dots is to prevent them from smearing when the bottle shape is pulled up.)
4. Chop up (or grate) the three green balls into small chunks and mix them together, adding a sprinkling of the baked black dots to the mix.

Forming the Bottle

5. Use about 3/4 of the jade mix to make the bottle. Put the rest of the clay aside for the stopper. Form a shallow bowl shape from the larger pile of chopped pieces, but don't do any additional conditioning, as this would make the greens streaky. Create a pinch bottle from this mix, following the instructions for a closed pinch pot in the chapter.
6. Use the short metal tube to shape the neck of the bottle around. Slip the tube into the opening, pull the clay gently up around the tube, and seal it at the top in order to give the bottle enough rigidity for shaping. When you are happy with the shape, pierce the top. Bake for 15 minutes at 265° F.
7. While the bottle is still warm, slice around the tube to make the neck of the bottle. Remove the tube.

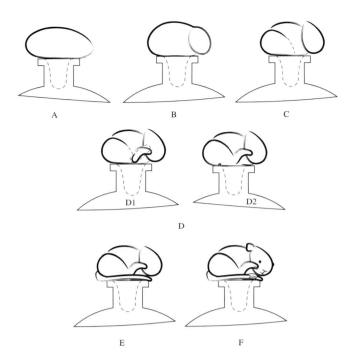

A. The starting stopper form, B. shaping the head, C. shaping the haunch,
D1. add the rear leg, D2. smooth out and detail the rear leg, E. add the tail,
F.
add the front foot, eyes, mouse, and nose.

8. Make a rim for the bottle by rolling out a snake of the jade mix, matching the thickness of the bottle, and long enough to form a ring that fits on top of it. Smooth the two ends of the ring together and press lightly into place; a touch of PVA glue will help it adhere.

9. Bake the bottle again and then sand and polish as desired.

Sculpting the Mouse Stopper

10. Form an egg shape, about 1/2" in diameter, and 3/4" long, from some of the remaining jade mix. Dust the bottle rim very lightly with cornstarch. Press the egg shape onto the rim (A). The bottle can now be used as a handle so you don't inadvertently squash the mouse in progress.

11. Squeeze the egg shape to slightly elongate the body of the mouse, then pinch one end to a blunt point to form the front of the mouse.

12. With the side of a blunt needle, indent slightly all around the front of the egg shape, approximately 1/4 of the body, from the pointed end to form the neck (B).

13. Twist the body away from you, as if the mouse is rolling over on to its far side, with the head bending slightly towards you.

14. With a needle, press a curved indentation on the near side to indicate the mouse's haunch (C). Continue the indent to the bottom of the body where it meets the bottle rim. This point should be approximately

half way between the neck and the rear end of the mouse.

15. Roll two 1/8" balls of different shades of jade clay together to form a 1/4" long mini-sausage. Mark the divisions between the toes in the same way as you did for the front paw. Slightly hollow out an area in front of the haunch line so the leg can be placed in position alongside the bottom of the body, flush with the haunch (D1). Smooth the leg to the haunch, making a little indent to suggest a joint. If space is short, the back leg can be lifted slightly as if scratching the ear (D2). The good news is that you don't need to do any legs on the other side as they are hidden under the body!

16. Roll out a 3/16" diameter ball of jade clay into a tapered sausage to use as the mouse's tail. Smooth the fatter end onto the mouse's rear end, and curve the tail around the near side of its body, finishing under the head (E).

17. Roll a 1/8" ball of jade clay for the front leg, stretch and flatten it slightly onto the tip of your index finger. Mark 4 divisions for the toes. Raise the mouse head enough to position the leg with the paw pointing forwards. Push down on the mouse body gently to help connect the paw. Curve it over the tail (F).

18. Use a blunt needle to make two eye sockets, and a sharper one to make a Y-shaped nose with a little mouth below. Roll tiny dots of black between your fingers for the eyes, bake, and place in the eye sockets.

19. Finally, for the ears, make two 1/16" diameter balls of jade clay and flatten them to make 2 thin disks. Press your knife blade against one side of each to make a small flat area. Pick up the disk and fold the flattened edge in half to form the ear. Attach it to the side of the head, using a needle to join and smooth it, shaping the ear as you do so. Repeat with the other ear.

Finishing

20. Carefully loosen the mouse from the bottle. Use either your finger and thumb on either side of the mouse's back, and if necessary, loosen underneath with a blade. Reapply cornstarch to the bottom of the stopper where it comes into contact with the bottle to prevent it sticking during baking. Replace the stopper loosely so as not to form an airtight seal.

21. Bake the whole piece again for 20 minutes. Clean up the underside of the mouse that you did not have access to before, especially around the front leg. Apply cornstarch as before and bake the whole piece again, without pushing the stopper down.

22. After baking give a final sanding and buffing and the piece is complete.

Polymer Clay: Creating Functional and Decorative Objects

PROJECT 2. BIRD HEAD FINGER PUPPET

Beginner/Intermediate
By Carol Zilliacus

The finished dimensions of each finger puppet depend on the size of your fingers, or those of the recipient. The outer dimensions of the puppet's head will average about 2" high and 1-1/2" in diameter.

Materials and Supplies

Fimo Soft
      Main color
      Small amounts in various colors
Kemper Lace Tool
PVA glue
Small circle cutter
3" x 4" piece of cloth for costume

(Photo: Nathan Watkins)

The Puppet Head

1. Condition the clay by running it through the pasta machine on the thickest setting at least 10 times. Roll a ball of clay about 1-1/2" in diameter and push a medium thickness, double-pointed, metal knitting needle through the center. Place the clay ball on your work surface and push the knitting needle through the clay so it sticks out on either end. Set the ball with the knitting needle parallel to the work surface.

2. Position the clay and knitting needle with one hand holding one end of the knitting needle toward the table. Gently roll the clay ball with the other hand; the opening of the ball will enlarge at the top, leaving the bottom edge opening small. Roll this way until the ball becomes conical and the hole is stretched large enough for your thumb to fit into it. Remove the needle.

3. Place the ball on your left thumb, if you are right handed, and on your right thumb if you are left handed. Keep the ball of clay on your thumb and press the top of your thumb on the work surface so the top of the cone is flattened. Take the clay off your thumb and round off the flattened end.

The Beak

4. Cut a small rectangle of clay for the bird's beak and flatten one end. Pull out a little clay at each side of the flattened end of the rectangle to make the flange where the beak is attached to the head of the bird. Shape the other end into a triangle shape. This will become the rest of the beak. Use a needle tool to draw a line indicating the upper and lower parts of the beak. Attach the beak near the top of the bird's head, then roll the needle on each of the flanges; this will attach the beak securely.

5. If you want your bird to have an open beak, slice the beak almost in half and carefully open the two layers. Be very careful not to cut it completely in half.

The Feathers

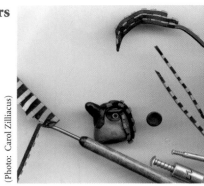

(Photo: Carol Zilliacus)

Cut strips of various colors of clay to make feathers.

6. Cut strips of various colors of clay to make feathers. Attach them at the top of the bird's head using a knitting needle to press the clay down. Carefully roll the needle over the entire length of the feather. Repeat, covering the entire head. A Kemper Lace Tool, or needle tool, can be used to draw texture lines.

The Bird's Crest

(Photo: Carol Zilliacus)

Cut one feather longer than the other two.

7. Cut three strips of clay for the feather on top of the bird's head. Cut one feather longer than the other two. Look at the drawing; see that the feathers are all joined. The top section of the feather is longer in the front. This is used to attach all of the feathers just above the beak. The bottom feather has a longer section at the end. This is used to attach all of the feathers to the back and underside of the bird's head. The middle feather is the part of the crest that relies on the other two to attach itself to the bird's head. Make different crests; look at the other finger puppet and notice its crest.

Eyes and Eyelids

(Photo: Carol Zilliacus)

The completed puppet head is ready to be cured in the oven.

8. Use a small circle cutter and a contrasting color to make the bird's eyes; attach them with your fingers. Roll small clay balls for the iris and pupils of the bird's eyes; and attach them with the Kemper Lace Tool. Cut another small circle in half for the bird's eyelids, attaching them by rolling the straight edge with a knitting needle. Then carefully bend the rest of the half circle over like an eyelid. Draw a line on them, keeping one of your fingers under it for support.

Finishing

9. Place your finger puppet bird head standing upright in the oven and cure for 30 minutes at 250° F to 265° F.

Bird Head Finger Puppet's Costume

10. Cut a plain piece of cloth, or an interesting pattern, about 3" long by 4" wide. Sew, iron, or glue the side seam together. Hem the bottom and finish the top by folding about 1/2" of the top edge inward with a running stitch. Pull the running stitch thread, evenly gathering the fabric so it fits around the bottom of the bird's head. Use PVA glue to attach the costume to the Bird Head Finger Puppet. Let the glue dry overnight before using.

PROJECT 3. WOVEN CONTAINER WITH LID

By Cindy Pack
Intermediate

Materials and Supplies

Fimo Polymer Clay
    3 oz. ecru
    2 oz. white
    3 oz. transparent
Pasta machine or roller
Kato NuBlade or sharp knife
Metal ruler
2" circle cutter
Round nose jewelry pliers
Cornstarch
Decorator chalks or powders, including gold
Fimo Gold Pulver powder
20-gauge craft wire
Black acrylic paint
Fancy yarns
1 charm

(Photo: Steve Pack)

Instructions

1. Condition the clay, roll each color into a log and twist all three together, stretching and folding several times until you have a pleasing pattern. Form a rectangular block, 4-1/2" long.

2. Slice 1/4" (6 mm) thick slices from the rectangular block and roll them through the pasta machine lengthwise until you get to the #5 setting (1/32" or .75 mm). Cut strips from the resulting sheet 1/4" wide and 5" to 6" long. Repeat these two steps until you have 30 strips, each 1/4". Lay 16 strips out vertically and begin weaving the rest through horizontally.

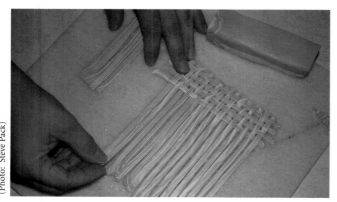

(Photo: Steve Pack)

Lay 16 strips out vertically; begin weaving the rest through horizontally.

3. Roll some of your leftover scraps through the pasta machine at the #3 setting (1/8" or 3 mm). Cut a 6" x 4" (10 x 15 cm) rectangle, lay the weave on top, and gently press together. Trim the edges so there is no overhang from the weave.

4. Decorate the woven finish with decorator chalks and gold powder. Stand the sheet upright so it is 4" tall. Butt the seams together and gently press until they stick together. Blend the joined edges to eliminate the seam. Roll out a rope, 1/2" (12 mm) in diameter and 5" (12.5 cm) long, and place it around the top inside edge, smoothing the seams.

5. Bake 35 minutes at 265° F. Let cool.

Completed cylinder with woven wall.

Wipe the pieces with a damp rag to remove any paint on the surface.

Bottom and Lid

6. Roll out a small clay sheet for the cylinder bottom, 1/8" (6 mm) thick, and cut a 2" (4.8 cm) circle. Press the cylinder onto the base firmly, taking care not to distort it. Roll out a rope of clay, 1/16" thick and 6" long, and lay it around the bottom of the cylinder.

7. To make the lid, roll a ball of scrap clay into a cone shape and cover it with a leftover woven layer of clay. Dust the pointed end and the cylinder rim with cornstarch. Insert the cone into the cylinder. Decorate the cone with chalks and gold powder. Cut a 3" length of wire and form a loop in the middle. Twist the ends and insert it into the cylinder lid.

8. Bake the assembled container for 35 minutes at 265° F. Let the piece cool. Carefully remove the lid while the cylinder is still warm but not hot.

Finishing

9. Brush black paint on both pieces and wait 3 to 5 minutes for it to dry. Wipe the pieces with a damp rag to remove any paint on the surface and add additional gold powder if needed. Let the covered container dry completely and tie fancy yarns and a charm to the wire to finish.

Chapter 5

Covering Existing Containers

Polymer clay, as you will soon discover, adheres to all kinds of objects made from materials such as glass, metal, wood, and plastic. It's easy to become captivated by the ease with which existing objects can become transformed by applying decorative surfaces of clay. Because the unbaked clay loves to stick to these materials, you may experience a sudden compulsion to cover everything in your home with it. Covering existing objects is a great way to become familiar with working with polymer clay, especially if the vessels you cover are attractive in the first place.

Here are some things you could start with: pens and pencils, glass objects, any size and kind of bottles, ceramic vessels, wood boxes, cardboard and papier-mâché containers, picture frames (except plastic), letter openers, drawer knobs, salt shakers, clocks, napkin rings and tableware, handles for your clay tools, finials for curtain rods and curtain pull-backs.

(Photo: Dorothy Greynolds)

Covering pens is a popular project for polymer clay artists. Artist Dorothy Greynolds *employs many decorative techniques including color blends, canes, and pure color to create her covered retractable pens.*

(Photo: Ben Shum)

Many different cane patterns have been applied to this glass wine goblet, leaving the top portion clear so it can still be used to drink from. 4" x 6-1/2". Artist: Wanda Shum.

(Photo: Vicki L. Domansky)

"Votive Candle Holder." Translucent clay blend to green lets the candle's light shine through the glass votive. The "fronds" of clay cut from leftover blend lend a whimsical note to this piece. 3-1/2". By Vicki Domansky.

Guidelines for Preparing Clay to Cover Objects

While you are creating, watch that you don't trap air bubbles between the support surface and the clay. Problems occur after firing. Little bubbles expand in the heat of the oven and become big, ugly bubbles during firing. If you don't plan properly, the clay will crack and detach from the glass or ceramic.

(Photo: Lypowy Studio/Toms River, NJ)

"Black Lacquer" by Matt Hamblen. This mirror is framed with black polymer clay that has been embellished with gold leaf, additional layers with tattered or torn edges. PVS glue is brushed on the clay that will attach to the mirror, and then the mirror is affixed to the clay. 11-1/2" x 10-1/2".

The following planning steps help eliminate potential problems:
—Eliminate air bubbles
—Use clay that is flexible after firing
—Thorough baking.

You can paint a vessel with PVA glue, such as Gem-Tac, before covering it. PVA is a thick glue that acts as a buffer between the polymer clay that contracts and expands at a slightly different rate than the two surfaces that contract and expand at different rates. Let the glue dry or tack up a bit before adding clay.

Metal, glass, and rigid plastic expand and shrink more quickly than polymer clay, and rates of shrinkage during cooling may also be significantly different. Due to variations in shrinkage, the clay may crack in firing, but you can often avoid this by using a thin layer of clay. On the other hand, if your clay layer isn't thick enough, the expanding glass will stretch it too thin and may cause cracks anyway. The keyword in this situation is "experiment."

Porous materials, such as cardboard and papier-mâché, usually need reinforcement to add strength when being covered with clay. One method is to coat the box with Liquid Sculpey (LS) or Translucent Liquid Sculpey (TLS) and bake the coated box for five or ten minutes. Then add another very thin film of TLS while it's still warm from the oven, and let the object cool before covering it with the final layer of clay. If you don't reinforce

cardboard or papier-mâché with Liquid Sculpey, you should at least coat the box first with white PVA glue to size it before you begin to decorate.

Glues

(Photos: Blaire Davis)

Artists: Cynthia Tinapple, Blaire Davis. *Maple bowl with inlaid polymer decoration. Originally, the inlay was bonded with a layer of glue in the channel. More recently, Cynthia began using liquid polymer clay as the bond for inlaying her designs in Blaire's bowls. 14".*

Glues that work for bonding clay and various materials are detailed in Chapter 2. The key factors to consider when selecting glue for the particular covering technique you are doing are:
1. Whether the surface to be covered is porous or nonporous.
2. Whether you have to apply heat to the bond (does the piece need to be baked after the adhesive is applied?).
3. Whether you need glue only for positioning or for permanent glue/polymer clay bonding.

Although polymer clay sticks easily to most surfaces, if you just stick it on the surface of most materials, it will peel away after baking. Instead, use glue that works as a "contact adhesive." A contact bond is when you apply glue to each surface and let it dry before attaching the two together. Cyanoacrylate "super" glues aren't good for this kind of work. Instead, use a contact adhesive such as E6000 or Goop.

Covering Process for Vessels

Start to cover an object by inverting it with the bottom up. It's easier to press the clay firmly on to the surface to be covered when the vessel is in this position. Use a sheet of 1/16" (3 mm) thick clay, draping it over the form. Smooth the clay and cut the sheet where it folds or

Getting Good Results

As already mentioned, condition your clay properly. All clay brands need conditioning, if only to wedge out the air bubbles that are a part of the manufacturing process.

Fimo, and CFC/Premo are the better clays to use for covering objects. Sculpey III, which is soft and flexible while unbaked, is far too brittle when cured, and it will crack if you handle the object too much.

Bake your item long enough so the clay is completely fired. Materials such as glass and wood must be thoroughly heated before the clay begins to cure. This means the firing time will be longer than when working with polymer clay alone.

Sheets of clay used for covering an existing form must be uniform, and don't have to be thicker than 1/16" (3 mm). There is no support provided by the addition of polymer clay to an existing vessel. All you are doing is coating the vessel's surface with decoration.

Polymer Clay: Creating Functional and Decorative Objects

A. To completely cover an object, invert the vessel and press the clay firmly on to the surface to be covered. Smooth and cut the sheet of clay where it folds or buckles, and match the cut edges and make butt joints making sure the clay layer retains a uniform thickness. B. Once you cover the vessel halfway, flip the piece right side up and work toward the top. C. After the surface is covered, apply your decoration to the base clay sheet. I've added a twisted coil to the rim and mold-formed butterfly wings to the body. Glass vase from Synicate Sales, butterfly angel wing mold from Amaco. 4-1/2"

buckles. Match the cut edges and form butt joints making sure the clay layer retains a uniform thickness. Smooth the seams with your fingertips or a brayer until they are no longer visible. Eliminate any air bubbles by piercing them with a sharp needle and pressing the clay firmly back onto the surface. Once you cover the vessel halfway, flip the piece right side up and work toward the top. After the surface is covered, apply your decoration to the base clay sheet.

"Bud Vases." The bases for these hanging vases are heat-proof test tubes. A base layer of clay is applied and then surface decoration including draped coils, wavy slices, cane slices, etc. 7" x 1". By Bonnie Merchant.

Covering a spherical form can be challenging because it is easy to deform or twist sections that have already been covered. The reason for this is that the heat of your hands softens the clay and the softened areas can be accidentally moved around. To eliminate this, place the vessel on a piece of paper or index card, and rotate the paper rather than the form; you won't need to touch the vessel as much when you move and turn it.

Preparing Non-porous Materials for Covering

Non-porous objects, like glass, metal, or bakable plastics, are best covered with glue, if the shape of the object is straight-sided. These materials may not need to be coated with anything before applying the clay if they

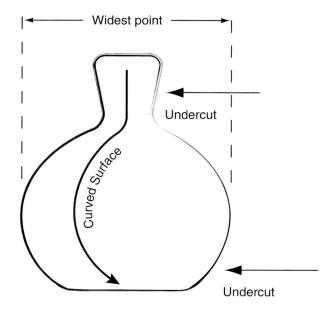

1. If you cover an object with a curved surface the undercuts may serve as mechanical bonds. With a mechanical bond there is less need to use glue to make the clay stick.
2. If you want to remove the clay after firing it on the round object you will have to cut it in half and reconnect it later.

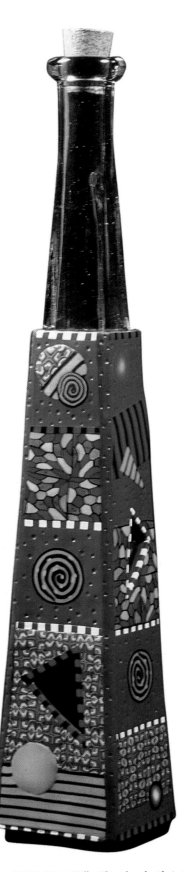

are curved in shape, like an urn, or a teapot. Although polymer clay does stick to smooth, nonporous surfaces before baking, the only bond that will be retained after curing is one that provides a "grip" to the vessel. The clay will continue to grip if there are "undercuts," such as these curves.

This "mechanical" connection between the clay and the base object secures the clay. It's possible to take advantage of the grip on a straight-sided vessel by extending the clay over the lip, trapping the vessel inside. With objects such as vases and round forms, there is less of a problem because the intrinsic shape of these objects often ensures a mechanical bond without reinforcement, such as glue.

PVC and other Pipe

Artists have reported mixed results in using PVC as a base for a clay vessel, although pipes with thicker walls are sturdier. If large, unsupported PVC supports slump when fired with polymer clay, supports can be easily made. If necessary, stuff wet newspaper inside the pipe to keep the pipe walls straight. Because PVC is so similar in chemical make up to polymer clay the two materials bond well.

Switch Plates (Plastic or Metal)

Linda Greer *created these simple, but elegant, switch plates covered with polymer clay, which is then carved and baked. After baking, the carved lines are filled with contrasting clay and the plates are re-baked.*

Switch plates are popular objects to make with polymer clay because they are quick and easy and the results are usually successful, even for beginners. Switch plates are made from many nonporous materials: ceramic, metal (unfinished or vinyl-coated) plastic, and nylon. Use UL-approved plate covers and test them before using them as support forms to make sure the material doesn't melt and the clay is compatible. Cover both front and back to make a finished edge, using a thinner layer of clay on the back. Put the clay-covered plate into a cold oven and bring the temperature to 200° F for 10 minutes before raising the temperature to 265° F for the rest of the time needed. After cooling, if the polymer clay layer doesn't feel secure, carefully remove it and create a contact bond with an adhesive such as E6000, then press the pieces

"Decanter #9." By Krista Wells. *This glass bottle is partially covered with various canes and patterns. The trapezoidal shape traps the clay on the glass, preventing it from slipping off. 2" x 2" x 12".*

Polymer Clay: Creating Functional and Decorative Objects

together again.

You can also use the base switch plate form as a support and remove it after baking. When you plan to do this, make sure the thickness of the finished polymer clay plate will accommodate the screws that affix it to the wall, and that the switch sticks out sufficiently to be used.

Preparing Porous Materials
Wood

(Photo: Jacqueline Gikow)

Before you cover a wood object, it's a good idea to heat the wood for about 15 minutes at 250° F to dry it out completely. This will eliminate any moisture in the wood and prevent it from expanding when you bake the covered piece. Painting the wood with PVA glue, like Gem-Tac, after heating, and before adding clay, will stabilize the bond. You can also paint wood with acrylic paint before covering it.

A method for covering a wood object with straight sides is to make thin, flat panels of polymer clay, and then apply them to the unfinished wood surface in a similar manner to woodworking veneer. Thinly coat the wood surface and the back of the clay panel with wood glue, and clamp it to the wood until the glue has dried. Make the panels slightly larger than the sides of the object, and trim them to fit. Applying baked panels is an easy method of combining polymer clay and wood. The clay panels can be made ultra-flat, and in handling, you leave no finger marks.

When you veneer an object not made of clay, it may help to put the piece in a cold oven and bring it up to the correct temperature before you start timing. Then turn off the oven and let the piece cool inside. This slower heating and cooling will help avoid cracking problems (since the underlying object expands and contracts at a different rate from the clay).

Terra Cotta and Bisque Ware

Terra cotta flowerpots or ceramic bisque ware should also be heated for 10 to 15 minutes in a medium oven to remove all moisture, the same way as wood, before applying clay. Once dry it can be covered in a similar manner to wood. If you expect the pot to get wet from use, however, it's imperative to use a sealer on it, both inside and out. Since terra cotta and bisque are both extremely porous, any water exposure makes them expand and then shrink when dry. Because of this, any polymer clay applied to these materials will eventually crack due to the constant expansion and contraction.

(Photo: Zelda)

The embellishments on this terra cotta pot were attached with PVA glue and then cured in the oven. Terra cotta should be prepared like wood for use with polymer clay. By Jacqueline Gikow.

Baking Covered Vessels

Whether your underlying vessel is porous or not, it is important to bake a clay-covered object long enough. Glass, for example, must reach the full oven temperature before the clay can even start to cure. Curing polymer clay on covered vessels takes a significant amount of time. Any ceramic or glass item covered with clay should be left in the oven for at least an hour at full temperature. Polymer clay gets stronger the longer you bake it, and it can withstand up to two hours of fusing time as long as the correct temperature is maintained.

(Photo: Roger Schreiber)

"Spoke." *The foundation for this footed bottle made* by Grant Diffendaffer *is a glass bottle that is covered with millefiori canes made of Fimo clay. 9".*

Papier-mâché, wood, and cardboard contain chemicals that can let off fumes, causing bubbling, cracking, or lifting when baked. To prevent these problems, heat the box first and let it cool before adding the clay.

Moving Forward

(Photo: Jodi Jones)

"Bottles of Hope" *is a special outreach program, sponsored by the Southern Connecticut Polymer Clay Guild, to bring a little beauty and hope into the lives of cancer patients. Diane Gregoire, a Rhode Island artist and cancer survivor, during treatment for her disease started the program. Bottles of Hope have been distributed to patients at hospitals and treatment centers in six states. From left to right: Candle bottle,* Jody Bishel; *Rose topped bottle,* Marie Segal; *faux wood and metal bottle,* Tracy Van Buskirk; *black and white pattern with pink rose,* Lucille Schacht; *Black and beige basket bottle,* Cassie Doyon. *2" to 3".*

Left to right: empty Coca-Cola bottle, bottle covered with faux jade, and bottle covered with abstract leaves.

When you first cover existing forms, the result will probably be a decorative object recognizable as the original. Did you cover a metal candy tin? What does it look like? If it still looks like a metal candy tin, only now it has a decoration on it, you're on your way, but you're not letting all your creativity out. What can you do to enhance the object you are covering? There are other options for making covered vessels besides simply reproducing the bottle or vase with a decorative surface cover. Apply the creativity you have snoozing in the background, and you can transform the appearance of an existing item into an entirely new vessel, unrecognizable from the original.

See what is possible to make using a bottle of Coca-Cola. This bottle is an icon in the United States, and even in the world. As attractive as the faux jade now covering this bottle is, it's still recognizable as a Coke bottle. In the third example, I've covered the bottle with abstract leaves that are only loosely joined. The Coke bottle inside provides a waterproof container, and the result is a useable vase.

Releasing a Covered Object

Once you have covered everything you can think of with clay (except, perhaps, your car), you may find yourself thinking, "Do I really need to leave that form inside?" You may find yourself curious as to what would happen if you removed the clay from the support beneath. After all you have found out it's sometimes hard to make the polymer clay stick anyway.

Start experimenting with different objects, planning to fire and separate the clay from the item. Think about what accommodations you have to make in your design so the seams you'll cut will be easily rejoined without destroying your design. Don't use glass vessels that have texture to which the clay might bond. You could dust a thin layer of talcum powder on a glass or metal surface so the clay will not stick to it. Metal leaf also works as a release agent to remove the clay from the covered item. Look at Chapter 7, which examines how to use existing forms as molds and supports, rather than a permanent structure.

(Photo: Patricia Kimle)

"Keeping Jar." Patti Kimle *applied a layer of clay to a glass form and baked it. After baking she cut the clay layer off using an angle cut and glued it back together with slow-setting cyanoacrylate glue. 7".*

(Photo: Judy Kuskin)

This is a mixed media vessel. The polymer clay base is made over a paper mold, which was removed after baking. The clay surface employs a Skinner blend and a crackle medium was added after baking. 5" x 13-1/2". By Judy Kuskin.

PROJECTS
PROJECT 1. CANE APPLIQUE CLOCK

(Photo: Barbara McGuire)

By Barbara McGuire
Beginner Project

Materials and Supplies

Assortment of square canes, either handmade
    or purchased
PVA glue
Wood clock base with an inset battery-run
    clock
Tissue blade
400, 600, and 800 grit wet sandpaper (optional)
X-Acto knife with #11 Blade

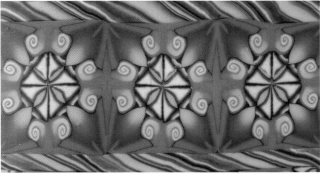

Instructions

1. Remove the clock and battery and coat the wood base with PVA glue. Allow the glue to dry. This makes a tacky surface for the clay to adhere to.

2. Cut a cane, or group of canes, into thin, even slices and apply them to the wood base, creating a pattern. You can work from the center outward or directionally from an edge. Position the canes lightly for placement, and when the clock is entirely covered, press them firmly into position.

3. Seams or gaps can be trimmed with a striped clay twist. Use a sharp blade to hollow out the hole where the clock will be inset.

4. Bake the clock base at 275° F for about 45 minutes. The wood must be completely heated before the clay will begin to cure.

5. Optional: When the clock is completely cool, you can wet sand it with 400, 600, and 800 grit wet sandpaper to even the cane seams and give the texture a smooth finish.

6. Set and insert the clock into the base.

PROJECT 2. JIGSAW PUZZLE HEART STOOL

Beginner/Intermediate

Fun with function! This little stool is comfortable for kids and for adults too–it's a great alternative to kneeling or sitting on the floor. In the center of the stool is a jigsaw puzzle that assembles and sets into the stool's center.

Materials and Supplies

Fimo polymer clay
> 10 oz. black
> 4 oz. silver
> 4 oz. indian red
> 2 oz. lemon yellow
> 4 oz. peppermint

Pasta machine or roller
Tissue blade
Wavy blade
Clay gun extruder
Needle tool
X-Acto knife
Tracing paper
Bamboo skewer or other thin, straight edge
Heart-shaped stool (available from Walnut Hollow)
PVA glue
Clay gun (optional)
Flecto Varathane Diamond Finish (optional)
Jeweler's saw (optional)

Preparation

1. Preheat the oven to 275° F and put the stool in to heat dry for 20 minutes. Let it cool and unscrew the legs from the seat.
2. Make one round and one square bullseye cane using red and black clay. Reduce the round cane to 1/2" in diameter. Keep the square cane larger as you will be using it in a variety of sizes. Reserve some of the red clay for the stool legs.
3. Make a gradient blend (refer to Chapter 3 for instructions) of the lemon yellow and peppermint clay. When the blend is smooth, roll it out to #3 on the pasta machine (1/16"). Set it aside.

The Stool Seat

4. Apply a layer of PVA to the stool seat. Let it get tacky, but not dry. Condition the black clay and roll it to #3 (1/16") and cover the seat with it. The clay should wrap around the bottom of the seat to create a mechanical bond. Make sure there are no air bubbles trapped between the clay and the wood.

5. Enlarge the template 200% and trace the inner heart line to the stool. Do this by piercing the line with your needle tool or a pin so you get a dotted line guide.
6. Extrude or roll a snake of clay about 1/8" in diameter and position it along the dotted line. Gently press it on the seat so it sticks but doesn't distort.
7. Bake the seat for about 15 minutes at 265° F.
8. Apply PVA glue to the black layer of clay on the outside of the clay coil. Roll out more black clay at #3 and layer it smoothly on the surface, again overlapping the bottom of the seat.
9. Roll the silver clay to #5 on the pasta machine and cut thin strips using the wavy blade. Spread some PVA glue down and apply the strips to the stool seat as shown in the color key.
10. Bake the seat for another 15 minutes.

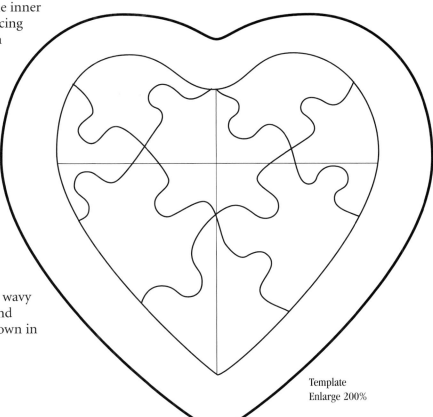

Template
Enlarge 200%

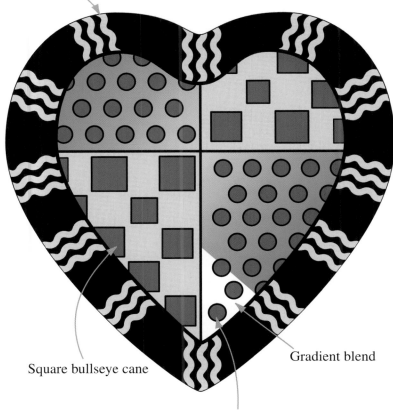

Cut with wavy blade

Square bullseye cane

Round bullseye cane

Gradient blend

Make the Jigsaw Puzzle Insert

11. Roll a sheet of black clay to #3 and cut it to the size of the inner heart shape on the template. Trace the four divisions from the enlarged template onto the clay.
12. Roll the rest of the silver clay to #3 on the pasta machine; cut it to the shapes shown on the template, and position on the black heart as indicated on the color key illustration.
13. Cut the color gradient clay to the shapes shown on the template, and position on the black heart as indicated on the color key illustration.
14. Indent the clay at the seams between the colors with the bamboo skewer. Roll or extrude a 1/32" coil of black clay and gently press it in the indentation.
15. Cut thin slices of the canes and arrange them as shown on the color key.
16. Carefully roll everything smooth, making sure not to distort the seams or trap any air bubbles. Trim neatly back to the correct size.
17. Incise the jigsaw lines onto this heart shape using a needle tool.

(Photo: Jacqueline Gikow)

Top: *finished seat ready for puzzle insert*
Lower left: *puzzle template with pattern*
Lower right: *graded clay placed on a sheet of black clay used as a backing layer.*

18. Bake at 265ºF for 15 minutes, Note: It's a good idea to bake this heart between two tiles to be sure it stays flat.

19. When the heart is cool, make sure it fits snugly inside the coil of clay on the stool, trimming as necessary. Then cut along the jigsaw shapes with a sharp knife or a jeweler's saw. Sand the edges of the puzzle pieces smooth.

The Stool Legs

20. Apply a layer of PVA to the each leg as you work on it. Cover the three legs with different colors of left-over clay: peppermint, red, and silver. Trim the clay back so the legs fit into the holes provided for them.

21. Insert the legs into the seat. Extrude or roll out 1/16" diameter, or less, coils of black clay and wrap them around each leg as illustrated in the finished example.

22. Bake the finished stool at 265° F for 45 minutes to an hour.

23. Leave as is or apply two light coats of Flecto Varathane Diamond Finish to protect the stool from handling. You can also glue the legs permanently into the seat using PVA wood glue.

(Photo: Jacqueline Gikow)

Intermediate

A wok is a large pan with a rounded bottom, used for stir-frying Asian foods. The cooking utensils for wok cooking are often made from bamboo. In this project I've added an additional Asian quality, using mokume gane, a metal pattern technique to cover the handles of the utensils. The silver mokume gane pattern is backed with deep blue clay, one of the traditional colors of Asian pottery decoration.

Materials and Supplies

Polyform polymer clay
    2 oz. ultramarine blue
    4 oz. translucent
Baking parchment
Roller or pasta machine
Cornstarch
Beacon Gem-Tac PVA glue
4 to 5 sheets of aluminum leaf
Soft paintbrush
Wide, soft paintbrush
Blunt tool handles
X-Acto knife
Tissue blade

Making Mokume Gane

This technique (pronounced Moe-koo-may Gah-nay) is an ancient metalworking technique developed in Japan by master swordsmiths. It's a technique that can be adapted to polymer clay with spectacular results. The name translates as "wood grain metal," which refers to one of the most popular patterns created with this technique.

The metal-forming technique involves soldering and stacking layers of different metals, rolling them thin, punching the surface and then slicing the dents off to reveal an effect that suggests metallic wood grain. The polymer clay version can include different colored clays, or a combination of colors, translucent clay, metal leaf, and paints.

Instructions

1. Roll out the translucent clay as thinly as possible. By hand, roll the clay between two sheets of baking parchment. With a pasta machine, dust both sides very lightly with cornstarch and sandwich the clay between 2 parchment sheets before running it through the rollers. Since translucent clay tends to be quite sticky, pay attention to the heat being generated by the pasta machine. If it seems to be making the clay too soft, put the clay in the refrigerator briefly.

2. Cut a square sheet of translucent, about 4" (10 cm) square and lay it on the parchment. Apply a sheet of aluminum leaf to the clay, carefully holding the leaf by the edges. Use a wide, soft paintbrush to brush down the leaf onto the clay surface and eliminate wrinkles and air pockets. Trim away any excess leaf around the edge to use in the next layer of leaf.

3. Cut the second sheet of translucent clay and press it onto the sheet of leaf. Roll the surface lightly to eliminate air bubbles but do not press too hard or the leaf will fracture. Continue building up alternating layers of thin clay sheet and leaf. Use scraps of leaf to fill in any spaces in the layers.

4. Build up five double layers, add a final layer of clay, and cut the block in half. Apply a sheet of leaf to the top of one half and stack the other on top so that you have about 11 layers of leaf in the sandwich.

5. Press dents into the block with various sized blunt tool ends, but don't press through the block of clay/leaf. Form small balls and ovals of translucent clay and press these into the dents so that they are filled with clay.

6. Turn the block over and press over it with your fingers, depressing the clay around the dents so you have a series of mounds on the clay surface.

7. Use your blade to shave off the top of the mounds and set these pieces aside for using as fillers later. Now take further horizontal slices, about 1/32" (1 mm) thick, from the raised areas. With each slice you will find that the leaf will be revealed in concentric but irregular rings, rather like wood grain or shot silk. These slices are used to decorate sheets of clay.

Covering the Wok Utensil Handles

8. Sand the wok utensils to remove any sharp corners and to create a slightly roughed-up surface on the handles.

9. Reserve a small piece of blue clay. Roll out the rest of the blue clay 1/16" (1.5 mm) thick and cut it in half, making sure each piece will cover one of the utensil handles. Cut slices from the mokume gane block and lay them on the blue sheet. Fill in any gaps with the smaller slices or translucent clay. Roll over the surface lightly to smooth it.

10. Apply a thin layer of PVA glue to the wood handles and let it tack up. Wrap each utensil handle with the layered clay, joining the edges cleanly and smoothly. Roll a thin coil of the plain blue clay and wrap it around the top of the handle to finish the edge.

11. Bake and let cool, sand, and buff the handles to a high shine to reveal the translucence.

Chapter 6

Boxes and Other Constructed Containers

(Photo: Bradley Miller)

"Universal Clock." Robyn Priestly *made this clock of overlapping circular slabs of colored clay that seem to float in front of the wall. The small circle with the moon on it is held on to the piece by the second hand—it really floats! The clock hangs from the built-in hanger on the clock insert housing. 6-3/4" square, center section about 4-3/4" diameter.*

Chapter 5 concentrated on making vessels by wrapping clay around a form that can be left in after baking. This chapter is about how to create successful, freestanding forms that don't need a permanent internal support. If you've ever looked through books about handmade slab pottery, you may have seen references to working with soft or stiff (leather hard) slabs. These distinctions are made because the suspension agent for clay is water. After wet clay is left exposed to the air for a while, it hardens, resulting in a firm slab that has more structure than a soft slab. This state is referred to as "leather hard."

Polymer clay, however, never gets leather hard. Since the composition of polymer clay includes a plastic compound as a suspension agent, it never dries out, although making thicker sheets of clay can help.

Rolling polymer clay out to the widest setting on the pasta machine results in the most even sheets. If you work with slabs larger than approximately 5", however, you'll need at least two layers, or 1/4" (12 mm), to avoid the warping that can occur during the firing process.

There are several ways to create boxes and other vessels from sheets of polymer clay. Slab working refers to a ceramic technique where clay is rolled flat, cut into the desired shapes, and then assembled into boxes, vases, or other objects. As a general definition, a sheet is uniformly thin and a slab is just a thick sheet. The term "slab" for making vessels is unattractive, seeming to imply that slab pots are either flat or undecorated. Of course, this is not true and slab-built pots can be exhilarating and lively. Some polymer clay artists refer to slabs as sheets, but the concept is the same. An infinite variety of shapes can be made with slabs.

(Photo: John Polak)

"Hairy." *This is a two-part container made from metallic Premo and Fimo clays. All the spines have silver foil tips. A temporary support was used during the first curing, and then removed for continued work. 4" x 6-1/2".* By Merrie Bucksbaum.

(Photo: Jeffrey Demain)

"Merlin Box." Arlene Summers *designed this exquisite box to showcase the handblown glass bead that is used as the knob.*

Sheets of clay can be joined in the raw state and then baked. As an alternative, you can cut clay sheets to the size and shape you want, bake them between two ceramic tiles or pieces of heat-treated glass (to keep them flat), and assemble them when cool. Depending on the effect you are looking for, your method would vary.

Start with a simple piece first with the goal of mastering construction of containers with straight-sided clay slabs using simple joins, such as cubes, cylinders, and ovals.

Rolling a Slab or Sheet

Forming sheets and slabs from conditioned clay can be done two ways. Anything that rolls, like an acrylic tube, a rolling pin (apply a sealer first because the clay will stick otherwise), or even a printing brayer will work. The other method is to use a pasta machine. For larger vessels, the pasta machine, which limits you to a 1/8" (6 mm) thickness is useful to make a smooth, even slab of clay that can be layered on top of one another to make thicker pieces.

If you are making slabs thicker than the 1/8" (6 mm) a pasta machine allows, or wider than a pasta machine can handle (usually about 5"), you can roll out the clay using guides on either side of your clay sheet. That will allow you to keep the clay even as you roll it out. Having

a variety of thicknesses on hand can be very helpful for simply making thicker sheets of clay or to even up layers.

Note: It's worth noting here that your pasta machine may not roll out perfect 1/8" or 1/16" sheets of clay. Because the pasta machine is made for making, well, pasta, it's not a precision machine for clay. You can hand-measure the slab thickness. On my Atlas machine, the thickest slab comes out a bit thinner than 1/8" and I compensate for that if needed.

Making Slabs Using Rolling Guides

Rolling guides are two sticks of any hard material that are used to keep a slab even while being rolled out to the correct thickness. Rolling guides can be made of a multitude of materials. The requirements are they must be a set (the same thickness) and they must be hard enough to withstand the pressure of your arms as you roll. Some possible materials include wood, rectangular brass tubing (found at art and hobby stores), and acrylic rods. Additionally, the hard cardboard backs of sketchpads can be made into versatile guides. Simply stack them to the height you need.

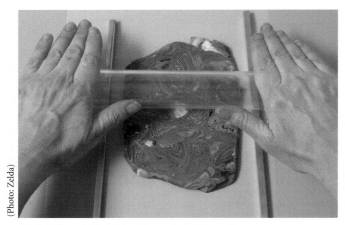

(Photo: Zelda)

Start in the middle, and roll towards the two ends.

To use the rolling guides, tape the two strips parallel to your workbench, close enough for the roller to span. Lay a sheet of waxed paper or tracing vellum down, a piece of clay flattened to near the desired thickness, and place it on the paper. Place your roller on the guides, in the center of the slab, and roll toward the two ends.

A quick way to roll out thin sheets of clay is with a smooth-sided, metal can (food or paint, for example). The seams on the ends will give you a thickness of a little less than 1/6" (3 mm), depending on the can seams, and you'll end up with a clay sheet width the height of the can.

Once you've rolled out your sheets and slabs of clay, you'll find a multitude of uses for them. A rolled out slab of clay gives you a flat surface, a marvelous vehicle for forming and decorating. Cutting shapes from a slab or sheet with a blade, shaped cutter, or fine needle tool can

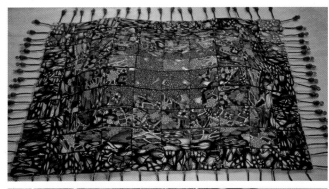

(Photo: Hertzel Yitzhak)

"Challah Cover." *The function of this piece is to cover traditional braided Sabbath bread. It is made from 100 panels of polished clay joined together with brass links. Its fringes are brass with glass and clay beads. 24" x 20". By Valerie Kanter.*

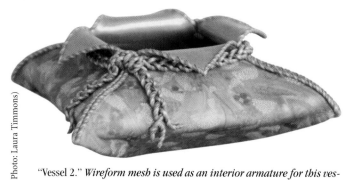

(Photo: Zelda)

A smooth-sided, metal can (food or paint, for example) can be used to roll thin slabs. You'll end up with a clay sheet width of however tall the can is.

make many shapes. Sheets of clay are pliant, and can be folded like leather into interesting sculptural forms, though unlike leather, sheets of polymer clay won't spring back to a flat sheet.

(Photo: Norman Watkins)

"Inro Bags." Carol Zilliacus works with slabs in combination with embellishment techniques to produce these small purses. These bags use two layers of different clay colors and the designs are developed either by cutting or carving through the first layer to reveal the second. Approximately 2".

Creating Boxes, Vases, and Other Objects from Clay Slabs

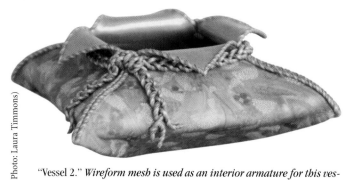

(Photo: Laura Timmons)

"Vessel 2." Wireform mesh is used as an interior armature for this vessel. The interior is gold metallic and was glazed. The exterior is a marbled pattern under layered canework. The ornamentation is layered polymer in blues, brown and gold, which is twisted and then braided. 3-1/2" x 7-1/2". By Laura Timmons.

Vessels that aren't shaped by other objects are challenging. The main goal is to make sure your construction doesn't collapse while it bakes, or before it has cooled. Two methods of working without any supports include using thicker slabs of clay or using WireForm between two slabs of 1/8" thick clay.

Supports for square boxes can be constructed from cardboard. Cylindrical vessels are easily kept round using two-ply Bristol board that has been bent into a round shape. With other shapes, you can gently stuff paper or pillow filling into areas that might sag. Keep the clay in these supportive structures until it has fully cooled. If the piece is complex or may collapse while you build it, construct and bake it in stages.

(Photo: Jacqueline Gikow)

"SeaBright #1." The walls of this box are constructed of multiple layers of clay. The pasta machine was a good choice to create the slabs because each layer is a different color. No supports were used in construction or baking. The legs are brass rods and the beads are wood. 4-1/2" x 9". By Jacqueline Gikow.

Your first attempt to build a square or rectangular form will introduce you to the problems involved in working with flat sheets of clay. Rolling the clay out on a sheet of vellum or parchment paper is the best way to begin. The clay will stick, but can be pulled off easily. The advantage of rolling out your clay on a piece of paper is that you will be able to move the clay sheets easily and without damage.

Whether you are making a rectangular, triangular, or cylindrical box, the requirements include a base and the sides. Aim for a uniform thickness when you roll out a sheet of clay. If you are making more than a 3" or 4" box, you will need at least a 1/4" (12 mm) thickness. After forming the sheets you need, set them aside for about 10 minutes to stiffen slightly before cutting the box sides.

Joining Slabs

Cut the ends of the slab perpendicular to the work surface.

After rolling out a slab, the next step is to cut it to size. It's important to hold the blade vertically when you cut so the slab's edges will be perpendicular to the sheet surface. The clay can be pulled slightly by the knife and special care is needed toward the end of the cut. A slight distortion of the form at the corners can be corrected with the fingers, but it is best avoided in the first place. An alternative method, which avoids distortion at the corners, is to cut in from each end of the slab, allowing the cuts to meet in the middle.

When assembling, the sides can either be stood on the base or around it. If you overlap the sides in a follow-the-leader pattern, you will get the maximum joint support for a box. The alternative system of butting the ends in pairs will produce a rectangular pot, although the sides are cut to the same width. If you want to have the pot look like its walls are raised from the surface on which the pot stands, you can cut an angled chamfer at its base. Doing this will cast a shadow at the bottom of the pot.

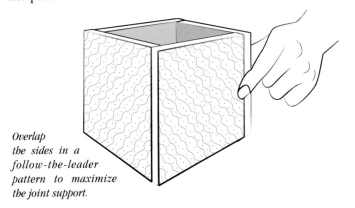

Overlap the sides in a follow-the-leader pattern to maximize the joint support.

(Photo: Louise Fischer-Cozzi)

Louise Fischer-Cozzi *created this small, slab-built box with feet. 3" x 4" x 4".*

Pinching the edges of the clay slabs gently until they stick together is the easiest way to join them. No bonding agent is necessary because the clay sticks easily to itself. While assembling the box, it is a good idea to have a heavy, smooth, and reliably vertical object handy so that the box can be rested against it. Set up the walls one by one, and use a modeling tool to smooth up the joints on the outside. A very fine roll of clay, about the thickness of a shoelace, can be added to the inside of each join and smoothed with a finger, but is not necessary.

Boxes

Something about boxes draws us irresistibly to them. We seem to be compelled to pick up a box and open it. Maybe a universal memory of childhood treasures in shoeboxes and tobacco tins entices us. Perhaps it's the toy-like movement of the hinge and catch, or the anticipation of the contents inside a hidden space.

Polymer clay vessels, cylinder, oval, square, triangular, etc., are reasonably easy to make. A straight-sided

(Photo: Margi Laurin)

Artist: Margi Laurin

This unusually-shaped box includes inlayed, pre-baked polymer tiles and other surface markings made using various tools including sandpaper and shaped wire stamps. To assemble, Margi temporarily held the box together with glue and used soft clay as "mortar," covering the seams with black and white striped coils. The lid of the box has a flange that sets in the top of the box. 5" x 2"

Polymer Clay: Creating Functional and Decorative Objects

cube begins with four rectangular sheets of clay cut from a larger sheet of clay. The clay was run through the pasta machine and layered so it's thick enough to support itself. The box is assembled before baking.

Make a Basic Box

(Photo: Zelda)

Measure the slabs using a ruler or a cardboard template so each rectangle is cut to the correct size.

You can either measure the slabs or use a cardboard template so each rectangle is cut to the correct size. For this vessel, the sheets are cut perpendicular to the table on all edges and joined by pinching the sheets together while smoothing the seam.

(Photo: Zelda)

Cut and attach the base. Notice the cut is angled. This will recess the base so the box will look like it is floating on the table surface.

The joined sides are placed on another sheet of clay. This will be the cube's base. Using a sharp blade, cut the base all around the sides and smooth the resulting seam.

The next step is to prepare the cover for the box. The cover will be a flat slab, similar to the walls, that overlaps the top edges. The cover is fired at the same time, but not attached to the box. The piece is cured in a preheated 275° F oven for 20 minutes.

When cool, a smaller sheet of clay that fits the size of the inside wall of the box is added to the cover so it will be held in place. The sheet is attached to the already-cured cover with Liquid Sculpey and baked again for 20 minutes.

A small sheet of clay that fits the inside wall size of the box is added to the cover.

(Photo: Zelda)

(Photo: Zelda)

The finished box was stamped with a relief pattern while being constructed. Brown acrylic paint was applied and rubbed off to give an antique look. 3" x 4-1/4" x 4-1/2".

Hinges, Hasps, and Finishing Touches

Adding a cover or lid to a vessel increases its mystery as well as its function. A cover can be as simple as a slab of clay sitting on top of a box to as complex as a pop-up hinge. A hasp, or catch, is a small detail that can be either invisible or add aesthetic interest to the front of a vessel.

(Photo: Steve Pack)

Cindy Pack *wove a "fabric" of clay for this covered jar and then attached it to a rolled out slab of clay. The jar is embellished with decorator chalks, yarns and beads, and antiqued with black acrylic paint. 4-1/2" x 2".*

(Photo: Louise Fischer-Cozzi)

"Green Box #4." This small vessel is enhanced by the addition of small feet that raise it off the table surface and a chunky handle. 3" x 4-1/2". By Louise Fischer-Cozzi.

Finishing touches on a vessel include things like adding feet, beveling the bottom edge of the vessel, and adding a decorative rim.

Hinges and Covers

Vessel using commercially available doll hinges. By Jacqueline Gikow.

(Photo: Zelda)

Man's first hinges, probably leather, vegetable or fabric straps or bands, are as effective now as they have ever been. The most common, most frequently used, and simplest hinges have all the components of every other hinge. It includes an odd number of tubular segments called "knuckles," a "seat" for the knuckles to sit in, and a close-fitting interior wire called a "hinge pin."

There is no "right" size or material for a hinge. You can use found materials and fashion hinges by hand or you can purchase commercial hinges. You can make hinges from wire, fabric, and even from polymer clay. Creating or picking the right hinge for a particular application is a personal choice that depends on the size, shape, and style of the object, and your aesthetics.

The satisfaction of making a working hinge lies in

the melding of art and engineering—a universal design principle taught as "form follows function" in the famous German Bauhaus school of the early nineteenth century. Do you want a hinge that can be seen? Should it be constructed from polymer clay, or is another material as, or more, appropriate? The multitude of small decisions you make ultimately result in a style that is unmistakably yours.

With this discussion, you can see there are a-million-and-one ways to hinge vessels. So, take a hinge from here and a catch from there, or make up your own variations and blend them with objects that will be as satisfying to use as they are to make.

Hinge Rules[3]

As varied as hinges may be, there are a number of universal "have-to's" that you can't ignore:
1. A hinge must be straight. This means the pin that the hinge rotates around cannot be bent. A hinge only works if it can rotate, and a curved pin will eventually break.
2. Build it correctly from the beginning so you don't have to fix it later. Once finished, a hinge is very difficult to repair. There should be no gaps between the knuckles, the spacing must be close together, and the pivot wire must be straight.
3. Close enough doesn't count. A poor fit will be obvious in a hinge. If it is too tight, the lid won't open; if the hinge is too loose, it will feel wobbly and sloppy.
4. Work step-by-step. This is a universal truth for all fabrication. Create your hinge following a logical plan.

Polymer Clay Hinges

Decide what kind of hinge you want before you fire your clay object because you need to decide how to construct it and where it will be seated. Following are three examples of polymer clay hinges, but many more can be developed using these as guides.

Every hinge is composed of the knuckles, a seat, and a hinge pin. Before you get scared off by these technical terms, let's define the elements. Knuckles are the individual tube sections of the hinge and, as indicated by the name of this hinge, there are three. The seat of a hinge is where the knuckles are attached. This area must be large enough to house the knuckles. Finally, the hinge pin is a piece of wire that runs through the knuckles to connect them and allow attached pieces to pivot.

Piano Hinge

A piano hinge is a simple, and the most frequently used, hinge. To construct this hinge, a clay tube, similar to a tube bead, is cut into three sections. The middle section is attached to one slab and the outer sections are attached to the other. The slices must be clean and straight (lightly sand the edges, if necessary), and

Polymer Clay: Creating Functional and Decorative Objects

reassemble in a close fit. Make sure the wire pin does not bend and finish the ends of the wire so they will not pull out of the hinge.

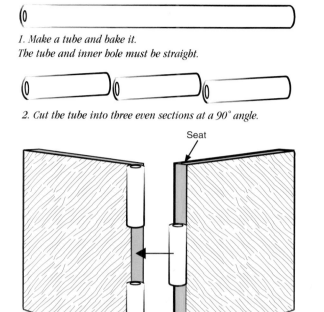

1. Make a tube and bake it.
The tube and inner hole must be straight.

2. Cut the tube into three even sections at a 90° angle.

3. Cut the hinge surfaces at an angle so there is a "seat" for the hinge sections to sit on (see above).
4. Using a thick cyanoacrylate glue, such as Surehold's Super Gel, attach two tube sections to the outer edges of one slab and the other to the center of the second slab.
The sections should fit closely when joined together. Make sure you don't glue the sections together.

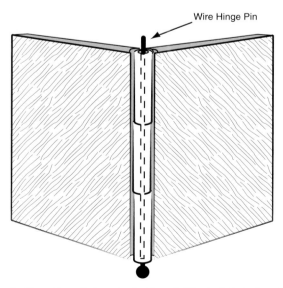

5. For the hinge pin, select a wire that loosely fills the hole in the tube and run it through the tube sections. Either bend the ends or glue a small bead on to stop the wire from coming out of the hinge.

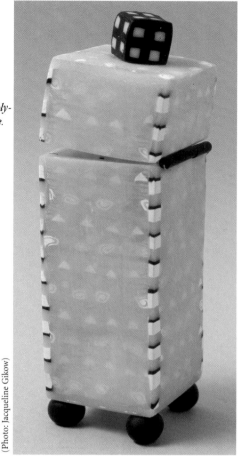

Footed box with a polymer clay piano hinge.
2-1/2" x 8".
By Jacqueline Gikow.

(Photo: Jacqueline Gikow)

Tube and Pin Hinges

This simplest of hinges is composed of a thin cylinder of polymer clay attached to one of the slabs to be hinged. A wire pin runs through the center and is connected, at both ends of the tube, to the other slab.

The tube used for this hinge must be straight and

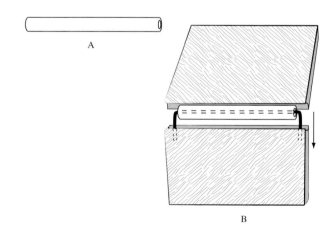

A. Make a tube and bake it. The tube and inner hole must be straight. Attach the tube to one of the slabs of clay.
B. Run the hinge pin through the clay tube and bend it at each end. You need to drill two holes in the clay slab that doesn't have the tube attached to it. Push the ends of the wire into the clay. Use cyanoacrylate glue to affix the wire inside the holes.

even, both inside and out. The diameter of the tube should be approximately the same as the thickness of the slabs being joined. The hole through the tube should be slightly wider than the "hinge pin" (the length of wire you will use as the pivot) but should not let the pin wiggle around too much. When connecting the two slabs, insert the hinge pin, making sure the hinge revolves freely. Bend the wire and insert the ends into the other slab.

Embedded Hinge

In an embedded hinge, both slabs of clay revolve around the hinge pin. This hinge is a bit tricky because the wire pivot is hidden inside the two slabs of clay. To

In this embedded hinge, both the lid and the side wall revolve around the hinge pin. This hinge is a bit tricky because the wire pivot is hidden inside the two slabs of clay. To assemble you drill a small hole in both slabs as illustrated. Then you must carefully slide the wire between the two pieces of clay to complete the hinge.

assemble, drill a small hole in both slabs as illustrated. You must carefully slide the wire between the two pieces of clay to complete the hinge.

Lids Without Hinges

Not every box needs to open like a clamshell, two units joined by a hinge. A simple approach is to make a lid that simply lifts off the base. Two elegant solutions include a lid that is flush to the box and a lid that overlaps the box.

With a flush lid, you create an interior lip, or "flange," either in the lid or the base, that prevents the lid from falling off the base. A flange is a thin frame that is best constructed after a preliminary baking so the container won't distort. Attach the flange, painting a coat of PVA and/or Liquid Sculpey between the two layers of clay. Brush cornstarch on the flange and container edge so it will not stick during baking. Finish baking, and when cool, sand the flange edge lightly with 600-grit sandpaper.

(Photo: Ben Shum)

"Petal Boxes." *Hand built polymer clay boxes* by Wanda Shum; *polymer clay veneer with transparent and metallic canes have a flange on the lid to keep them in place. 3" x 1-3/4".*

For a vessel where the lid overlaps the box, build the container first and fire it. When it is cool, construct the lid as a shallow box that will slip over the container. Dust the inside of the lid and the outside of the box with cornstarch or wrap a piece of vellum around the outside

(Photo: Robert Groh)

"Good View." *3" x 8".* By Debbie Jackson.

Polymer Clay: Creating Functional and Decorative Objects

of the vessel so the pieces won't stick together during firing. Depending on the shape of the cover, you may have to fill the box with polyester fiber filling or construct a paper support for the lid when you fire it.

Hasps

Hasps or catches can be as simple as a lid with a snug fit or as complicated as a hidden mechanical device. Regardless of the complexity of a catch, it should always be easy to understand and operate, and simple to construct. While not all boxes need catches, they can add sophistication and improve the function of a piece. Most catches are made toward the end of the construction process. As a rule, catches are positioned directly opposite the hinge, but sometimes an unexpected off-center catch can provide an interesting detail.

Friction catches are part of the construction of containers with a snug fitting, flush, interior flange closure. Simple friction keeps the lid attached to the holder. Longer flanges, ones that extend further down the inside wall, will have more friction than shorter ones because there is more surface leaning against the box interior. The same principle of friction also holds for a lid that slides over the box edge (see Photo 6-18).

Dimple Catches

Another simple catch idea is the "dimple" catch. It consists of a small, raised dot on the flange and a corre-

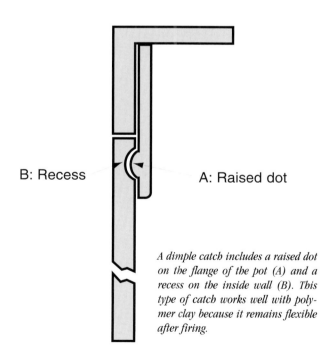

B: Recess   A: Raised dot

A dimple catch includes a raised dot on the flange of the pot (A) and a recess on the inside wall (B). This type of catch works well with polymer clay because it remains flexible after firing.

sponding recess on the interior of the box, making the two pieces want to stay together, rather than separate. This catch is an excellent solution for polymer clay

because of the clay's intrinsic flexibility when completely fired.

Hook Hasps

A hook hasp includes a trigger, a hook, and a "snag."

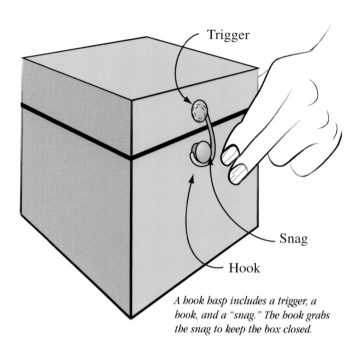

Trigger

Snag

Hook

A hook hasp includes a trigger, a hook, and a "snag." The hook grabs the snag to keep the box closed.

The hook grabs the snag to keep the box closed, and releasing the hook from the snag allows the lid to be opened. It's possible to make a hook hasp from polymer clay with a coil of clay. Because this catch will get a lot of use, the clay should be one of the more durable and flexible brands. Fimo Classic and Premo are good choices for this. If you mix a small amount of Super Elasticlay in the clay roll it will become more flexible and less apt to break. Roll or extrude a coil of clay in a diameter that is in proportion to the size of your container.

Make the hook and trigger first. The hook should consist of a loop at one end and a hook at the other end of the clay coil. The trigger can be as simple as a section of the clay coil attached to the lid or a fancy shape with a hole large enough for the hook to fit through. Bake these pieces not attached to the vessel at 265° F for about 15 minutes and let them cool.

Slip the hook over the trigger and glue the trigger to the lid of the pot. Let this construction dry until the cold bond is strong enough to hold together while making the snag. Then cut another section of the clay extrusion for the snag, and attach it to the box as shown in the illustration. Guidelines for determining the size of the snag will be provided by observing the scale of the box. Practically speaking, the snag must have, like the trigger, an opening large enough for the hook to fit into. When assembled, bake the box for the final time.

The Rim

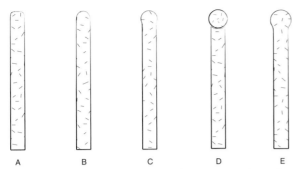

A reinforced rim is not only a cosmetic enhancement, it also makes a box stronger. These cross-sections show some possibilities for different rims on a vessel.
A. Slightly rounded rim, B. Hemisphere shape, C. Rim pressed down and rounded, D. Coil added to top of rim, E. Coil blended in at top of rim.

(Photo: Zelda)

"SeaBright #2." The walls of this box are constructed of multiple layers of translucent and opaque clay enhanced by mokume gane embellishment. The legs are made from aluminum tubing. The circular lid sits flush with the top layer of clay and is held in place by an angular inside cut. 5" x 5-1/2". By Jacqueline Gikow.

There is a split second of drama with almost every box or container when the lid is lifted for the first time to reveal the interior. Whether large or small, boxes are monolithic forms, objects characterized by their mass. If a massive-looking box is opened to reveal construction that seems inadequate, it may spoil the power of the object. Likewise, if a delicate form is opened to reveal a clunky construction, another illusion may be lost.

There are good reasons not to make container walls too thick and several ways to thicken the rim so the container doesn't look flimsy. In addition to being a cosmetic enhancement, a reinforced rim makes a box stronger, providing a longer life expectancy even without thicker walls. You can add a clay strip, coiling it on the inside top of the box, or roll the edge to either the inside or outside of the rim. Just pushing the edge down to compress and thicken it will result in the illusion of substantial mass. Sometimes thickening the edge doubles as a surface decoration or molding.

Even if a container doesn't have a lid, its rim should be finished simply because it looks more elegant. An uneven or ragged rim can ruin the effect of a container that took many hours of intricate work. There's nothing wrong with rims that haven't been squared off, but at the very least, sand and smooth them so the result is intentional-looking.

Down Under

I'm not speaking of the other side of the world. Instead, I'm referring to the base of a vessel. The least considered part of a container is often its base. The way the box rests on a surface should be contemplated from both practical and aesthetic perspectives—consider them when you are designing your next piece. Should the walls run straight to the table? Should they be rounded, or angled? Would adding feet to the box change it for the better … or worse? What about adding a base? Will it help or hinder the container? How tall should it be? Should you attach the base to the box or make a separate pedestal from which the box can be removed? You may be surprised that there are so many decisions to make, or ideas to sift through, weigh, and discard.

The simplest way to finish a box is to leave the straight edges of the walls flush with the table surface it sits on. What would the effect be if you rounded the bottom edges? Alternatively, what would the box look like with the bottom edge of the box trimmed at a 30°, or 45° angle?

If you add feet or a base to a vessel you will change its character and introduce a unique personality to it. Feet can be amusing, graceful, clunky, simple, or complex. You can make each one the same color and shape, or each one a different color and shape. When a vessel is elevated, it looks very different than when it sits prosaically on a table.

When you construct vessels with more complicated forms, the reasons for adding a base or attaching feet grow. If your box isn't constructed with a flush base, for example, it needs something to balance it so it will stand. Often a pedestal or tripod of some sort will be the most appropriate support.

PROJECT 1. SLASH-DECORATED SLAB BOX

By Louise Fischer Cozzi
Beginner
3" x 4" x 4" high

(Photo: Louise Fischer-Cozzi)

Materials and Supplies

Polymer Clay
　4 oz. red
　4 oz. pink
Acrylic paint (optional)
Cyanoacrylate glue such as
　Zap-a-Gap
Linoleum carving tool
　with #2 blade
Pasta machine
Sharp knife or long blade
Head pin (optional)

Instructions

1. Mix and/or condition 4 oz. of your favorite red and 4 oz. of your favorite pink.
2. Roll out 2 slabs of pink. Place 1/2 on top of each other, rolling a bit to connect and use as one slab. Reserve these slabs, and any excess.
3. With the excess clay, roll out a slab each of red and pink to #5 on the pasta machine. Place the pink on top of the red. Roll the slab through the pasta maker at #6 (fine setting). With a linoleum or fine wood carving tool, cut a pattern of three parallel slashes. Then carve three slashes perpendicular to the first. Continue the pattern, being careful to remove excess clay from the slab. When this slab is completely carved, run it through the pasta machine at #6 to display the color underneath.
4. Trim the pink slab to a rectilinear shape. Cover with the patterned red and pink sheet and roll lightly to join. If you choose to decorate the inside of the box, turn slab over and use acrylic paint to paint veins on the inside. Slice slab in half horizontally and then about 1/3 of the way in vertically. These are the four walls for the box.
5. Miter the edges of the sidepieces at a 45° angle, pinch them together and place the box form on a slab of clay reserved for the bottom. Attach the sides to the bottom.
6. Roll a short snake about 3/8" (9 mm) in diameter and cut four small feet for the box from it, but don't attach them yet.
7. Cut the lid to desired shape. Glue a polymer roll on top to act as handle, securing with a head pin through top of box.
8. Bake for 20–30 minutes, according to manufacturer's instructions. When cool, glue the feet to the box base. If desired, sand and buff.

(Photo: Jacqueline Gikow)

By Karen Goulet
Beginner/Intermediate

These lacy bowls will enhance any party setting or dress up your coffee table. You can also fill them with wrapped candy or nuts in their shells. The bowls in the photograph are varied in size: 4-1/2" to 5-1/2" diameter by 1-1/2" to 2" high.

Materials and Supplies

Polymer clay
Rolling pin, plexiglas tube, or brayer for rolling
Vellum or wax paper
Small flowerpot or glass jar
Cheesecloth or soft, lightweight muslin

Instructions:

1. Make canes in your choice of colors, patterns, and shapes: round, square, triangular, etc. You can use all one shaped cane or a variety. An alternative is to use ready-made canes such as Amaco Friendly Clay Designer Squares. Your choice of cane shapes will affect the finished shape of the bowl.

The canes in the photograph are made from the following colors and clay brands:
The mint green, bordeaux red and gray cane bowl is made from Fimo.
The red, yellow and blue cane bowl is made from Premo.
The purple and green cane bowl made from Sculpey III.

2. Cut the canes into slices, about a 1/4", or slightly larger.

3. Lay the canes out on wax paper or vellum as close as possible to each other. Then lay another sheet of wax paper on top and use a rolling pin to blend the slices together into a solid sheet. At some point, you have to also use your fingers to press the slices together. Don't roll the sheet too thin or it will break easily, even after baking.

Note: Round slices are a little more difficult to work with; you may not get all the spaces out, but this can be a "planned feature" to the bowl, giving it some extra character.

4. Once the desired sheet is made, gently peel it off the wax paper. Invert the flowerpot or jar and drape the sheet over it. The shape of your support will also affect the final shape of the bowl. Then pinch/fold the clay as desired. Follow the "natural" flow of the clay as it drapes rather than forcing it into a specific shape. It's also a good idea to put something, like a piece of cheesecloth or muslin, between the clay and object so it doesn't pick up marks or a gloss from the object.

5. Bake according to the manufacturer's instructions and leave the bowl to completely cool in the oven before removing it. No sanding or finishing is necessary.

Project 3. Hinged Vessel

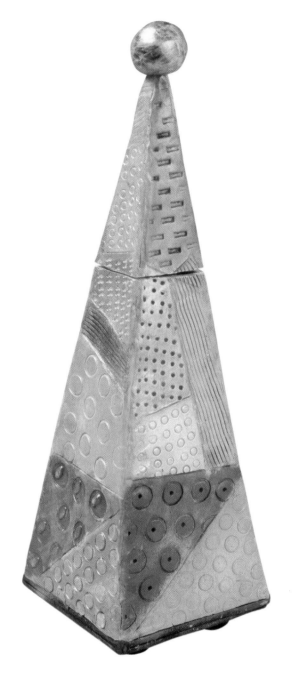

Intermediate/Advanced
2 1/2" square x 7-1/2" tall

Materials and Supplies

10 oz. Premo White
2 oz. Premo Black
Gel cyanoacrylate glue such as SureHold
Pasta machine, and roller or brayer
Sharp knife or long blade
An inexpensive, retractable ball-point pen that can
     be taken apart
Colored, decorative powders, pastels, markers,
     interference paints, etc.
1/2" thin brass hinge
Needle tool
Straight edge
Thin piece of wire (18-gauge)

Instructions

1. Roll out the white clay at the second largest pasta machine setting. Divide in half and roll two layers together. Repeat with the black clay.
2. Enlarge the vessel template (next page) 200% and cut 4 side shapes from the white slab.
3. Use a straight edge to mark divisions in each panel side as in the finished example.
4. Take the pen apart and use the various parts to fill in the areas with patterns (see finished photo). The ink tip makes small holes, the opposite end of the ink barrel makes small circles the outside barrel portion makes large circles, and the spring can be rolled to make stripes.
5. Once the entire vessel is patterned, apply various decorative colors to the different areas.

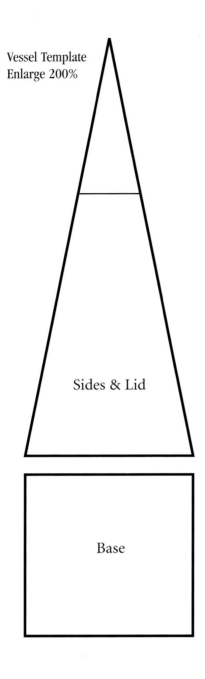

Vessel Template
Enlarge 200%

Sides & Lid

Base

the clay ball firmly on the point of the lid.
11. Roll 4 small balls of clay, bake and attach them with PVA glue to the vessel as feet. If you recess them under the base, the box will look as if it is floating on the table.
12. Bake again for 20 minutes.

Attaching the Hinge

13. Select one side of the vessel as the back and cut a slot that the hinge pin will fit in when mounted inside the vessel. The cylinders should be flush when at a 90° angle.

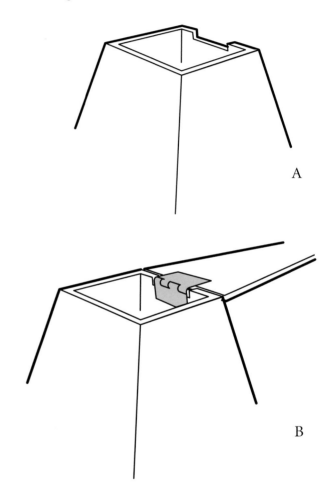

A

B

Assembling the Vessel

6. Carefully assemble the four sides and then firmly place the form on the black slab. Trim around perpendicular to the work surface.
7. Using a needle tool, incise a groove on the vessel at the position indicated on the template. This is the dividing line for what will become the vessel lid.
8. Place the vessel in the oven and bake for 20 minutes at 275° F.
9. When the vessel is cool, cut along the groove on the vessel to separate the lid from the base.
10. Re-assemble the pen. Roll a ball of black clay and pierce a hole, using the point end of the pen, taking care not to distort the ball. Widen the hole and set

14. Glue one wing of the brass hinge on the inside of the base.
15. Glue one wing of the brass hinge on the inside of the lid.
16. Lightly coat the container with Varathane or lacquer to seal it. This is important because the powders you added will come off on your hands otherwise.

Chapter 7

Mold Making for Polymer Clay Vessels

People have used molds to shape clay since the second century B.C. Some of the earliest clay containers were made by smearing a layer of clay onto the inside of a basket and then burning the basket away to leave a hardened clay shell. Ancient one-piece terra cotta molds have been found in China, Greece, Rome, the Middle East, and the Americas.

(Photo: John Polak)

Merrie Buchsbaum *made these* "Scented Herb Polymer Lamps" *using a paper mold. Herbal inclusions in the translucent clay provide color, texture, and an appealing aroma when the bulb warms the clay. Sizes 10-18" x 7-10"*

You'll never look at anything the same way again once you get into mold making! Forget about being intimidated—molds are easy to make. Even the ones that seem complicated only need a bit more preparation than a simple push-mold.

Polymer clay is easily cast into three-dimensional shapes and you can also make molds out of polymer clay. Almost any textured surface or intricate shape can be reproduced in polymer clay simply by pressing it against the object to be duplicated.

Let's start with some definitions:
• A *model* is the three-dimensional object you make a mold of (also called a master model).
• A *mold* is the impression taken of the model.

• A *casting material* is both:
  a) A material you make the mold from.
  b) A material that reproduces the original model from the mold.
• A *release agent* is a substance that prevents one material from sticking to another—in this case the mold and the model or the casting.
• A *casting* is the reproduction of the original three-dimensional object from which you made a mold.

Watch out for Undercuts!

The main things to look out for when making molds or taking impressions are undercuts. Undercuts are negative spaces that create an overhang in a solid form.

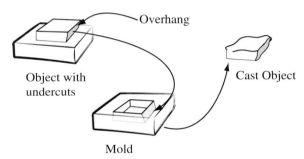

A. Models and molds must have no undercuts or the polymer clay will not be able to release without being distorted. Undercuts are negative spaces that create an overhang in a solid form. If you cast a model that has undercuts the mold will not release the model. Instead it will either stay caught in the mold or you will have to break the mold to get it out.

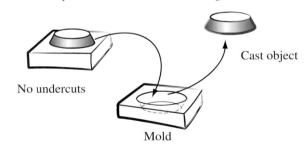

B. If the model has no undercut the mold will release the model.

Undercuts are caused two ways:
1. If the model you are casting has indents that curve under or twist in some way it will get caught and not release the mold. Examine your model for undercuts and fill them in with clay before making your mold.
2. If you are making a mold and you make the mold divide over the halfway point it will get caught and not release the model.

It takes time to learn to find and eliminate undercuts either in the model or the mold. When you look straight down at your tile model, every edge of the design should slope out at an angle. After a few frustrating times of having to start over, you will begin to recognize where to fill in or divide the forms.

Found Molds

Saucers, bowls and plates from the kitchen are examples of items that can be used as molds for polymer clay. River rocks are another potential mold, as are cardboard tubes, crumpled aluminum foil, even light bulbs.

Emi Fukishima

Emi formed this vessel over a large rock and cut it in half to make a base and cover. A second baking bonded the embellishments with the first layer.

(Photo: Krause)

(Photo: Jacqueline Gikow)

Bowls made with canes using a found mold as a support. By Lucille Schacht.

(Photo: Roger Scheber)

"Ghost Diary." Judy Kuskin *formed this vessel over a round ceramic flower vase. After firing, the polymer clay was split in half and removed from the vase. Decorative elements hide the seams. The vessel is highly textured with a patina of burnt umber acrylic paint for the organic look. 6" x 5-3/4"*

You saw in Chapter 5 that glass, ceramic, and metal rarely stick to cured polymer clay so hollow forms with rich, colorful, and textural surfaces can be made using these materials. Found molds of this type are used either as hump molds or drape molds. If you use a bowl, for example, the clay will drape into it and you can then push the clay to the bowl's surface to get the interior

impression. If you turn the bowl upside down you would drape the clay over it and form it closely to the outer surface. In the case of the drape mold, the casting will come right out after firing because the small amount of shrinkage in polymer clay will draw the clay inward, away from the bowl. With a hump mold, it's necessary to remove the vessel form while the clay is still somewhat soft from the heat.

Spherical or undulating shapes can be used as a mold if you cut the clay in half at the sides after firing. You can hide the resulting seam by applying decorative elements to it and incorporating them into the finished vessel.

(Photo: Zelda)

Background: An assortment of cardboard cylinders. Foreground: A water-color brush holder made from a thin paper towel cardboard tube.

Cardboard cylinders and tube vases can be used as tall, straight-sided molds. I have a collection of tubes from paper towels, kitchen wraps such as firing parchment, and bathroom tissue. I've also collected larger diameter cardboard cylinders from bolts of fabric, rolled up carpets, oatmeal boxes, and shipping tubes. Cardboard should be covered with aluminum foil or 100 percent cotton rag vellum as a mold release. The advantage of using aluminum foil or vellum with cardboard molds is that they are thin and the clay will easily slide off after firing.

(Photo: Krause)

"Animal Augury #1 and #2." By Nan Roche. *A core vessel was made from polymer clay and baked. The top pieces are sculpted animal heads. The surface design is mokume gane and stamps. A necklace of small tube beads of polymer clay adorns each animal. The base of each vessel is impressed with a basket pattern mold. The pieces are treated with bronze powder and patinas. Approximately 7-1/2" x 2-1/2".*

Core Molds

A core mold is a form unique to polymer clay. Because polymer clay can be refired any number of times, you can completely cover a core, cut the clay apart after firing, and rejoin it, hiding the seams. Some core molds include rocks, crumpled up aluminum foil smoothed with clay on top to fill the creases, and light bulbs.

(Photo: Zelda)

Clay covering a rock. Left and center is the clay split in half with the top removed. Don't worry about cracks when you do this—that's why glue was invented. Right: a first layer after it was split, removed from the rock, then glued back together. The shell will be used for further development of a vessel.

(Photo: Zelda)

Here is one of the rock coverings finished as a fish vessel. This could be used to hold pens and pencils, brushes and other tools, or even flowers.

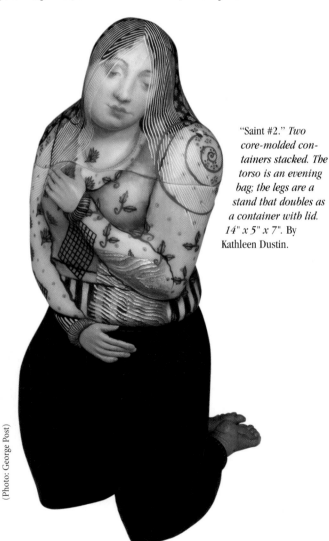

"Saint #2." *Two core-molded containers stacked. The torso is an evening bag; the legs are a stand that doubles as a container with lid. 14" x 5" x 7". By Kathleen Dustin.*

(Photo: George Post)

Before firing, mark the clay at the widest point of the rock. While the clay is still warm from firing, cut all the way through the division and remove the clay from the rock. If you want to add a second layer, you can re-fire the pieces on the rock or separately. Add a flange or hinge to connect the pieces and a hasp to keep it closed. If you want the vessel to stand you can build a base.

Although not strictly a found mold, compacted aluminum foil covered with scrap polymer clay is a good replacement for a rock mold. Fired and sanded, it can be used again and again. The advantage of this mold is you can decide on the size and shape you want. Make sure there are no undercuts and fill in any you find.

Light Bulb Core Molds

Burned out light bulbs can be used to make spherical vessels and the fun is in making them look like anything but a light bulb. To make a vessel using a light bulb as a mold:

1. Cover it with a thin (1/16" to 1/8") layer of polymer clay. The clay can extend almost all the way to the metal end.
2. After you fire the clay and bulb, break the glass away from the screw end, carefully pick up the clay-covered bulb, and squeeze it to break up the glass.

(Photo: William Sacco)

"Autumn Cairn." *This molded vessel uses a floodlight bulb with tin foil and newspaper for the mold. The bulb was removed after the first curing. The vessel is constructed with a mixture of stone and translucent clays, which were textured with rough grit sandpaper. 4-1/2" x 4" x 5-1/2". By Diane Villano.*

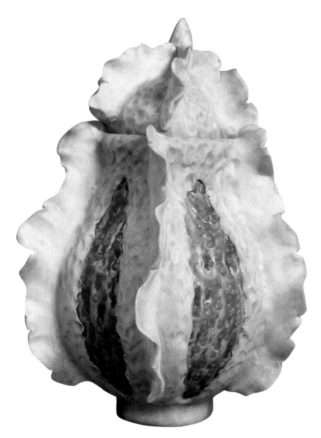

(Photo: Daniel Buckley)

"Organic Vessel." Jodi Bishel *made this vessel by covering a lightbulb, which was removed after firing. Blue-green embellishment is applies under the white leaf motifs.*

(Photo: Zelda)

Here the screw end is broken off and some glass shaken out. A hammer covered with cloth is used so there is a minimum of stress put on the thin clay.

3. Continue squeezing and dumping out the bits of glass until all have been removed. You can use a paintbrush to brush out fine bits of glass.
4. Finally, rinse the clay interior with water. Once you have the basic vessel you can add on to it in any way you want.

Polymer Clay: Creating Functional and Decorative Objects

Stuff to Make Molds From

Little press molds with objects in front.

Molds for polymer clay can be made from household items: jewelry, toys, screwdriver tips, bolts (make great stripes), fancy buttons, bracelets, wooden shapes, bits of filigree, netting or fabric, combs, charms, and more!

Molds can be cast from objects or textures in just about any material: plastic, glass, fired polymer clay, sheets of copper foil you have textured, plasticine or non-firing oil clay, ceramic or air-drying clay (make the mold while clay model is wet or leather hard), or soft, carveable sculpture materials.

Polymer Clay Molds

Polymer clay is ideal for molds because of its ability to take impressions. Hard-sided polymer clay molds can be made with Fimo, Premo, and Sculpey III. Sculpey Super ElastiClay yields a flexible, soft-sided mold. Releasing agents such as cornstarch, ArmorAll, silicon spray, or spray vegetable oil should be used between your model or casting and the mold. If what you are making a mold of is not made of polymer clay it can be fired in the mold, otherwise remove the model before firing.

Cured polymer clay becomes more resilient and less apt to crack with longer firing times at the correct temperature. Feel free to bake your mold for an hour or even longer.

One Piece Polymer Clay Molds

Push- or press-molds are the simplest kind of mold, and often the most useful. Small molds work well for reproducing beads, coins or appliqués. Larger polymer clay press-molds are great for making tiles, texture sheets, and applied decorations.

Foreground: the master model. Background: press-mold.

When you make a push- or press-mold, only the front and sides of an object are molded and the castings have a flat back. Remember to apply a mold release to the mold and clay before firing.

Whatever size item you are casting, all you need to make a polymer clay press-mold is scrap clay and mold release. These instructions show you how to make your own tile mold using polymer clay and then how to make reproductions from those molds.

These three tiles are from the finished mold. The tile on the left is translucent clay with interference gold powder laid into some of the depressions on the tiles. The right tile is custom mixed blue clay. I cut out the large leaf and replaced it by inlaying green clay into that shape. I took extra care to place the inlaid green clay over the leaf. Green metallic powder was brushed into some of the depressions. 4" square.

1. Brush the object you are making a mold from with cornstarch, brush off the excess, and set it on a flat surface. Condition enough clay to cover the tile model and take an impression. This 3" tile mold took about 8 oz. of clay for the mold, so you can see how the cost of using polymer clay escalates as you start making larger molds. Brush cornstarch over the surface that will cover the model.
2. Press the powdered surface of the mold clay firmly onto the tile, working the clay down to the flat surface. Don't let it move around or you will get a dou-

ble impression. When you are sure the clay is firmly pressed down all over the model, set it in the refrigerator for a few minutes. If your model is made from polymer clay, remove it from the mold before firing; otherwise you can leave the model in the mold.

3. To make a casting, brush the inside of the mold lightly with cornstarch. Roll out enough clay to cover the mold cavity. It should be slightly thicker than the mold interior, but with a smaller diameter so it does not overflow the mold cavity too much.

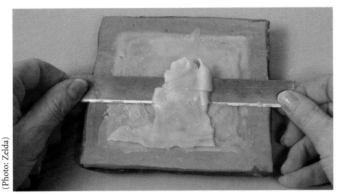

(Photo: Zelda)

When the model is correctly set in the clay trim the mold so the "face" of it is relatively flat. Be sure the model is only covered to a center parting line. Press a couple dents into the flat face so the next half of the mold can be aligned correctly. The dents should be clear and have slanted sides.

4. Press the disk firmly into the mold, pushing it in all around. Again, be careful the clay doesn't shift in the mold or you will get a double image. If necessary, trim the back with a tissue blade to remove excess clay. If the blade drags through the clay, try setting the mold and clay in the refrigerator for a bit and clean your blade. Make sure you are using a sharp blade.

5. Gently remove the casting and smooth the back edges. If the clay distorts, simply push it back into place. Fire the casting (in this case the tile), and do any finishing necessary.

Two-Piece Polymer Clay Molds

Two-part molds are not difficult to make from polymer clay and are extremely useful for duplicating small, three-dimensional objects. You saw how much clay was needed for a small tile mold, so making molds from polymer clay can get pretty expensive if you start making two-piece molds of any large size.

This demonstration shows how to make and use two-piece polymer clay molds. In this example I'm using a handle purchased from a hardware store.

Making the Mold

1. Dust the model with cornstarch or talc and tap off any excess.

2. Condition enough scrap clay to cover the entire model 1/2" thick. Separate the clay into two equal piles and roll each to 1/2" thick.

3. Place the slab on a piece of paper on the tile or surface you're going to use for firing and cover the model half way up, to the widest point. Remove the model. If the imprint didn't come out right, squish the clay back into a blob, powder your model again and start over.

4. Remove the model from the mold and bake the mold at 265°-275° F for an hour.

5. Re-powder the model and place it back into the baked mold. Powder the mold face as well.

6. Pick up the rest of the conditioned clay, press it over the exposed part of the model, making sure it fits snugly to the model and baked mold part and fill in the dents. (If the imprint didn't come out right, squish the clay back into a blob, powder your model again and start over.) Don't blend the raw clay into the baked mold; just make sure it's a tight fit.

7. Bake the second half of the mold at 265° F for an hour. Voila! You've got a two-piece mold that will duplicate the original.

(Photo: Zelda)

Left to right: the original handle model, half the finished mold with raised positioning nodes, the other mold half with positioning dents and a casting in it. Notice the flashing at the edges of the casting still in the mold. At the far right the casting has been removed from the mold and the flashing trimmed away

Making the Casting

8. To take a casting, powder the mold halves generously and tap off the excess.
   a. If you are making a hollow casting condition enough clay to make a 1/8" to 1/4" shell and press it firmly into each half of the mold.
   b. If your casting will be solid, like this handle, fill each half completely.

9. Press the two mold pieces together firmly. If you take off one of the mold halves there should be slight flashing at the mold joining where the casting squished together. It's a good idea to remove the casting from the mold instead of firing it in the mold.

Super ElastiClay Molds

PolyForm Super ElastiClay is a strange polymer clay because it remains rubbery and can be twisted and pulled without breaking after curing. This quality makes it perfect for molds of objects that may have some *small* undercuts in them and texture sheets. Super ElastiClay molds are made the same way as 1- and 2-piece polymer clay molds.

Super ElastiClay can be used to make thin texture sheets able to pass through the pasta machine. For strong texture sheets use a layer of Liquid Sculpey as a backing to the Super ElastiClay. Float a thin layer of Liquid Sculpey on a piece of glass or tile and cure it. Roll a thin sheet of Super ElastiClay with your pasta machine, adhere it to the cured Liquid Sculpey, and texture it with various tools and/or stamps. Bake the textured sheet. Use it by dusting the sheet with cornstarch and running it through the pasta machine under a sheet of raw clay.

(Photo: Jeanne Sturdevant)

"In Celebration of Women's Friendships." *For this vessel,* Jeanne Sturdevant *made positive and negative ElastiClay molds from the relief surface of a painting. She draped thin impressions from these molds over a panty hose covered bowl and as each figure was added, she sculpted connecting details. The outside surface was cured and additional impressions of the figure completed the inside. The base was created over a smaller bowl, and one repeat of the figure was used. 7-1/2" x 3-1/2".*

Plaster Molds

Plaster molds have been in common use since the eighteenth century. Dry plaster (calcium sulfate) is a white powdered substance that becomes hard when mixed with water. The most commonly used, Number 1 Pottery Plaster, also called Plaster of Paris or casting plaster, usually comes from clay suppliers in 50 to 100 pound (22.7 to 45.4 kg) bags. You can also purchase smaller amounts. Your local hardware or paint supply store probably carries plaster in 5 or 10 pound quantities.

For molding hollow vessels or objects larger than three inches, plaster is a better choice than polymer clay because it is a lot less expensive. Additionally, plaster picks up finer details than polymer clay. The disadvantage is that it is somewhat fragile and can chip easily.

Store dry plaster in a dry place, as its shelf life is limited by its tendency to absorb moisture. Double-bag and seal tightly if you plan to keep the plaster for a long time.

(Photo: Krause)

"Molded Clock." *Plaster molds were made to cast the clock wheels and other embellishments. An edition of 25 castings is planned. Sculpey was used for casting. The finished clock was assembled using transparent Liquid Sculpey as an adhesive. The clock was hand-buffed using clear shoe polish! 7-1/2" x 2-1/2"* By James Gilbert.

Mixing Plaster

The materials needed for mixing plaster are waterproof rubber or latex gloves, a mixing bucket and, if you are measuring the plaster, a scale.

You can measure the plaster and water for casting your molds by using a ratio of sixty percent plaster to forty percent water by weight. For molds less than six inches, preparing the plaster this way can be impractical because of the small amount of materials needed.

Creative Plaster Mixing

Luckily, there is an alternative, foolproof plaster-mixing method for those of us who are averse to making precise measurements. This method is called the "island" method of plaster mixing.

The island method of mixing doesn't require you to weigh the plaster; you'll learn instead how to "guesti-mate" the amount of water and plaster needed.

Sift or filter plaster into water slowly and evenly. Do not drop handfuls of plaster directly into the water. Wait to add more until the islands of plaster that form sink.

Mix the plaster mixture until it feels like extra heavy cream (your finger should leave a shallow path if you rake it over the surface). Plaster is caustic and should not be in contact with skin for long, so wear a waterproof glove to mix the plaster.

In the beginning, you may find your molds are too soft, but after a few times you'll get a sense of how much plaster is needed.

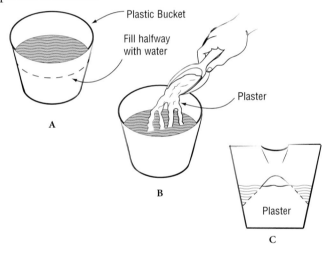

The "island" method of mixing plaster.
A. Fill a plastic bucket halfway or less with water, depending on the amount of plaster you need.
B. Slowly sprinkle the dry plaster into the water. Remember, do not add water to plaster. You must always add plaster to water. Don't dump the plaster into the water; sift it slowly in, a small amount at a time.
C. Stop adding plaster when the islands no longer sink quickly into the water, but sit on its surface for 15 seconds or more. Let the container sit until the plaster has fully absorbed all of the water. Do not mix. This mixture will not set unless it is agitated. After water has been fully absorbed into the plaster, mix with your gloved hand to blend the mixture. The longer you blend the mixture, the faster it will set.

Mold Releases

If your model is made from ceramic polymer clay, you won't need a mold release to cast your mold because the water in ceramic clay and the oil in polymer clay act

as a release. If the clay is dry, baked, or fired, though, a release will be needed. Models in other materials—glass, metal, wood, etc., will also need a mold release. Some releases include silica spray, petroleum jelly, or mold soap (available at ceramic suppliers). I've also used sprays for cooking, such as Pam. ArmorAll would probably work as well.

Cleaning up after working with plaster is a chore, but it is a chore better done right after casting than to wait until the next time you want to make a mold. If you have coated the bucket with petroleum jelly the task will be somewhat easier. If you clean up immediately after casting you'll find you are less reluctant to make the next mold. Here is the procedure for cleaning up plaster:
1. Always pour any excess plaster into a waste bucket, allow it to harden, break it up, and discard it.
2. Never pour liquid plaster down a sink drain because it will harden in the pipes.
3. Clean your gloves, mixing bucket, and tools immediately in a clean bucket of water. If you wait, the hardened plaster will be more difficult to remove.
4. Allow the plaster that you've rinsed off from your gloves, mixing bucket, and tools to set up in the bottom, pour off the water, and throw away any solid plaster.

One-Piece Plaster Press-Molds

Making a one-piece plaster mold is similar to making it from polymer clay. The major difference is that you need a mold form to hold the liquid plaster until it sets up, whereas polymer clay is hand-formed. Place the model on a level, non-porous surface such as ceramic tile. Be sure the model adheres firmly to the surface so it won't float up when you pour plaster over it. Place the

For a quick and easy plaster mold form you can make a collet of a slab of clay. Water-based clay is more suitable than polymer clay for this because it is less expensive.

mold form around it and pour the plaster.

After pouring the plaster let it set up for about 20 to 30 minutes and then remove the mold form. Remove the model and let the plaster dry completely before using it. You can speed up the drying somewhat by setting it in an oven at 250° F for a few hours.

Two-Piece Plaster Press-Molds

To make a two-piece mold, bury the model in clay so only the top half is exposed, place it model up on a smooth surface, and place a mold form around it.

Pour the plaster slowly into your mold form and avoid splashing. To help the plaster settle into the crevices of the model, jiggle the work surface gently. If you run your hand along the model it will help remove any air bubbles on the surface. As the plaster sets it will start to feel warm.

(Photo: Zelda)

Master model in clay set in the mold form ready for casting the top half.

Remove the mold form, clay support and casting any time after the plaster starts to cool off. Separate the clay and plaster and remove the model. Smooth out any bumps and fill in any air bubbles that were trapped in the mold while casting. Smooth the top of the mold half and press 3 or 4 indents in it. Remove the model. Smooth the bottom of the plaster so it will sit flat on the casting surface again.

To cast the second half of the mold, set the first plaster half so the cavity opening is facing up. Apply mold release to the mold and model, replace the model and replace the mold form. Repeat the steps for the first mold half, and when it has set for 20 to 30 minutes again remove the two pieces from the mold form. Clean up both molds.

(Photo: Zelda)

Clockwise from left: Master model, 2 mold parts, and casting using the mold as a main form for creating a teapot. The great thing about molds is that the finished object doesn't have to be an exact duplicate of the original.

Let the plaster mold dry completely before using it. When a plaster mold is dry, it will no longer feel cool to the touch. Examine the mold.

Vessel Supports

Some objects may be built over a supporting structure. A supporting structure could be an armature, but not if the support will be removed from the clay after or before firing. A support differs from a mold as well, in that the clay doesn't reproduce the mold shape.

Paper or paper pulp, such as papier-mache and Creative Paperclay can be made into supports that will fit under a clay form like a drape mold. Paperclay, especially, is quick drying and can easily be sanded to a smooth surface.

Many wire meshes, available in hardware or art/craft stores, can also be used as supports. I use chicken wire covered with aluminum foil for some support forms. Chicken wire is not the best choice for intricate forms because it's unwieldy to work with, but it does provide support for vessels I make from multiple shapes, like the leaves in the vase on the book's cover. 1/4" plain weave hardware cloth makes good straight-sided molds. WireForm, a sculptor's wire mesh, is available in various meshes and weaves, as well as gauges that are pliable but strong, making it useful for supports that require complex curves or surfaces.

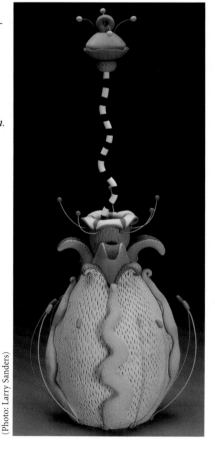

"Green Vase." This unique vase was formed over an egg-shaped, glass form. It has carved patterns that are the result of layering black clay under chartreuse. The polymer clay flower that sits in the vase opening uses a wire armature to support the stem. The flower finishes the vase as a sculpture as well as a functional vase. 16" x 8". By Rebecca Zimmerman.

(Photo: Larry Sanders)

Working with WireForm

WireForm mesh from Amaco Products, is a great support and armature material. WireForm mesh was designed by an artist to replace traditional chicken wire and plaster sculpture armatures. Made of aluminum, brass, copper, or steel, this mesh is lightweight and rust-proof. There are two types: One is woven just like window screen (except that it's made from copper, brass, etc.) and the other is produced from a sheet of metal, into which holes have been punched. Each row is offset so if you pull from the opposite sides, the holes open and the metal easily stretches in all directions.

A popular method of working with WireForm is using it as an armature with the mesh cut the shape you need and embedded between two slabs of clay. For this to be successful, it's usually best to sketch out your design first and make a template. The mesh can be cut with scissors or an X-Acto blade. You can use it free hand or make angled edges to bend the corners neatly into a box shape. A clay form using WireForm is quite rigid after curing.

Clockwise from upper left: Clay shape with WireForm to be embedded, Liquid Sculpey spread over WireForm, second layer of clay added, shaped leaf.

(Photo: Jacqueline Gikow)

Cut the mesh about 1/2" smaller than the shape you need. Lay the mesh on a slab of clay at least 1/16" (1.5 mm) thick so the mesh texture doesn't show through and roll it into the clay. Brush a thin layer of Liquid Sculpey on the mesh to ensure the clay and mesh bond. Place a second slab of clay on top and roll smooth, being careful not to trap any air bubbles. Trim the clay to the template shape and size, and you have a strong, bendable slab of clay. When your clay/mesh/clay sandwich is complete, you can stretch or bend it into the shape you want. Take a look at Diane Dunville's lamps in Chapter 8 to see more examples of WireForm use with polymer clay.

New Materials and Special Techniques

We don't often link art with technology, but just as computer technology keeps expanding, so do the arts and crafts material manufacturers in their ongoing quest for new materials to challenge and inspire creativity. The adaptability of polymer clay continues to be exploited as artists push the edges of its perceived limitations.

Sculpey SuperFlex

Sculpey SuperFlex is a new polymer clay product for which there is room for experimentation. It is soft, pliable, and remains bendable, flexible, and virtually indestructible even after firing. Sculpey SuperFlex is available in eight colors and should be cured in a preheated oven at 275° F for 20 minutes.

(Photo: Jacqueline Gikow)

This woven SuperFlex pouch resulted from Tricia Echeagaray's experiments with extruded clay-blending that produces a rainbow effect.

Patricia Echeagaray experimented with making SuperFlex into fiber by extruding it with a clay gun into fine strands. Once fired, this flexible string can be used for many fiber-oriented projects. You can crochet, knit, weave, and macramé with these strands.

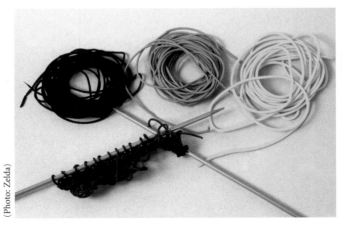

(Photo: Zelda)

Various color extrusions and a knitting sample.

Making SuperFlex Fiber

By Patricia Echeagaray

1. Select the clay gun die with the diameter "thread" you want to make, and mix the color you want the thread to be. The smallest diameter die will yield about eight yards of "thread" for every inch of clay in your extruder. Line a 9" x 12" firing pan with a piece of lightweight card stock (index card weight). Keep a stack of additional card stock next to the pan.

(Photo: Zelda)

Extrude the clay onto the first sheet in the pan.

2. Extrude the clay onto the first sheet in the pan, running a continuous thread back and forth across the card stock without letting the SuperFlex touch itself. When the sheet is full, set another sheet on top without breaking the extrusion. Continue extruding onto this new sheet of stock. Make as many layers as necessary until you've emptied the clay gun.

Tip: To join the threads, overlap the ends about 1/2" and squeeze them gently until they stick together. Then roll the overlap to blend and even out the thickness.

3. Fire the thread within an hour of extrusion to avoid having the polymer plasticizer leach into the paper. If this happens the finished thread will be dry and weaker than it should be.

Liquid Sculpey (LS)

PolyForm Products developed Liquid Sculpey at least 20 years ago, but it has only recently made its way to the artist's market. Liquid Sculpey is a pourable, brushable form of polymer clay. It isn't of much use in creating structural forms, but it can be an invaluable aid for embellishment, sealing, and repairing flaws. Liquid Sculpey comes in two formulas, opaque and translucent. The only difference is opaque Liquid Sculpey has titanium to make it white. Liquid Sculpey can be colored to blend in with the clay it is joining, and you can make patinas and color washes, fill in carved areas, or use it as grout to fill in between polymer clay "mosaic" tiles. It can be brushed onto the inside (or outside) of a vessel to add strength to a thin construction.

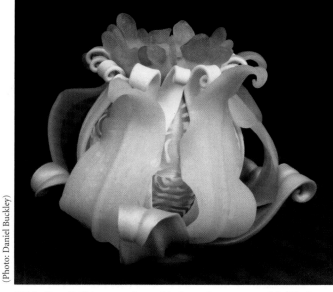

(Photo: Daniel Buckley)

"White Vessel" This covered vessel is formed over a round lightbulb and fired. The clay is removed, glued together, glazed on the inside with opaque LS, and rebaked. 4-3/4" x 3". By Jodi Bishel.

Although you can use Liquid Sculpey to join sections of clay together, it is not an adhesive. It remains fluid until fired. While you can use it to join flat surfaces, it will pool at the bottom of a vertical seam. To attach vertical sections together you need to apply PVA to hold the pieces in place through the firing phase.

The easiest way to dispense Liquid Sculpey is to pour it into a wide-mouthed squeeze bottle and squeeze out what you need. It is also convenient to have a glue syringe filled with LS around too. Mixing on a disposable palette or keeping pre-mixed colored LS in covered containers helps keep the mess under control. Baby wipes are handy for small clean ups and wiping brushes and tools. Larger clean-ups are best done with mineral spirits.

Liquid Sculpey is formulated to cure at 300° F but also cures well at normal PC temperatures of 265° F to 275° F. As with regular clays, the fumes of Liquid Sculpey are not toxic unless it burns. Liquid Sculpey produces a strong odor when baked normally, and leaves oilier residue than the regular clay. For that reason, good ventilation when using LS is even more important than usual.

> ***WARNING!** Do not put wet thinner or turpentine in your oven. Solvents are flammable so let them dry or better yet, use Sculpey Diluent to make color washes. You can paint on raw or baked clay. Don't mix water-based colors with TLS because the moisture in them turns to steam in the oven and it will puff it up—or worse, explode.*

(Photo: Zelda)

Liquid Sculpey can be colored with various pigments and oil paints. Here, I dropped thinned, colored TLS onto these disks and drew a bamboo skewer through to make the marbled designs.

Polymer Clay on a Potter's Wheel

Although slab, coil, and pinch construction are the most commonly used techniques with polymer clay, there are new methods emerging every day. A relatively new application for polymer clay, the potter's wheel, is beginning to catch clay artists' attention. The potter's wheel is a flat disk that revolves horizontally on a pivot. There isn't enough space here to give instruction on how to throw; the best way is to learn with ceramic clay before starting to throw polymer clay vessels. However, if you know how to use wheel, it's not a great transition from ceramic clay to polymer clay.

The main difference between making polymer clay vessels and ceramic ones on a potter's wheel is that ceramic clay is lubricated with water and polymer clay is lubricated with a water-based lubricant gel. Periodical lubrication with the gel is needed to allow your hands to slide smoothly over the surface of the clay.

Polymer Clay on a Lathe

A lathe is used to turn wood stock into round objects. The shapes you can turn vary, but they all have one thing in common and that is that they are variations of cylindrical shapes: rods, domes, cones etc. Polymer clay can easily be turned on a wood lathe. Wood lathes are expensive, so unless you know someone who works with wood turning it may be difficult to get access to one of these great pieces of equipment. Take a look at craft schools in your area to see if wood turning courses are taught.

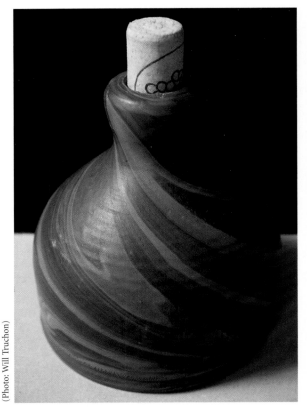

(Photo: Will Truchon)

Wheel-thrown polymer clay bottle. A lump of clay was made by stacking different colors, resulting in this swirled pattern. 6" tall. By Will Truchon.

(Photo: Eston Mansfield)

This vessel combines wood and polymer clay both worked on a wood lathe. Artist: Laura Mehr

PROJECTS
PROJECT 1. FAUX RAKU BOWL

Raku pottery was developed in Japan over four hundred years ago as the Ceremonial Tea Ware of the Zen Buddhist masters. Raku is valued because it is believed that the Spirit of the Maker is embodied in the form and revealed at the foot, which is traditionally left unglazed. It is believed that if we are alert to ourselves when contemplating the raku form, we will recognize in it our own spirit and meaning. Raku items are often used in the Japanese tea ceremony.

Raku is pottery apart from utility or function and must be approached with different criteria in mind, like a painting or a symphony. This bowl, constructed with WireForm and embellished with raku colors selected from powdered pigments and metallics, is modeled after this philosophy. Center yourself while making the form and reveal your spirit with the colors of raku. 7" diameter.

Materials and Supplies

All Premo clay
- 6 oz. black
- 3 oz. transparent
- 3 oz. turquoise

Translucent Liquid Sculpey (TLS)

Pigment and metallic powders
  (Pinks, green, blues and purples are common colors that appear in the raku firing process. It's your piece—use the colors you like).

WireForm mesh, 8-1/2" square

X-Acto knife with sharp #11 blades

Stiff Kato NuBlade cutter

Pasta machine or rolling pin

Flecto Diamond Finish Varathane

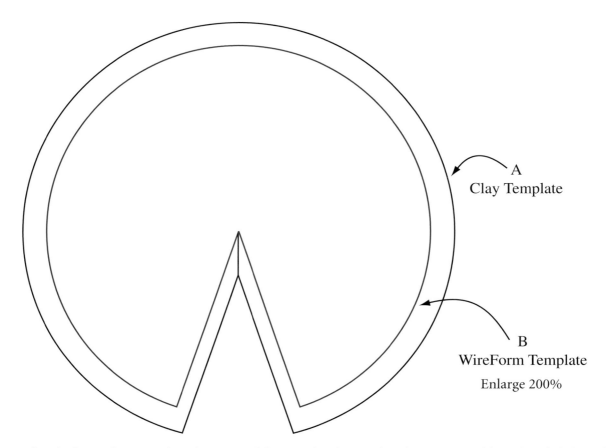

A

Clay Template

B

WireForm Template

Enlarge 200%

A. The outer circle is the clay template. Notice the wedge cutout and the cutting line that extends to the center point of the circle. Include them when you cut the clay layers. B. The inner circle is the WireForm template.

Instructions

1. Enlarge the templates 200 percent.
2. Mix together and condition the transparent and turquoise clay and roll it out to about 1/16" (1.5 mm, #3 on an Atlas pasta machine). Make a slab slightly larger than 9" square and cut it to the large template circle size.
3. Condition and roll out the black clay following the directions in step 2.
4. Cut the WireForm following the inner circle of the template. Center the WireForm on the turquoise circle and roll it flat, but not pressing so hard that it distorts the circle. Spread a thin layer of Liquid Sculpey over the WireForm.
5. Roll the black circle over the WireForm and turquoise clay to form a sandwich, matching the wedge cuts as the template indicates.
6. Carefully, slowly, and gently form the clay/WireForm/ clay sandwich into a bowl. First connect the two wedges so you have a wide cone.
7. Then, beginning with the bottom, pleat the WireForm as shown in the finished example. As the bowl bottom becomes rounded, work upward rippling the top edges.

8. When the bowl is shaped the way you want, set it aside to let it cool for awhile. Then texture the outer black surface with any abstract texture you like. I simply pressed a stylus repeatedly into the clay.
9. Dip a small, soft brush into the powders and shake off the excess. Start at one corner and brush the powders on the surface of the clay. Don't just dust them on, but don't mash so hard that you lose the texture. Vary the width and general shape of the colors. Remember the raku effect is random and unpredictable.
10. Bake the bowl for 20 minutes at 275°F and let it cool.
11. Decide whether you want a glossy surface or a matte surface or a mixture. I've used Translucent Liquid Sculpey brushed on where I want the matte finish.
12. Roll a coil of clay, about 1/2" in diameter, in black clay to raise the bowl off the table. Form the coil into a circle, brush some TLS on the top, and attach it to the bowl.
13. Fire the bowl again for 20 minutes. When the bowl is cool, coat the rest of the powders and pigments with Flecto Diamond Finish Varathane.

PROJECT 2. TEAPOT

Jody Bishel designed this project using a standard-sized light bulb as a mold, tinting the surface with Liquid Sculpey. The result is a teapot that is both short and "sweet."

(Photo: Daniel Buckley)

Materials and Supplies

Premo polymer clay
    4 oz. pearl
        Pea-sized ball of green pearl and red pearl
Transparent Liquid Sculpey
PVC coated craft wire, about 14"
Midnight Pearls gold mica powder
1 standard light bulb (40/60/75 watt—no halogen bulbs)
1" wooden ball knob
1/4" flat brush for TLS, 1 soft brush for polymer varnish
Waxed paper cups
Pasta machine

Tissue blade and X-Acto knife with #11 blade
Lace remnants, antique buttons
Oven tray
Cornstarch packing peanuts
400 grit wet/dry sandpaper
Brown paper grocery bag
Goggles and work gloves
Heavy scissors
Superglue gel
Square of waxed paper
Flecto Varathane Elite Diamond Floor Finish IPN or other polymer-friendly finish
Paint thinner

Constructing the teapot body

1. Condition the pearl Premo and cover the light bulb with a sheet rolled out at the #4 setting on the pasta machine (1/16" thick). Leave 3/8" of glass uncovered at the screw-end of the bulb. Shape the craft wire for the handle armature by pressing 1-3/4" at the center against an uncovered light bulb or shape the curve with your fingers. Press the wire lightly in place on the clay-covered bulb. Don't push it so deeply into the clay that it goes through to the glass.

2. Cover the bulb with a second layer of clay, leaving the ends of the craft wire sticking out. Don't try to finish shaping the handle yet. To make the foot, roll out a sheet of clay at the widest setting on the pasta machine (1/8" thick) and cut a strip 3-3/4" x 1/4". Join the ends to form a ring. Dampen the edge with TLS and press it into place at the bottom of the clay-covered bulb. Decorate the teapot by pressing the lace and buttons into the clay. If they stick to the clay too much, dust them with baby powder as a mold release.

Constructing the Spout

3. Use cornstarch peanuts to create the open interior of the spout. After baking, they will dissolve away with warm water. Start with two peanuts and join them to form a spout shape by moistening the ends with water and pressing them together. Continue adding more peanuts. You can trim them with a tissue blade and sand them gently to get the shape you want. Cover the peanuts with a sheet of #4 (1/16") clay. The result will be a bit lumpy but that will be covered with a second layer of clay later. The spout should be a little smaller than you want the finished spout to be.

Constructing the Lid

4. Cover slightly over half of the wooden ball knob with #4 (1/16") clay and texture it with the lace and buttons. Put all the parts on a tray and bake at 275°F for a half-hour.

Breaking out the Bulb

5. Put on goggles and work gloves.
6. Place the cooled, clay-covered bulb, clay-end first, into the grocery bag. Gather the bag opening around the screw-end of the bulb. Hold the screw end firmly with one hand and give the uncovered glass between the screw-end and the clay a sharp whack with the scissors handles or the back of a heavy knife.
7. After you hear the glass break, carefully pick the clay-covered bulb out of the bag. Most of the bulb will still be inside the clay. Squeeze the clay to crack the glass and dump the loose shards into the bag. Keep squeezing and dumping until all the glass is out. Do not use your fingers to check for remaining shards! Rinse the teapot body well with running water and dry with paper towels. Tape up the bag of broken glass and dispose of it safely.

Assembling the Teapot and Lid

8. Trim the top of the teapot and bevel the inside of the edge. Moisten the area with a little Translucent Liquid Sculpey (TLS). Roll out a 1/4" thick snake and join the ends to form a ring of clay to fit the teapot opening. Press and blend the ring onto the teapot to form the finished edge.
9. Make another smaller ring to fit inside the teapot, 1/8" down from the edge and press it into place to form a ridge to support the lid. Look at a ceramic teapot or sugar bowl if this step is unclear.

10. Twist the two sections of craft wire around each other and shape the handle armature. Cover with pearl clay to make a 3/8" thick handle. Blend the ends into the teapot body and smooth well.
11. Remove the cornstarch peanuts from the spout by melting them in a bowl of warm water. Dry the spout thoroughly and trim it to fit the teapot. Since the teapot is for decoration only, I don't cut an opening between the bowl and the spout, but you could if you wanted to. Use a few dots of the super glue to hold the spout in place on the teapot. Brush a little clear TLS between the spout and adjoining teapot to help the new clay to stick. Add a snake of clay along the seam and blend the spout into the body of the teapot. Add more clay where needed to smooth out the spout and refine the shape.
12. Cover the whole spout with a final layer of #4 (1/16") pearl clay. Decorate with the lace and buttons.
13. Remove the cooled clay dome from the wooden bead. Moisten the edge with uncolored TLS. Cut a strip of Pearl clay 1/8" thick x 1/4" high and form a ring to fit the bottom edge of the dome. Attach and blend it into the dome. Roll a 1/8" snake of clay and apply it along the line where the dome and ring have been joined. Roll a small ball of pearl clay and attach it with a little TLS to make the knob on top of the lid. Bake the teapot and lid for 20 minutes at 275°F.

Glazing the Teapot with Tinted TLS

14. Wet-sand any uneven spots in the handle or lip with 400 grit sandpaper and dry well.
15. In a waxed paper cup, mix 2 tablespoons TLS with a pea-sized lump of Midnight Pearl gold mica powder. If you choose to glaze the interior of the teapot and lid, do that first by pouring a generous amount of tinted TLS into the teapot and spreading it with a brush. Up-end the teapot on a piece of waxed paper for ten minutes to let the extra TLS drain out. Fold the waxed paper to pour the TLS back into the cup. Brush TLS inside the spout and lid. You can continue with the outside glazing but it is easier to bake the teapot for 10 minutes at 275°F to set the TLS.
16. When the teapot is cool again, paint the tinted TLS over the textured areas. It should be thick enough to settle into the details and darken them while leaving a thinner glaze over the high areas. Excess TLS can be wiped away with a paper towel. Clean tools and brushes with paint thinner.

Adding the Roses

17. Mix a soft green and pink by blending the green pearl and red pearl with some pearl Premo. The roses are made by compressing small balls of clay to make petals. Roll the first petal to create the spiral center of the rose and build out from there with more petals. The leaves are made simply by forming a flat teardrop shape with the fingers. Apply the roses with a little uncolored TLS to help them stick where there isn't already TLS glaze. Position the leaves and press vein lines in them with the back of the X-Acto blade or other tool.

18. Bake the teapot and lid for 15 minutes at 300°F. When the teapot comes out of the oven, it will have a soft matte look and the Midnight Pearls will be muted. If you like that, you're done. To bring out the color and sparkle of the mica flakes, clean the teapot with rubbing alcohol and finish with Flecto Varathane or your favorite polymer-friendly varnish.

PROJECT 3.

HANGING VESSEL WITH LIQUID SCULPEY TRANSFER

(Photo: Jacqueline Gikow)

Jacqueline Gikow
5-1/2" x 4" x 1-1/2"

Materials and Supplies

10 oz. Premo polymer clay
    5 oz. white
    4 oz. ecru
    1 oz. fuchsia
12 oz. scrap clay
Translucent Liquid Sculpey (TLS)
Sculpey Diluent
NSI Wild Wire, 20-gauge, brown
ArmorAll for mold release
Clear filament thread (bearing weight—1 lb.)
7" clear acrylic ornament holder
    (available from National Artcraft)
Various stamping or texture tools
Pasta machine or roller
X-Acto knife
Tissue blade

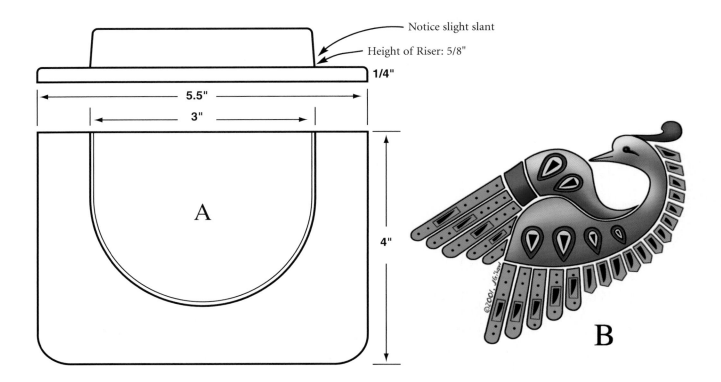

Notice slight slant

Height of Riser: 5/8"

1/4"

5.5"

3"

A

4"

B

Instructions

Make the Hump Mold

1. Enlarge the template **A** 150 percent. Refer to the measurements with the illustration when building your mold.
2. Condition and roll out a 5/8" thick slab of scrap clay (or as many sheets as it takes to reach that thickness with your pasta machine) and cut it to the triangular shape of the inner template. Angle the sides out slightly as shown in the cross-section.
3. Condition, roll out, and roll together 2 layers of clay at the largest setting of your pasta machine (or hand-roll a 1/4" thick slab) of scrap clay. Cut it to the shape of the outside template shape.
4. Center the two pieces of clay as shown in the cross-section and roll together. Slightly round the edges of both shapes. Fire for an hour, let cool, and sand.

Make the Transfer Image

5. Make two photocopies of the Phoenix motif (**B**), the holder with a stand.
6. Mix about 2/3 TLS with 1/3 Sculpey Diluent. Spread a thin coat of TLS over your image and bake it for about 15 minutes at 300° F.
7. Soak the images in water, rub the paper off the back, and let them dry.

Make the Vessel

8. Condition and roll out a slab of clay, 1/4" thick (or 2 sheets at the largest pasta machine setting). Spray ArmorAll lightly on the mold.
9. Lay the slab of clay over the mold, fitting it closely to the shape. Cut around the edges of the mold and smooth the edges of the clay.
10. (Optional) Texture the outer surface of the form.
11. Apply a thin layer of TLS to the back of the image, press it to the clay at the center of the raised portion, and bake for 30 minutes.
12. After the first half of the vessel is done repeat steps 9–11 for the second half.
13. (Optional) If you want the vessel to hold water, join the two halves with TLS, add a thin strip of clay around the edges, and re-bake.
14. Drill small, matching holes through both halves of the top and bottom of each side of the vessel. Use the 20-gauge wire to join the sides and bottom, wrapping it through the holes and around the outer edge.
15. Cut a 10" length of clear filament and tie it through each top hole. Hang the vessel from the acrylic stand.

Part III
TECHNIQUE APPLICATIONS

Chapter 8

Polymer Clay and the Literary Life

A Primer of Polymer Clay for Reading, Writing, and Miscellaneous Accessories

The history of civilization can be divided into two eras: before and after the invention of writing. Before the age of writing, communities practiced an oral tradition. As our ability to write emerged, history, law, and literature developed, and in their wake, the evolution of books. Creating art for reading and writing fascinates artists in many mediums, including polymer clay artists. In this chapter you'll use polymer clay for making books, writing instruments, and even postcards.

The word *biblos* (book) was originally applied to papyrus scrolls, which were stored rolled in protective tubes or wrappings. Books have been through many changes in form over the centuries, from the early scrolls to the new electronic model. Artists have started to look at book forms as a source of inspiration, recapturing the excitement of handling and reading books. Even the simplest book binding techniques can produce interesting results if you incorporate unusual combinations of color, pattern, and texture. Polymer clay is an excellent medium for bookbinding because its many colors can be made into patterns, and because its clay-like consistency adapts well to applied textures. Further, polymer clay's unique characteristic of flexibility lends itself well to making thin, but durable sheets that function like paper.

Writing implements have also evolved through the years. Who doesn't use a pen daily? At a coffee shop, or wherever ideas come up, do you jot them down on a computer? No; you use a pencil or pen. Writing instruments are everywhere and for a good reason. Nothing beats the feel of a personal touch.

(Photo: Hertzel Yitzhak)

Millefiori Pens by Valerie Kanter. *Two styles of pens use the millefiori technique.*

Azurite Frog Paperweight by Henrietta Scott. *Chunks of green and gold Premo coated with paint were mixed into various shades of blue. A large glass marble was covered with a sheet of this mixture. The frog on top was sculpted after the first baking. 1-3/4".*

(Photo: Archie Miles)

(Photo: Brad Miller)

Mini Books. *Codex-bound books with polymer clay covers and paper pages. Embellished with marbling, mokume gane, transfers, found objects, leaf impressions. 1-1/2" x 2". By Robyn Priestly.*

(Photo: Liv Ames)

Deborah Anderson crafted these Miniature Purse Business Card Holders. *Approximately 3-1/2" x 3-1/2".*

Additional possibilities for polymer clay craft objects related to literary use include business card holders, sealing wax stamps, rulers, paper folders, and envelope openers.

Making Books

The book projects in this chapter draw on folding styles from two civilizations: Eastern and Western. Eastern structures employ accordion folding and variations, Western civilization relies mostly on the codex, or folio system. The accordion, simple, beautiful, and versatile, is the most common among fold books. A codex book is more complex in terms of binding, but just as exciting to experiment with.

Accordion Books

The accordion book structure developed from the scroll. Since scrolls were both bulky to store and cumbersome to read, creasing the scroll into flat sections and pasting it between hard covers resulted in a form that was easier to access and store. An accordion book consists of a long zigzag-folded strip, or several smaller, pasted-together strips, of paper. Once you pick the size of your book, you can begin making the various pieces.

Accordion Page Folding

Let's say you wanted a finished book measuring 4" x 6". Cut a single piece of paper the height of your book,

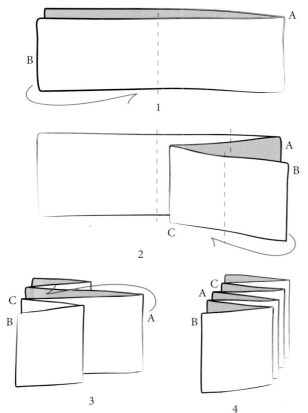

Accordion Fold
1. Fold the paper in half lengthwise and then fold each end (B) back towards the first fold (A).
2. Repeat, folding the end (B) towards the second fold (C). Do the same with the other half of the paper.
3. Fold the middle section fold to match the other edges.
4. The final accordion fold.

6", and as many times the width of your book as you want. A book with four pages requires a length four times the width of each page (For example, 16" will make four, 4" wide pages.) If you are not using paper that is the length you need for the entire book, use multiples of four to make it easier to fold your pages. Each time you want more than four pages for a book, you can attach another length of paper 16" long, which will make the book an additional four pages long.

The easiest way to fold perfect accordion pages is to begin folding from the center of your sheet of paper. First, fold a long sheet of paper in half. Then fold end (B) into the centerfold (A), using the center crease as a guide. Make a sharp crease line at each new fold that will match the paper edges (B). Then reverse the centerfold (A) and bring it even with the folds (C) and edges (B). You should have a mountain/valley fold sequence with each flat surface, the size of your book page. Continue folding in half until all the flat pages are the desired size of your book.

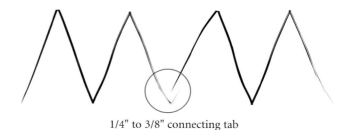

1/4" to 3/8" connecting tab

If your paper isn't long enough to fold the accordion to the size you want, you can extend it by connecting two or more additional sheets.

If your paper isn't long enough to fold the accordion to the size you want, you can extend it using 2 pieces of paper the size you need. On one, allow an extra 1/4" to 3/8" at one end. Crease along this point and fold over. Then fold both accordions as shown above and paste the small hinge of paper to the back of the second fold as shown. The additional paper sections should be attached at an edge of what will be considered the front of the book, not at the spine.

Polymer Clay Covers for Paper Pages

An accordion book cover that will support regular use can be made from polymer clay. A cover made from a thicker sheet of clay is sturdier than a cover made with a thinner one. Make the cover from either Premo or Fimo–clays that remains flexible after firing. If you usually use Sculpey III, mix in another, more flexible clay so it isn't too brittle.

Roll out two sheets of clay 1/8" thick and decorate them on one side as desired. If you are adding canes or another decorative layer, roll the clay to 1/16". Re-roll to 1/8" after decorating. Cut each sheet to the size of your book pages.

Note: you aren't limited to square- or rectangular-shaped books. Experiment with odd shapes, or even tearing an edge or even using scissors for a decorative edge to make your book covers.

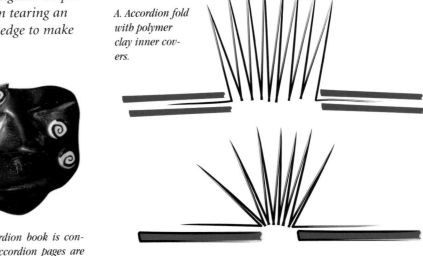

(Photo: Don Felton)

A. Accordion fold with polymer clay inner covers.

"Map of the Mind" by Dayle Doroshow. *This accordion book is constructed from ivory and black clay canes. The accordion pages are imprinted with a map of the universe. 3" x 2-3/4".*

B. Fan book: glue back folds together.

If your book covers are flat, baking them between two heavy, flat surfaces will prevent them from warping. Two 8" or 9" square tiles will work for many book sizes. Fire the covers for about 20 to 30 minutes at the manufacturer's recommended temperature and let them cool. With PVA glue such as Beacon Gem-Tac, glue the end pages from the paper accordion to the polymer covers as shown and let them dry. Below are a few other ways to attach the pages to the covers.

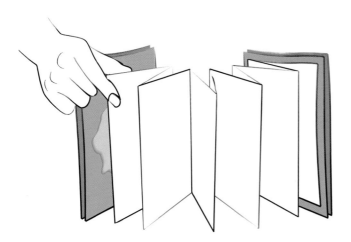

Attach the end pages of the accordion fold to the polymer covers using PVA glue.

You can add an inner polymer clay liner and hide the paper edges (A) or glue the back edges of the accordion pages together (B). This is called a "fan" book. Because the edges are glued together in a fan book, you no longer have access to the back of the paper in the book.

(Photo: Brad Miller)

"Botanica Book-Pyramid" by Robyn Priestly. *A set of nesting polymer clay pyramids with a book in the center. Books are accordion-folded with paper contents and polymer covers. 5-1/2" x 7".*

Polymer Clay: Creating Functional and Decorative Objects

Making an Accordion Book with Polymer Clay Pages

"See-thru Book." This accordion book has paper-thin pages and is hinged together with handcrafted lock-rings. 2-1/2" x 4". By Jacqueline Gikow.

It isn't possible to fold a strip of polymer clay into an accordion and have it open and close like a piece of paper. But that won't stop us from using polymer clay for accordion pages! Polymer clay accordion pages are made separately and hinged together. Because of this, it's not necessary to work in multiples of four and there are many ways to attach the pages together so they will fold into an accordion. One option is to use fabric strips as hinges. Polymer clay pages can be joined using fabric, ribbon, string, grommets, and even lock rings.

A Flexible Hinge

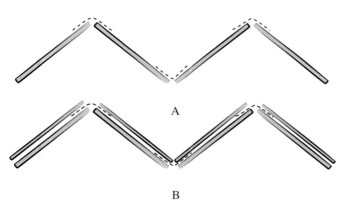

A. A visible fabric hinge is made by gluing a thin strip of fabric to one side of the clay panels. This can be quite attractive if you use a fabric pattern that complements your clay pattern or color.
B. Alternatively, you can hide the hinge by sandwiching it between two sheets of clay.

A polymer clay accordion book with a flexible fabric hinge can be made two ways: either you can leave the hinge visible, or you can hide the hinge. To hide the hinge you'll need to double the number of pages so the fabric or whatever you make your hinge out of can be sandwiched between them. The clay should be rolled to the thinnest setting on the pasta machine (usually number seven) before cutting each "page." The pages can be left plain for later writing or decorating, or a decorative surface can be created while you make the book.

Making Codex Books

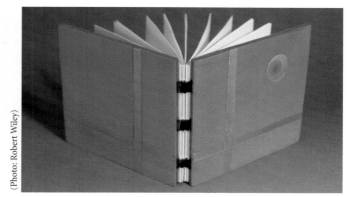

"Sunrise." Polymer clay covers and paper signatures are bound with an exposed spine sewing technique. 3" x 1/2". By Robert Wiley.

Historically, bookbinding did not exist in the manner of today until the codex style began to replace the scroll, roughly 2,000 years ago. The codex book form originated in the Eastern Mediterranean area. Examples of Egyptian Coptic-style bindings can be dated to about the second century, from fragments of bound papyrus texts.

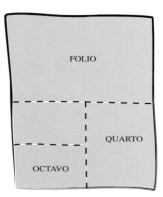

These are the parts of a traditional codex book.

The physical parts of a Western book form a structure that is essentially unchanged for hundreds of years.

Each time a piece of paper is folded in half it results in smaller pages which are given different names: folio, quarto, and octavo. The full size of the paper affects the page size of all three divisions.

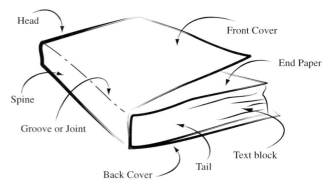

Each folded section of paper is given a different name: folio, quarto, and octavo.

A codex book form consists of sections called "signatures," sewn together to form the book block. Signature is the name for the assembled, folded, and sewn set of pages. The smallest signature is a single, cut and folded, sheet of paper that has two leaves and four pages (front and back). Books usually consist of several signatures.

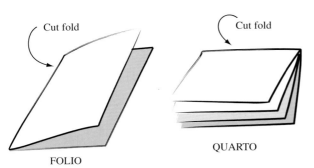

(Photo: Barbara McGuire)

Barbara McGuire's *journals are inlaid abstract paintings of cane slices and rolled clay. The collage effect is a result of layering small bits of color over a solid sheet and then passing it through the pasta machine until the color is stretched to create a "wash" effect. Inclusions such as gold leaf, and texture such as stamped impressions are a part of the overall surface treatment. The individual face cane slice is also stretched and manipulated to the desired expression.*

Cut fold

Cut fold

FOLIO

QUARTO

Don't cut folds

OCTAVO

Folding a signature from a single sheet of paper.
A. Fold the paper in half. The top and bottom edges must line up exactly. Flatten the fold with a bone folder or the side of a pencil. Cut the folded edge with a sharp knife.
B. Repeat this two more times for subsequent divisions (quarto and octavo), but don't cut the edge fold of the third repeat (C).
At this point eight leaves make up the signature. Four folios, quartos or octavos, resulting in 16 pages, are usually the standard numbers for a signature.

Even the simplest book can be both functional and attractive. The easiest codex book to make is a pamphlet. This simple pamphlet project covers all the steps for making any traditional codex book. The basic principle can be demonstrated with a signature made from a single sheet of paper.

Sew the Signature

Punch 3, 5, or 7 holes at the signature fold. Run the thread through one of the center holes and continue sewing a running stitch.

Whether your book has one or many signatures, it's still necessary to sew each one. To do this, mark 3 to 7 hole positions on the center inside fold of the signature. Larger books need more positions. Thread a tapestry needle with string or yarn, four times the height of the signature. Starting in the middle, sew a running stitch to one end. Reverse the direction and sew back to the middle. Repeat for the other end.

To make the signature edges even, use a triangle set to the folded edge and trim off a small amount of the other three sides.

Adding a Polymer Clay Cover to Paper Pages

Preparing a codex book cover in polymer clay is similar to the one illustrated for the accordion. You'll need a front and a back cover, but don't attach the pages to the covers just yet. Here are a few new ways you can bind your paper pages with polymer clay.

(Photo: Zelda)

This codex-style journal contains four signatures of different paper types. The pages have been bound with a polymer clay cover. 5-3/4" x 5-3/4" x 5/8". By Jacqueline Gikow.

Books With Polymer Clay Pages

This polymer clay sketchbook combines scrap clay and thin white clay on each leaf, which serves as the sketching area. A small fan book is attached to the front cover, and the binding uses three binder rings. 5" x 5" x 1/2". By Jacqueline Gikow.

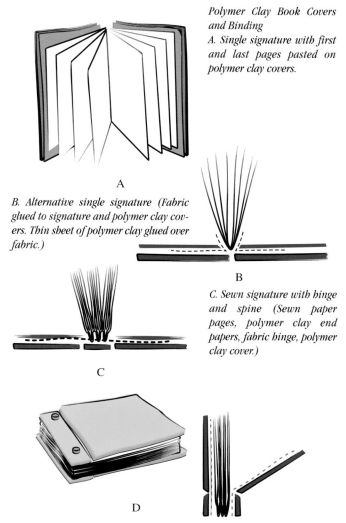

Polymer Clay Book Covers and Binding
A. Single signature with first and last pages pasted on polymer clay covers.

A

B. Alternative single signature (Fabric glued to signature and polymer clay covers. Thin sheet of polymer clay glued over fabric.)

B

C. Sewn signature with hinge and spine (Sewn paper pages, polymer clay end papers, fabric hinge, polymer clay cover.)

C

D

D. Album with split covers and post holders (Multiple signatures, fabric hinge, polymer cover.) Note: this will work with polymer clay pages also.

Because polymer clay is quite strong even when thin, it's an excellent medium for making books. It's possible to make books that can be written in, to design the pages as completed stories, or create folios of related works of art. Begin by determining how many pages the book will contain, and then roll out the desired number of paper-thin sheets of clay.

Making paper-thin sheets of clay requires some care. As you are working, give the clay sheets time to cool before running each through progressively thinner settings on the pasta machine. Very thin pages are often easier to control if you hand roll the clay. Don't handle the clay pages a lot because that may cause them to warp during baking. Decorating can be done either before or after cutting the pages and before or after baking.

Cut the sheets of clay to the desired size, lay them on a flat baking surface, and place them in the oven at the manufacturer's recommended temperature for about 20 to 30 minutes. You can stack them in layers in the oven by placing them on sheets of tracing paper or vellum.

Because these pages are paper-thin, longer baking may cause some clay colors to darken. Make sure the oven temperature stays steady so the clay doesn't burn or warp. Let the fired clay cool, and then get ready to bind the pages together.

Binding Polymer Clay Pages

There are many alternatives to binding books with polymer clay pages, just as with paper. Binding polymer clay books in traditional codex style is also quite similar to binding paper books. The difference is that you don't have signatures to sew together.

Cut a strip of muslin or other lightweight fabric the same height as the book and 2" wider than the spine. Stack the clay pages and align the back edges. This will be the bound edge. Apply a coat of Liquid Sculpey to the clay page edges and carefully center the fabric over them. Pull the fabric taut over the spine and use a straight edge to tack it firmly to the edges of the pages. Then glue the flaps of fabric to the beginning and ending page with

PVA. Re-bake the text block for about 15 minutes and let it cool.

To attach the book pages to the covers, cut another piece of fabric about 3" wider than the spine and slightly shorter. Attach it to the spine and covers of the book with PVA glue, and let it dry. Refer to Illustration below to see what this looks like in a cross-section.

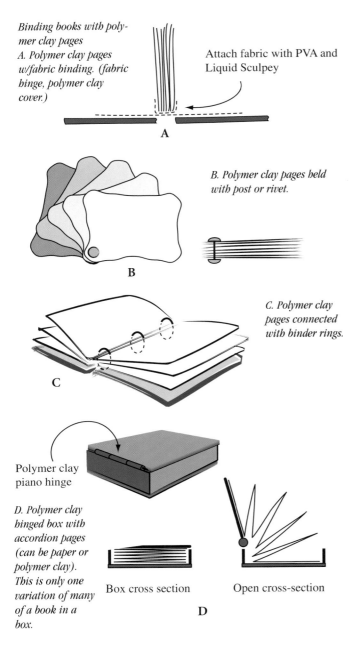

Binding books with polymer clay pages
A. Polymer clay pages w/fabric binding. (fabric hinge, polymer clay cover.)

Attach fabric with PVA and Liquid Sculpey

A

B. Polymer clay pages held with post or rivet.

B

C. Polymer clay pages connected with binder rings.

C

Polymer clay piano hinge

D. Polymer clay hinged box with accordion pages (can be paper or polymer clay). This is only one variation of many of a book in a box.

Box cross section

Open cross-section

D

Terry Lee Czechowski
"Dance Fan." *Polymer clay stamped and mixed media. 2" x 6".*

"That 'C' Word" by Terry Lee Czechowski. *Fan book with polymer clay covers, coffee filter pockets, cardstock. 5" x 7".*

The explosion in book arts in the last decade has resulted from artists exploring nontraditional, as well as traditional bookbinding. Books have become means of expression and enable artists to combine visual arts and thoughts in an individual work. The polymer clay medium is proving to be an important material in contributing to the new growth of the book arts.

Writing

The history of writing instruments by which humans have recorded and conveyed thoughts, feelings and grocery lists, is the history of civilization itself.

Among our early ancestors' first inventions was the handy sharpened stone—that all-purpose skinning and killing tool that was adapted into the first writing instrument and used to keep records of hunting trips and events in daily life such as the planting of crops.

The earliest means of writing that resemble the pens and inks as we know them today were found among the

Artists' Books

Most of us think of books as the objects found sitting on a library shelf or displayed in a bookstore, but the range is much greater than that. Books can vary in size, shape, and style, and structure is almost synonymous with technique. There are so many options it would be impossible to cover them in one chapter.

Polymer Clay: Creating Functional and Decorative Objects

(Photo: Vicki Domansky)

"Dragon Pen." Vicki Domansky's *pen is covered with a layer of metallic green polymer clay sculpted in the shape of the dragon and textured with scales. The dragonhead serves as a cap, and was made after covering the end of the baked pen with aluminum foil. The pen cap features eyes and fangs of glow-in-the-dark polymer clay.*

(Photo: Zelda)

Bic Stic pens covered with a layer of patterned clay and then embellished with leaf-motif canes. By Elizabeth Campbell.

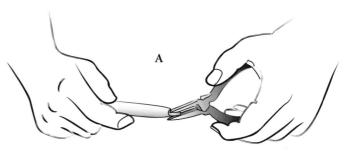

A. *Use needlenose pliers to remove the pen cartridge before you start to cover and decorate the pen. When the pen is completed, re-insert the pen cartridge into its holder, again using the needle nose pliers.*

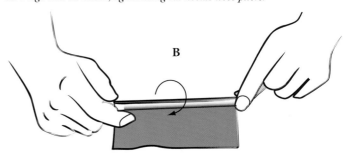

B. *Place the pen at the straight edge of a slab of clay and carefully, but firmly roll it around to meet the other end. Trim off the extra clay and roll the pen to eliminate the seam.*

Greeks, who employed a writing stylus made of either metal, bone or ivory to place marks upon wax-coated tablets. The Chinese invented and perfected "Indian Ink," a mixture of soot from pine smoke, lamp oil mixed with donkey-skin gelatin, and musk, which came into common use in around 1200 B.C.

Pens have a long history. From quill pens to fountain pens to ball-point pens and pens with fiber tips and even electronic pens, many variations have been created over the years. The writing instrument that was predominant for the longest period in history (over one thousand years) was the quill pen, made from a bird feather. It was introduced around A.D. 700. The principle of ball-point pens, the most common pen in use, dates from the late nineteenth century and is still used today. The only real difference these days is in the holders for the ink source, which can be as varied as the creative mind can imagine. And that is what makes polymer clay a perfect material for pens.

Traditional pencils are made with a wooden case and a lead that runs through the center. Pencil "lead" is not the metal we call lead, but a mixture of graphite (carbon) for blackness, and "China Clay" (the same clay used to make cups and saucers). The ratios of one to the other are varied for hardness. The leads are baked in a kiln and we use the term "grades" to describe hardness. A numbering system indicates how hard or soft the lead is. HB is the zero point, with hardness and softness increasing in either direction: 2B is a soft black, while 2H is a harder black. As with pens, any innovations we have seen have been new designs and decorations for the pencil "casing."

Ball-point Pens

Learning to cover ball-point pens with polymer clay isn't difficult. I'm using plain, old Bic Stic pens for this demonstration, but you could also use the more expensive metal pens. The Bic Stic, made of PVC, will withstand the firing process. Don't use clear plastic-cased pens as they melt when heated.

Remove the ink cartridge from the pen with a needle nose pliers. The cartridge is attached to the tip, so don't let the pliers slip and pull out the tiny metal point.

Roll the clay to #3 on a pasta machine (1/16") if you want a thick pen and to #5 if you want the pen to be thin, and trim the slab to the length of the pen. Cut one edge of the clay straight and lay it along the edge of a piece of plain paper. Set your pen parallel to the front edge of the clay sheet and use the paper to pull the clay up over the pen. This will keep the clay from stretching out of shape. Roll the paper/clay over the pen and smooth it to the pen from end to end.

Pull the paper away and continue to roll the clay forward. When it reaches all around, it will leave a cutting guide mark. Cut just inside that line, and roll the pen forward again to pick up the rest of this strip that you've cut. Make sure that these two edges touch, but don't overlap. If the clay overlaps, the uneven bump will make it difficult to reshape the cylinder. Roll the pen on its side until the seam disappears.

If extra clay has extruded over either end of the pen, trim it off. It's a good idea to leave both ends of the pen open until you have released any trapped air bubbles. The pen may require several cycles through this rolling and shaping before it looks right to you. After you bake the pen, replace the ink cartridge.

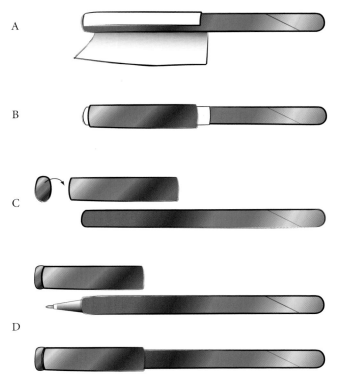

Make a pen cover
A. Wrap a strip of freezer (dull side on pen) or tracing paper, 2" wide and several inches long, tightly around the pen barrel. Wrap the paper twice around so the cap fits tightly. Tape the paper tightly to itself using masking tape or a dab of PVA.
B. Wrap a 1-1/2" to 2" wide sheet of clay (the same thickness or thinner than your pen) around the freezer paper until clay meets clay and cut to fit. Match the seams carefully and smooth them by rolling on a flat surface. Trim the ends evenly. Bake the tube on the pen for 20 minutes and let it cool.
C. Remove the tube and paper from the pen. You may need to run a needle tool between the cap and paper to loosen it. Brush some TLS onto the top of one end of the tube and flatten a small ball of clay onto it. Make sure you have total contact between the flattened ball and cap. Decorate the cap as you wish. Bake the finished cap for 30 minutes. When it cools test the cap for fit. If it's too loose, brush some TLS on the inside edge of the cap and bake again.

If you want, you can also make a cover for the pen. Just wrap a small piece of tracing paper around the top end of the pen. Wrap that with a layer of clay cut to the size you want, and wrap it around the pen. The tracing paper gives you just enough room to pull the pen out.

This is just a beginning exercise. You can get as exotic as you want with covered pens. I've seen them dressed up as cute "critters," elegant as marble, and as funky as the imagination can go.

Making Pencils

If you make the pencil thin enough it will work in a pencil sharpener. Thicker pencils have to be sharpened with a razor blade or X-Acto knife. By Jacqueline Gikow.

Polymer clay pencils are made in a similar manner to pens and are almost as easy to make. Instead of covering a plastic case, however, you cover the actual mark-maker; in this case the round stick of graphite (often referred to as "pencil lead"). Pencils are made entirely of polymer clay apart from the graphite and can be sharpened like a wood pencil. Graphite sticks are quite fragile, even the thicker ones, so work carefully when applying the clay layer.

You'll find plain graphite sticks at art supply shops and stationery stores. HB and 2B grades (softness) are good choices for a general use pencil. They are usually available in lengths of about 6" and about 1/16" (1.5 mm) in diameter, similar to that in an ordinary wooden pencil.

As with other covered items, coating the graphite with PVA glue is recommended to aid the bond. While the clay will stick to the graphite when it is raw, it may pull away from it after it is fired. Keep the clay rolled tightly against the graphite to prevent this.

About 1/4 oz. of polymer clay is the best quantity if you want to be able to sharpen your pencil in a commercial sharpener. Roll the clay into a ball about 1" (25 mm) diameter, lay it on your work surface, and pierce it with the graphite stick, straight down the center, the way you would a large bead. Push the graphite through until it is centered, turn the clay with graphite on its side, and roll gently, as shown, until the ball becomes cylindrical, and spreads out along the lead. If the clay works away from the lead, stop rolling and squeeze it back on firmly, then continue.

To make your pencil even, you can roll it under a piece of glass or Plexiglas. Keep the rolling surface parallel to the working surface, place your hands on the glass, and roll gently back and forth. This technique is great for smoothing out coils or snakes of clay as well.

Polymer Clay: Creating Functional and Decorative Objects

A. Roll the clay into a ball, lay it on your work surface, and pierce it with the graphite stick, straight down the center, the way you would a large bead. Push the graphite through until it is centered, turn the clay with graphite on its side, and roll gently, as shown, until the ball becomes cylindrical, and spreads out along the lead.

A

B. When the clay is extended to the full length of the graphite, measure the diameter to make sure it will fit into a pencil sharpener. Thicker pencils can be sharpened with a knife. Shape the front of the pencil into a point so it can be started in the pencil sharpener easily.

B

When the clay is extended the full length of the graphite, measure the diameter to determine it's not too thick to fit into a pencil sharpener. If you make it thicker, it will need to be sharpened with a knife. Trim the ends if they extend past the lead and pinch the clay into a point at one end of the lead, which will make it easier to sharpen later. Apply a disk of clay to the end, or add decorative elements, to keep the lead from pushing out when the pencil is sharpened.

Bake the pencil for about 30 minutes or longer. When it is cool, carefully sharpen it. Because of the nature of polymer clay, these pencils flex when sharpening and in use, so be careful when handling them.

(Photo: Zelda)

Even out the surface of your pencil by rolling it under a smooth, flat surface. Clear Plexiglas lets you see what's happening.

Cards, Cards, Cards

Tarot and other fortune-telling cards are said to hold the secrets of our present and future. Business or calling cards are great items to leave with potential customers or

(Photo: Krause)

"Chaos Cards." Dayle Doroshow *created these decks of artist's tool cards with instructions to inspire, guide, or jumpstart a stalled project. Transfers, oil and acrylic paints, carving, handset type, and embossing powders. 2" x 3-1/4".*

just with a friend. With flat objects made from polymer clay, the key to success is in a long curing time. The longer you bake it (at the correct temperature, not high or low) the more flexible it becomes, and that translates to less of a potential for damage.

Sending Postcards Through the Mail

Postcards are containers of words, of pictures, of texture and surface. The artwork is the container; the writing is the filling.

(Photo: Zelda)

You can actually send these postcards through the mail. On the top postcard, two slices of a transparent and black windowpane cane were rolled to #7 on the pasta machine and then rolled by hand onto the violet sheet. The bottom card is made from scrap clay with two pieces of white clay rolled onto the back for areas to write a message and an address. Approximately 4" x 6". By Jacqueline Gikow.

Did you know you could send a postcard made completely of polymer clay through the mail just like a regular postcard? You must follow the Post Office's size guidelines when sending polymer clay postcards, but that doesn't mean your postcards have to be rectangular and boring in shape. The maximum size of a regular postcard is 6" long, 4-1/4" high, and the thickness of an index card and it costs twenty-one cents to mail. More than likely a postcard made of polymer clay will exceed these measurements. Instead, follow the letter or large envelope rates for first-class mail. Each piece must weigh 13 ounces or less, or they can be sent as Priority Mail. Check with the Post Office for the exact cost. When your cards are addressed and ready to mail, take them to the Post Office to have them hand-stamped. Although polymer clay is flexible enough to endure the rigors of mail delivery, it won't withstand the abuse of an automated handler.

Reading and Writing Accessories

Polymer clay can be used for more than pens and pencils. Use your imagination to consider bookends, inkwells, paperclip holders, pencil cups, stamp holders, stationery holders, and more.

These objects can be made using many of the techniques covered in Part II of this book. An inkwell can be equally attractive whether made by covering an existing small bottle, by making a pinch bottle with a closure, or using a mold for shaping the form. You can make objects that reflect your style to enrich your reading and writing life, rather than settling for what a store has to offer.

"Stamp Dispenser." Red pearl and black Premo clay make up this slab-built pot that is decorated with bullseye canes and thin coils of black clay. The lid connects to the vessel by an inner spindle, which is used to hold the stamps in place. By Jacqueline Gikow.

(Photo: Zelda)

"Butterfly Bowls." Made from polymer clay canes, the wings of this butterfly are shaped in a bowl form to function as a paperclip/thumbtack holder. 3" x 3" x 3". By Jacqueline Gikow.

(Photo: Zelda)

Polymer Clay: Creating Functional and Decorative Objects

PROJECTS

PROJECT 1. MAKING A POSTCARD

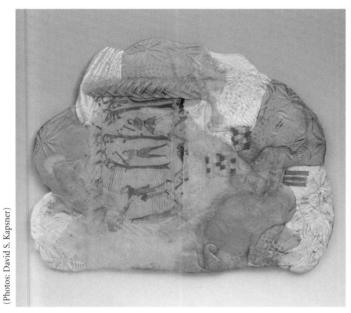

(Photos: David S. Kapsner)

by Linda Goff

Beginner

Postcard (front and back) Approximately 4" x 6".

Materials and Supplies

Premo clay in various colors (use translucent sparingly)
Pasta machine
Sharp knife
Waxed or plain paper
Assorted embellishing materials

Instructions

1. Run a sheet of clay (any color or blend of colors) through your pasta machine on the #3 setting. You can use some translucent but not a lot—it is more brittle than other colors.
2. Cut the sheet into a geometric or organic shape about 4-1/2" x 6" and set it onto a piece of wax paper or plain paper. Even if you are making a rectangular card, I recommend forming it without sharp corners, so your card won't break in transit.

Decoration

3. Once you have the clay sheet base, the rest is pure fun! Add thin slices of canes, mokume gane, clay scraps. Add a copier or magazine transfer. Punch a few holes in the clay or cut ragged edges with paper scissors. Texture the surface with rubber stamps, leather tools, patterned materials, or rough textured fabric. Make a leaf, flower, or branch imprint. Rub some metallic powder in to accentuate your textures. After you're finished with one side, turn the card over and decorate the other side. Decorate the whole card as a piece of art, or leave space to write on. Your recipient will love it either way.
4. But wait! Remember to leave a section of smooth, light-colored clay on one side for the address and stamp.
5. Bake at 275° F for 30 minutes. For other clays, follow usual baking instructions.

PROJECT 2. INDEX CARD BOX

(Photo: Mary Cairns)

by Judy Kuskin
Intermediate

The polymer box displayed here is called "Palestine and Israel: Inside the Same Box." It is constructed of strips of polymer clay imprinted with Arabic and Hebrew proverbs using a photocopy transfer technique. The image on the cover is also a photocopy transfer. The sticks on the lid are used on the edges of the box for both decorative and structural purposes. The box you create will be similar in construction but your choices of photocopy transfer and sticks will affect the final form. 4-1/2" x 8-1/2".

Materials and Supplies

12 oz. 00 translucent Art Fimo

One pea-sized piece each of yellow and green polymer clay

Narrow, straight twigs cut to the following lengths (skewers can be used but will give a different effect):

Twelve 4" long for corners of box

Four 6" long and four 4" long for bottom edge of box

Two 8" long and two 7" long for top of box

Waxed linen cording

Photocopy of an image you like, approximately 5" x 3" for top of box

Photocopied text (from magazine or newspaper) for sides of box (I like to use foreign language text to add intrigue!)

3 sheets acetate (used for overhead projectors or copy machines)

Cyanoacrylic glue such as Zap-a-Gap

Pasta machine and/or roller

Q-tips

Rubbing alcohol

Sharp knife

3" x 5" index cards (or handmade paper cut to size)

Instructions

Box sides and bottom

1. Mix a pea-sized piece of yellow polymer clay with 4 oz. of 00 translucent Fimo to create a lovely translucent yellow.

2. Mix a pea-sized piece of green polymer clay with 4 oz. of 00 translucent Fimo to create a lovely translucent green.

3. Roll a sheet of each color on #4 on the pasta machine and cut to 5" x 7".

4. Photocopy the text image onto a piece of acetate. Lay the acetate on the photocopy machine glass, printed side up, and make a photocopy of that. You will now have a mirror image of the text photocopied onto paper.

5. Lay the paper photocopy with the mirror image text, print side down, on the yellow sheet of polymer and burnish well with a roller.

6. Dip a Q-tip into rubbing alcohol and rub over the back of the paper. You will see the image emerge through the saturated paper.

7. Let the photocopy image rest on the clay for 15 minutes and remove paper. Bake as directed for 00 Fimo translucent. Your text will now be permanently adhered to the clay and it will be in the original orientation. (If you don't reverse the text image using the acetate first, you will end up with mirror image text on the clay.)

8. Repeat steps 4 through 6 with a 5" x 7" sheet of green clay.

9. Cut the yellow and green sheets of clay, with the text imprinted on them, into 3/8" strips.

10. Make the four sides of the box by weaving the strips in a standard over-one, under-one pattern. Make two of the woven sides 4" x 6" and two woven sides 4" x 4".

11. Roll two sheets of translucent on #1 on the pasta machine for the bottom of the box. Layer them together and cut to 4" x 6".

12. Make four bundles of three 4" sticks for the corners of the box. Tie the bundles together at either end with the waxed linen cord.

13. Make two bundles of two 6" sticks and two bundles of two 4" sticks. Tie the bundles together at either end with the waxed linen cord.

14. Assemble the four sides and the bottom of the box, gluing the bundled sticks on the corners and bottom edges to hide the seams.

Lid of Box

1. Roll out a 4 oz. piece of 00 translucent Fimo to #4 on the pasta machine for the box lid. Cut to 4" x 6".

2. Roll the photocopy image you selected for the top of your box, print side down, on the sheet of clay.

Burnish it well with a roller and rub with a Q-tip dipped in rubbing alcohol. Let it rest for 15 minutes and remove the paper photocopy. The image should be transferred to the clay. Bake as directed for 00 Fimo translucent.

3. Roll a flat sheet of 00 translucent at #4, and cut to 5" x 7". Center the image transfer sheet of clay on top of this sheet.

4. Arrange some strips of the text transfers around the photo until you get a pleasing combination and glue to the bottom sheet. The strips should lie flush around the image (not woven), resulting in one smooth surface. (Lid A.)

5. Roll out another sheet of 00 translucent on #4 on the pasta machine and cut to the same size as the lid you made in Step 3. (Lid B.) Bake the two lid sections separately.

6. Make a frame of two 7" sticks and two 8" sticks which fits snugly around the lid you just made. Overlap the sticks at the corners and tie with the waxed linen cording, leaving a long piece of cord at each corner.

7. Arrange the stick frame around lid B and glue the corner strings firmly onto the top of lid B to hold the frame in place.

8. Glue lid A on top of lid B. Put index cards in the box and you're ready for a day's work.

EBONY & IVORY TRIANGULAR CONCERTINA BOOK

(Photo: Zelda)

Beginner/Intermediate

This triangular concertina features accordion-folded pages with polymer clay covers. It looks complicated, but it's quite simple to do.

Concertina books are accordion-style books traditionally used for Buddhist sutras, or calligraphy and painting albums. Concertinas aren't limited to rectangular shapes; they can be just about any size and shape you want. A painter friend of mine uses concertinas to do quick sketches from live models resulting in a ribbon of lyrical sketches. 5-1/2" triangle

Materials and Supplies

Premo polymer clay
  2 oz. translucent
  2 oz. white
  2 oz. ivory (or mix 1 ecru + 1 white)
  2 oz. black
Paper: 36" long x 5" high (You can use paper that comes on a roll or connect smaller sheets of paper as illustrated in the chapter)
Ribbon: Grosgrain or satin ribbon
Pasta machine or roller
Sharp knife
PVA glue
Scrap paper for pasting
Waxed paper
Metal straight edge
Bone folder or similar tool
Book press or large, heavy weight

Instructions

Cover

1. Condition and roll out the black clay to #1 (1/8") on the pasta machine, and trim it to 5-1/2" square.
2. Mix the white, translucent, and ivory clays as described in the Faux Ivory instructions on the next page.
3. Make a cane from part of the ivory and the scrap from the black clay. You can either make the one shown in the finished example, or you can make one you prefer.
4. Slice pieces off each of the 4 sides (not the top and bottom) from the "chunk" of ivory. Lay the slices on top of the black clay and roll them together to join. Make sure you completely blend the seams from the pieces.
5. Optional: You can draw designs in the ivory with a needle, make light scratches for a "damaged," antique look.
6. Cut the square in half diagonally as shown at right.
7. Wrap a thin piece of clay around the edges of each triangle.
8. Fire for about 30 minutes at 275° F.
9. Optional: Rub a patina of dark brown paint into the crevices, then wipe most of it off with a paper towel. After the paint dries, rub the clay with fine steel wool (#000) and buff slightly for a light sheen.

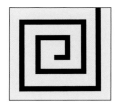

Cane profile

This is the design in the book above. You can use this template, or use your own creativity to design the covers your own way. At the top is the profile of the cane I used in the center circle.

Pages

10. Start with the text paper stretched in front of you horizontally. Holding one end against the work surface, fold the paper down to make a diagonal fold (B). Be especially careful that the corner is perfect and that the edges match perfectly at the left side.

Note: Small errors multiply in fold books. It is especially important that you be as meticulous as possible or monstrous gaps will appear by the end.

11. Now fold the long end of the paper up (C). Again, the corner must be perfect and the left side must match.

12. Continue to fold along the diagonal until you're finished (D). Be careful at each step to have the edges match and the corners perfect. If you have any excess paper at the end, trim it to the edge of the last triangle.

Assemble the Book

13. Paste each end triangle from the paper onto the center of the inside polymer book cover.

14. Place a piece of waxed paper between the glued papers and the rest of the book and weight it down overnight until completely dry.

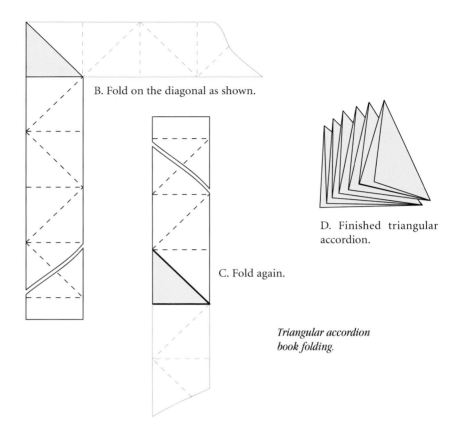

B. Fold on the diagonal as shown.

C. Fold again.

D. Finished triangular accordion.

Triangular accordion book folding.

Faux Ivory

1. Condition the translucent, ivory, and white clay and press each into a flat sheet. You can do this with the pasta machine, but using your hands will make the thickness a little irregular, which will result in a more natural look.

2. Lay one sheet on top of the other and cut into 4 quarters. Stack the 4 sheets. You now have a striped block with 8 layers.

3. Press and flatten the block with your hands, then cut it into 4 quarters again and stack again. Now there are 32 layers. Repeat this twice more.

Note: You won't be able to see the layers very well, but the translucent will change color during firing and they'll become more obvious. These layers form the grain of the ivory.

Chapter 9

Diversions, Entertainment, and Pastimes

Introduction

In this chapter we'll use polymer clay to create a variety of games, musical instruments, and toys that will challenge you to expand your polymer clay abilities and delight you with the results. From games to musical instruments to toys, here are ideas that will spark your "claymagination"!

Define a board game in terms of vessels? In practical terms, a board game holds the game pieces. But, it's also something that holds our attention. So do toys. Something about toys fascinates everyone, not just children. And polymer clay toys have their own unique charm.

Most of the musical instruments discussed in this chapter hold air, and without the vehicle (vessel) that holds it, there would be no sound at all. Of course musical instruments can also hold and emit sound by vibration. Just look at the drum by polymer clay artist Cynthia Tinapple and her woodworker husband David.

Well, there's the justification. But whatever the reasons, the objects in this chapter are here for just what the chapter title mentions—for diversion, entertainment, and passing the time. Enjoy!

Games

(Photo: Jacqueline Gikow)

"Board on a Wire." *This chess set consists of a board constructed from polymer clay and coiled Wild Wire. The wire was coiled into tight springs and connects each round playing surface piece to the board. The surface pieces are stamped with a texture, different for each color. The playing pieces are color-coordinated with the playing board. 9" x 1".*

Games exist in many categories and take many forms. From board games, to card games, to puzzles, and more, the potential exists to use polymer clay creatively in designing many of them. With so many choices, where should we start? Board games are probably the easiest to demonstrate, and can yield some exciting results.

The histories of the major board games played today are from all over the world. People have played games

using a board surface since before the 1500s. A few Western board game favorites include Backgammon (England, 1600s), Checkers, Chess (descended from Shaturanga, India circa. A.D. 650-850). Chinese Checkers (descended from an older Chinese game, Victorian, around 1880), Go (China, fourth or sixth century), Monopoly (USA, 1934), and Parcheesi (national game of India, fourth century) complete this partial list.

Making Board Games

Most board game surfaces are wood or cardboard, decorated with two contrasting colored, alternatively arranged squares. Tiles or a painted surface can be used to make up the board as well. Most playing pieces are simply round disks.

Making a game board is a great way to experiment with color and shape. Although game boards traditionally are square, who says they must be? Who says they must be flat? What would a tiered, or perhaps a freeform, chessboard look like?

Color and pattern can be interestingly used on a traditional square board as well. Why not use two contrast-

(Photo: Zelda)

This small checker/chess board is hinged to a container that stores the game pieces. The feet are guilded wood drawer pulls. 5" x 2-1/2".

ing square canes for the board? It makes an easy, yet striking game board. I like a millefiori cane that contrasts with the solid color slab for the alternating squares on the board, but two canes could be used as well.

A chess or checkerboard is traditionally a grid of eight by eight squares. Marking a sheet of graph paper with eight squares across and down is a good way to

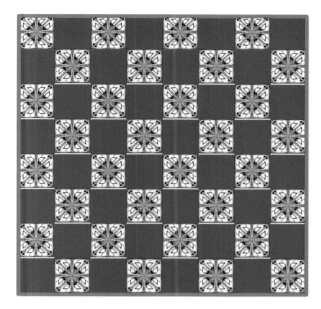

Using a square cane with a contrasting solid color for the board results in a striking game board. A chess or checkerboard is traditionally a grid of eight by eight squares.

Either mark a sheet of graph paper with eight squares across and down or blow up this illustration to the size you wish. A slab of clay should be used as the base.

measure, or blow up the illustration to the size you wish. The best way to proceed is to use a 1/8" slab of clay as the base, laying the alternating canes on top. The cane slices should be about 1/8" thick. To finish, run a 1/4" x 1/8" strip of clay around the outside of the board. You could even put the board on top of a shallow box and attach a hinge as was described in Chapter 6 to have a place to keep the playing pieces.

Game Pieces

"Board on a Wire." *The playing pieces assembled on the chessboard.*

Playing pieces for board games can be as simple as round, flat disks, or as complex as your imagination takes you. Checker playing pieces are the easiest to make

because you are making the same shape for all. Although checkers are traditionally round disks, you could experiment with different shapes. An interesting variation would be to make contrasting canes the size of a playing piece. Chess pieces, on the other hand, can be a lot of fun because of the different playing pieces. Think about different approaches, from realistic to abstract. Polymer clay lends itself to either version or anywhere in-between.

Tanagram

Here's another great game to make with polymer clay. Originating in China prior to the eighteenth century, little is known of the true origins of the Tanagram puzzle. The Chinese called this centuries-old game the "Seven-Board of Cunning" because only an exceptionally determined player would attempt its amazing and challenging puzzles. During the nineteenth century and to this day Tanagram puzzles continue to be popular all over the world.

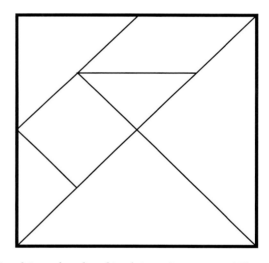

This template can be enlarged to whatever size you want. A 3" square is great for taking on a trip; the most practical size is 5" square.
A. Roll out a slab of clay to 1/8" thickness (pasta machine #1) and set it on a piece of paper and then on a ceramic tile so you won't have to move it when you put it in the oven. This will prevent warping.
B. Lay the template on the clay square and mark the divisions so you can cut the shapes. Don't move them apart, however.
C. Fire for 30 minutes according to the manufacturer's recommendation. Lay another tile on top of the clay to keep it flat while baking.
D. When the clay comes out of the oven, let it cool slightly and then make sure the pieces come apart. If they stick together cut through at the original lines again.
E. When the pieces are totally cool, sand the outer edges.

The Tanagram puzzle is similar to the Western jigsaw puzzle with one key distinction: It is unlimited in its range of solutions. Tanagram puzzles are squares divided into seven pieces of varying size and geometry. The objective of the puzzle is to compose a pictogram using all seven pieces. The game is restricted to two dimensions, and by the number and shape of the pieces. You can make more than 1,500 different designs.

The Tanagram puzzle is best made with a solid color or subtle pattern because it's easier to see the pictograms if there is no pattern obscuring them.

Here are five Tanagram solutions to try.

"Djembe with Polymer Inlay." Artists: Cynthia Tinapple and Blair Davis. *Blair made the oak drum from more than one hundred precisely cut and glued pieces of wood. Cynthia added the polymer clay inlay. Firing this expanse of inlay was tricky. The design was made in one 8" x 10" flat sheet that was cut into four 2" x 10" strips so that the pattern never repeats. The drumhead was commercially purchased.*

Music

Music is a primal love of people in all cultures. So there are ancient drums, harps and whistles in Asia that look very similar to ancient instruments in Africa, Europe and the Americas. Many modern instruments are refinements of these very primitive instruments. Musical instruments are the tools of musicians, just as are the tools we use for creating with polymer clay. Musical art gets expressed in intangible ways; the sound is ethereal and vanishes after is has been expressed. Working with polymer clay to create some of these instruments, we have the better of two worlds. We can create the tangible and then express the intangible.

(Photo: Kim Kauffman)

"Art Kazoos™". Artist: Lynn D.T. Hershberger. *Metal kazoos are covered with brightly colored and patterned polymer clay and applied canes. Each kazoo has a matching stand. Approximately 5".*

Musical Instruments

Many musical instruments adapt well to crafting with polymer clay. Enclose two small, round light bulbs with clay; break the glass after baking, and you have a set of maracas. A pinch pot becomes a whistle and cylinders of clay are versatile as wind and rhythm instruments.

(Photo: Zelda)

"Little Tooter Bird." *This basic whistle was embellished both before and after firing. I used Wild Wire for the tail feathers here because the colors are anodized which makes them safe to use in the oven. The legs are piano wire. The beak, which acts as a mouthpiece, was added after the whistle was tooting. 3" x 9". ©2001 Jacqueline Gikow.*

Whip up a Whistle

Although clay has been used to make bells, rattles, drums, horns, and even stringed instruments, most ceramic musical instruments are whistles. Whistles, in one form or another, have been for centuries an impor-

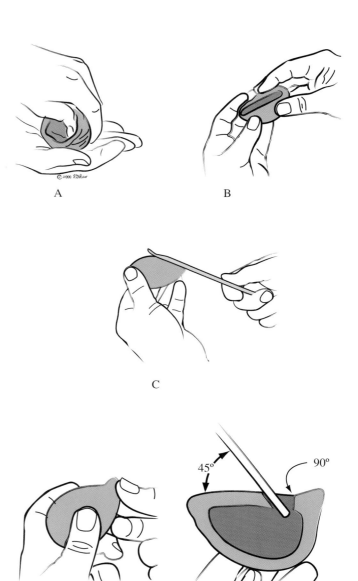

A. Make a pinch pot from a 2" ball of clay. Keep the wall thickness as uniform as possible. The size of the pinch pot you make determines the tone of the whistle; the smaller the inside chamber, the higher the tone.

B. Press the open edges together and seal them. The closed form should resemble a three-cornered pillow and the seam must be airtight.

C. Smooth the seam using your fingers or a clay tool. Shape the whistle, but keep your first whistles simple. Use your fingers to push, pinch, or pull, use a small paddle, or roll it on your work surface to move the clay into the general form of a design. You should also start forming a tip or stem that will become the site for creating the whistling parts. Extra clay can be added if needed. This is also the time to add any decorative attachments.

D. Form the tip by lightly pushing the clay in and up in front of the hole you just made. This makes the form a bit thicker here and facilitates forming the air slot.

E. When you get the shape you want, form the whistle wedge. About 1/2" from the tip, pierce the sealed form with a 3/8" dowel or the blunt end of the needle tool handle at about a 45° angle. Don't push it all the way through. Pull the dowel out at the same angle you pushed it in to make a clean, sharp wedge to split the air. Check to see that the hole you just made is not plugged. After forming the wedge, don't mess with it!

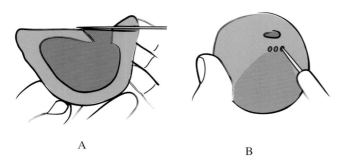

A   B

A. Insert a needle tool through the thick ridge on the tip until it just touches the far edge of the hole to make the initial air slot guide hole. It is critical to make the air slot parallel to the thin edge of the wedge. And don't wiggle the tool up and down!

B. Working at eye level, make 3 or 4 more holes parallel to the first guide hole. The floor of the air slot must be even with the thin edge of the wedge (edge of hole across from the air slot). If you do not keep the tool parallel to the top surface of the whistle body as you pierce the ridge, you won't get a peep! This air passage must be a slot, not a round hole.

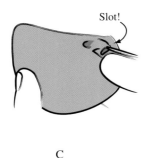

Slot!

C

C. Complete the slot by gently inserting the needle tool in one of the guide holes and moving it side to side. Don't move it up and down like a seesaw. Enlarging the hole by moving side to side clears out the little bits of clay separating the guide holes, and this creates the slot. The ridge is like a little bridge, and it forms the roof of the air slot. This slot directs the air across the wedge and creates the dynamics that produce the sound. Be sure the slot is clean and clear of clay debris.

D. Try out the whistle by carefully putting your lips on the end of the slot and blowing. Do not hang your lip over the slot, and be very gentle because the clay is still soft and can easily be distorted. If the whistle doesn't work now, it won't miraculously start after it's fired.

D

tant part of the global music culture. Called a "hsuan" in China, in France a "cou cou," in Italy, the word for a whistle can be traced to the word "Ocarina" ("sweet little goose"). The pitch of the sound produced in a whistle varies with the size. Small whistles produce penetrating, bird-like sounds and larger vessels produce soft, mellow, deep-pitched sounds. Adding tone holes produces scaling through which you can produce a few notes, up to a span of two octaves.

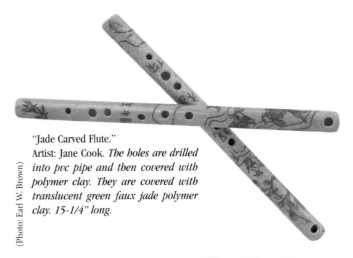

"Jade Carved Flute."
Artist: Jane Cook. *The holes are drilled into pvc pipe and then covered with polymer clay. They are covered with translucent green faux jade polymer clay. 15-1/4" long.*

(Photo: Earl W. Brown)

Flirt with a Flute

One of the most ancient and widespread of musical instruments is the flute. During the early eighteenth century, the flute rose to be the most popular of wind instruments. Almost every culture on Earth has some sort of flute. Flutes are considered "aerophones," a category of instruments that make sounds as air vibrates through a tube.

The flute is used by different cultures for different things: For performance, for pleasure, for courtship, or for meditation. It is easily played and no lessons are needed. You don't have to be able to read music or know about keys (I don't), to be able to play your own music and find your own song.

The width and length of the tube through which the air travels determine the shape of the sound wave. The longer the tube is, the longer the sound wave is, which means the deeper the sound. If a tube of one length produces the sound of C, then a tube twice as long will pro-

Hole Size

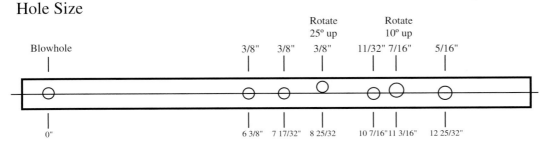

The finger hole positions for this flute are a distance from the center of the blowhole. This diagram is not in scale so just follow the measurements indicated.

Hole Distance

duce a sound one octave lower.

A good diameter for a flute is 3/4" on the inside. Covering a 3/4" dowel is a great way to get this diameter. The tube length should be about 15-9/16". If your oven is small, try laying the flute in at an angle when you fire it.

This chart shows the size of each hole and the distance from its center to the blowhole of the flute tube—again, measured with the flute cap off. You can use the distance measurements to make a pattern on a piece of paper, ruler, or dowel, which you can then place against your flute pieces. Two holes are slightly offset as shown, for easier fingering.

Orchestral flutes are usually made from metal or wood and craftspeople have brought about a resurgence of interest in handmade flutes, creating them in other materials and reviving older types of flutes.

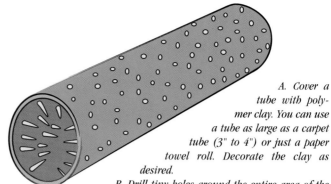

A. Cover a tube with polymer clay. You can use a tube as large as a carpet tube (3" to 4") or just a paper towel roll. Decorate the clay as desired.

B. Drill tiny holes around the entire area of the baked tube. If you are using smaller tubes from toilet paper or wrapping paper, then all you need to do is poke holes with a needle tool or other sharp instrument.

C. Insert flat-headed nails into the holes. When you look into the tube, you should see a maze of nails. If you are using a smaller tube, you can stick toothpicks through the holes you poked earlier. Then plug up one end of the tube and re-bake.

D. After sealing one end of the tube, put sunflower seeds, rice, corn kernels, or a combination of all three, into the tube. You will hear just how much material is necessary to achieve the desired sound. Also, you don't want to make the rainstick too heavy, so take it easy on the filling. Then seal the other end of the tube and bake again.

Now, all that's left to do is to play your rainstick and wait for the thunder.

(Photo: Zelda)

"Millennium." *This rainstick was made over a paper towel cardboard core that was removed after baking. 11-1/2" x 1-3/4".*

Rattle a Rainstick

Legend has it that the Chilean Indians invented the rainstick to make rainy weather. From the windswept hillsides and barrancas beneath the Andes, artisans with burros collect dead and dried cactus that might otherwise be used for firewood. The thorns are then pressed into the hollow cactus shafts. Pebbles cascading over the thorns create the sound of this ancient instrument that is still heard in the music of the Andes.

A polymer clay rainstick can easily be formed around a wooden dowel, which is removed after baking. Depending on the sound you want, insert sections of wire, nails, or wooden pegs into the tube. Then fill the cylinder with pebbles, hard seeds, beans, sand, rice, or tiny shells. The sounds created when pebbles or beads hit the nails or pegs inside the tube mimic the sound of rain falling on the leaves.

Toys

(Photo: Norman Watkins)

"Puppet Tribe." Artist: Carol Zilliacus. *Bird and Elephant finger puppets with decorative dress. The sizes of the puppet heads vary, with the elephant head being the largest at 1-1/2" x 1-1/4". The overall sizes of the puppets with costume are 7-1/2" x 8-1/2".*

From the beginning of humankind, children had playthings or toys. Natural objects such as sticks, cones, bones, seed pods, smooth stones were, with a little imagination, the toys of children long ago. The spinning top, an early ancestor of the yo-yo, may have derived its original form from seedpods or gourds. Balls, dolls, pull toys, and spinning tops are basic toys in nearly every culture. Carved limestone push or pull toys have been found as part of Persian culture as early as the twelfth century B.C. Bruegel's famous painting "Children's Games"

(1560) shows children playing with toys, most of which are still used in their original form today. Until the late eighteenth century, most toys were handcrafted.

"Polymer Doll Lamps." Artist: Petra. *Petra makes these little working lamps that are the perfect accessory for a dollhouse. Techniques used include millefiori, Mokume gane, and canes. She covers templates for the shades and bakes on the template. The bases are beads and a light bulb is threaded through the base. Once in a doll's house the lamps can be plugged into a universal outlet that most dollhouses have for their lighting. There are three sizes: 1", 1-1/2", and 2". These are all able to be used in 1/12th scale dolls houses.*

In the twentieth century, toys have evolved from simple wood or cloth to new materials of mass production. The shelves are lined with plastic, robotic (batteries not included), electronically enhanced, computer voiced toys. Toys of today lack the warmth and value of the often handcrafted toys of yesteryear. In rebellion, many seek out simple handcrafted toys and playthings. Craftspeople all over the world are producing a fine assortment of toys. Handcrafted yo-yos and kaleidoscopes, for example are two toys that are an enjoyable challenge for artists to make.

"Silver Lace" *and* "Blue Swirl" *Kaleidoscopes. The scopes are covered with a sheet of clay, much like covering a pen with polymer. The mirrors are held in place by friction and reinforced with polymer clay.* "Silver Lace" *9" x 1.5" diameter,* "Blue Swirl" *12.5" x 2" diameter. By Linda Geer.*

Kaleidoscopes

Sir David Brewster, a Scottish physicist and natural philosopher, invented the kaleidoscope. His invention of the kaleidoscope was one result of his notable light-polarization studies. His tube-like instrument contained

"Ivory Coast." Artist: Dotty McMillan. *The case of this scope is made entirely of polymer clay. The main feature on this scope is an old photograph transfer of an elephant along with antique (faux) ivory fragments that are set off by textured and antiqued black clay. The optics are surface mirrors and the object wheels feature dichroic glass and glass gems. 10" x 2-1/2".*

loose pieces of glass and other objects that were reflected by mirrors and/or lenses set at different angles to create various symmetrical patterns when viewed through one end of the tube. Brewster's term for this new instrument, "kaleidoscope," came from the Greek words meaning, "beautiful form to see." By the late 1880s, the use of kaleidoscopes had become a legitimate pastime, earning prominent positions in Victorian parlors.

The three-mirror kaleidoscope system can be arranged in any form of triangle, so long as the sum of the three angles equals 180°. It produces a continuous field of honeycomb-like patterns. The 60°-60°-60° equilateral triangle is the most common, but a 90°-45°-45° triangle evokes a more interesting, if unusual, symmetry.

How Kaleidoscopes Work

The mirrors inside the kaleidoscope reflect what you have at the end of it, creating an image. When you change or move the end piece by rotating the case, the image changes.

The heart of a kaleidoscope is the mirror within, but the exterior of a kaleidoscope is where the polymer artist can be creative. Although a kaleidoscope's chamber is very important, the exterior case is what catches the eye first. A polymer clay case can be made in a cylinder or other shape. It can be carved, made with patterned clay, such as faux finishes or semi-precious stone. You can apply millefiori and mokume gane decorations, metallic powders, paints, and more.

Polymer Clay Kaleidoscope Case

A kaleidoscope case is easily made by covering a cylinder of cardboard or glass, since these can be removed after baking. A good size for a beginning kaleidoscope is 8" in length and wide enough to make an open cylinder, about 2-1/2" in diameter. Alternatively, you could cover the kaleidoscope mirror chamber itself and end up with a triangular kaleidoscope.

You'll also need three 1/8" thick Plexiglas disks the size of the interior of the clay cylinder, as well as three strips of mirror 7-1/2" long by 2" high.

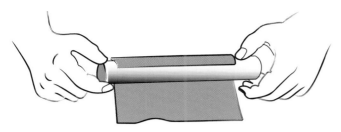

Place the cylindrical support at the straight edge of a slab of clay and carefully, but firmly roll it around to meet the other end. Trim off the extra clay and roll the cylinder to eliminate the seam.

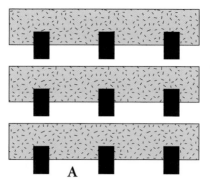

A. Cut three stripes of mirror, each 1-1/2" x 8". Using black electrical or plastic tape, place 3 strips of tape on the back of the mirror, about 1" long across one edge of each of the mirror strips.

A. A good size for a beginning kaleidoscope is 8" x 2-1/2". When you insert the mirror assembly you may have to add some packing material so the mirrors don't move around.

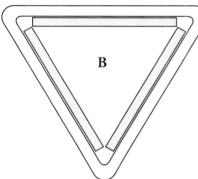

B. Alternatively, you could cover the kaleidoscope mirror chamber itself and end up with a triangular kaleidoscope.

B. Next, stand two of the strips on end on the tabletop. Put two edges together (one edge will have tape on it, the other will not) and hold the strips in a wide V shape with an overlap of about the thickness of the mirror and tape the two edges together. Then place the third strip at the open end of the "V," and tape it to the other two sides as shown.

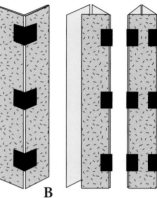

Finally, place a clear, Plexiglas disk where the mirrors stop, near the top of the open end of the clay cylinder. Place beads and things between the mirror cap and the Plexiglas and attach the other disk to the end of the cylinder with PVA glue. Experiment with a different number and type of things inside, and then permanently affix the disk.

Whirling, Twirling, and Other Active Toys

Mobiles, pinwheels (whirligigs), wind chimes, wind (weather) vanes, tops, and wind toys are only a few things that can be created from polymer clay. Some move, some are musical, and all enchant the viewer.

Because their only purpose is to delight and amuse us, whirling, twirling, and wind toys seem to appeal to everyone. As with children, our eyes light up, smiles widen into grins, and grins become outright laughter. No matter how sophisticated we are, moving toys remind all of us of simple pleasures.

To make the ivory, stack different thicknesses of the colors. Cut the stack in half, compress by rolling it out by hand, and then restack. Repeat this process until the lines are very thin. Then marble the mixture lightly until some of the striations are blended and some are still in stripes.

The Kaleidoscope Chamber

To make the interior chamber of the kaleidoscope, lay the mirror pieces on a work surface, reflective side down with about a 1/8" (3 mm) gap between them. Place three pieces of tape horizontally across the mirrors with the extra tape hanging over one side.

Fold the mirrors into a triangular prism with the reflective sides on the inside. Use the extra tape to wind around it. One edge of each mirror overlaps the edge of the next mirror consistently around the prism.

If the kaleidoscope is round, fit the mirrors in the cylinder, packing foam pieces around the outside of the mirrors to keep them in place.

(Photo: Jacqueline Gikow)

"Twirling Tops." The magical whirling tops shown here are deceptively easy to make. Polymer clay is used throughout with embellishments of patterned clay and image transfers. 3" x 3".

PROJECTS
PROJECT 1. PHENOMENAL PINWHEEL

Intermediate/Advanced

This project seems complicated because it's long, but it just has lots of steps. You'll soon see it's a snap!

Materials and Supplies

2 oz. Fimo in your choice of color or colors
Metallic powders, paints, foils, gold threads, etc., for decorating
3 to 4 mm seed or polymer bead—hole of bead must fit loosely around T-pin
Cyanoacrylate glue such as Surehold "Plastic Surgery"
PVA glue
1/8" diameter x 12" to 16" dowel
1" finishing nail
2" T-pin
X-Acto knife
Toothpicks
Cornstarch
Pasta machine (optional) or rolling pin
Work surface that you can tap a nail or pin into
Acrylic paint (optional)

The Pinwheel Head

1. Condition and run your clay through the pasta machine at progressively smaller thicknesses until you've gotten to #6 or #7 on your pasta machine. (If you do this by hand, you want a paper-thin sheet of clay.) Lightly dust a sheet of vellum with cornstarch and lay the clay on it. Powder the top of the clay, set a piece of vellum on top, and roll the clay out with a roller so it is slightly thinner than the #7 pasta setting. Cut a square about 5-1/2" square and discard the scraps (Polyclay dusted with cornstarch is not useable again).

2. Decorate both sides of the clay as desired and lightly roll to flatten.

3. Set the clay sheet on a flat-bottomed baking sheet or a tile and set a tile on top to make sure the sheet stays flat. Bake at 265° F for 30 minutes. Let the clay cool.

4. Enlarge the template 200 percent to 5" square and place the full-size copy on the baked clay sheet. Trace the outline, marking the diagonals and circles, and cut out the shape.

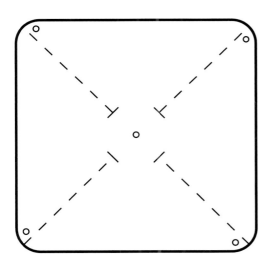

Pinwheel Template
Enlarge 200%
Will be a 5" square

5. Pierce a hole in the center of the square and the corner holes with the finishing nail.

6. Set the clay square on the flat work surface and tap the finishing nail into the center hole to hold the square in place. Put a small amount of cyanoacrylate glue around the center hole, but not in the hole. Fold over each of the pinwheel tips, one at a time, slipping the end hole over the work board nail. Hold each clay tip in the glue until it sets (about a minute). Set aside to completely cure the glue.

The Handle and Spin Connector

7. Condition enough clay to make a coil; 1/2" diameter x 1-1/2" long. This will connect the pinwheel to the handle and allow it to spin freely.

8. Bend the coil at a 90° angle at the middle.

9. Apply PVA glue (or Liquid Sculpey) to one end of the dowel and poke a hole with it into one end of the coil, rotating the dowel as you push. It might be a good idea to start with a mid-sized knitting needle first so you don't distort the connector. Leave the dowel in the clay, packing the clay tightly around the inserted end to hold it in place.

10. Pierce a hole, using the finishing nail, all the way through the horizontal part of the clay snake. Rotate the nail as you do this so you don't distort the clay. Make sure the hole is large enough by inserting your T-pin through it. The pin should fit easily in the hole. If the hole is too tight, your pinwheel won't spin freely. Set the clay piece and handle aside.

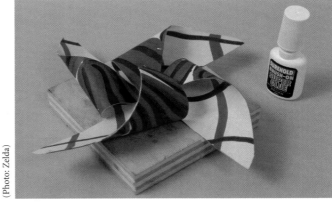

Set the pinwheel square on a flat work surface and tap the finishing nail into the center hole to hold the square in place. I've made a reusable tool using a 3/4" x 4" piece of plywood. ©2001 Jacqueline Gikow

(Photo: Zelda)

11. (Optional) If you want to decorate the rest of the handle with clay, spread a light coat of PVA glue on it and let it get tacky before adding clay to the dowel.

12. Make a 1/2" diameter, or square, flat bead of clay to sit at the front of the pinwheel head (see finished pinwheels). It should be about 1/4" thick. Alternatively, slice a section from an existing cane. Insert the T-pin into this bead, embedding the head in the clay. The "T" of the T-pin shouldn't be visible at the front of the bead.

13. Make a small (1/2") conical bead and pierce a hole halfway through the length of the bead.
14. Bake the dowel, the flat bead, and the small conical bead in a preheated oven at 265° F for 30 minutes.
15. When the dowel has cooled, test the pinwheel head by slipping it onto the T-pin, inserting it in the hole in the connector, and blowing on the pinwheel a few times to see if it spins.
16. Optional: If you haven't completely covered the dowel with clay, finish it with paint, stain, wire wrapping, or other decoration.

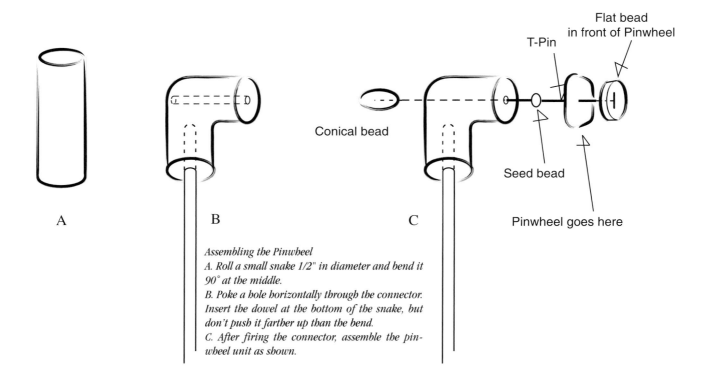

A

B

C

Conical bead

T-Pin

Flat bead in front of Pinwheel

Seed bead

Pinwheel goes here

Assembling the Pinwheel
A. Roll a small snake 1/2" in diameter and bend it 90° at the middle.
B. Poke a hole horizontally through the connector. Insert the dowel at the bottom of the snake, but don't push it farther up than the bend.
C. After firing the connector, assemble the pinwheel unit as shown.

Assembling the Pinwheel

17. Using the illustration above as a guide, insert the T-pin (along with the clay shape attached to it) through the hole in the pinwheel. Next, slip the seed bead onto the T-pin. Then insert the pin into the hole in the clay connector. About 1/4" of the T-pin should protrude from the back of the connector. If too much protrudes, cut off the excess with wire cutters.
18. Insert the protruding T-pin into the cone bead and make sure the pinwheel turns freely. Then, using cyanoacrylate glue, glue the cone bead permanently in place on the end of it.
19. Now go find some wind.

PROJECT 2. CRYPTIC CHINESE CHECKERS

Intermediate

Chinese checkers is the same game as Halma, an old Chinese game reinvented by the Victorians, and transformed into a star-shaped board in America. The objective of Chinese checkers is to move your marbles across the board to the star point directly opposite. The game gets interesting when there are lots of pieces in the center requiring a player to strategically move around them. The player who moves all the marbles across the board first, wins.

This star-shaped, polymer Chinese checkerboard and playing pieces are easy to make. You'll create six blended color shapes to construct it, just to give you a challenge.

12" diameter

(Photo: Jacqueline Gikow)

This Chinese checkers set will give you hours of pleasure. 12". Star-shaped Chinese checkers game, 12".

Materials and Supplies

Premo polymer clay
2 oz. red
2 oz. blue
2 oz. green
2 oz. yellow
2 oz. orange
2 oz. purple
10 oz. white
10 oz. black
Large amount of scrap polymer clay
    (Note: you can use any color if you
    don't have scrap clay)
Cornstarch
Dull straight edge
Sharp knife
Marbles (optional)
Paper for cutting templates
Pasta machine or rolling pin
Wet-dry sanding paper 400 and 600 grit

Instructions:

1. Enlarge the circular and diamond-shaped template 200 percent. The final dimensions of the game board will be 1/2" x 12" in diameter.
2. Condition and roll out two slabs of clay. Make one from your scrap clay that is 1/4" thick. Make the other, 1/8" thick from black. Make the slabs large enough to cut a 12" disk from and use the template as a guide.
3. Assemble the base by layering the scrap clay disk over the black. Make sure you don't trap air holes between the layers. Smooth the outer edges of the playing board base. Set the base aside.
4. Make color blends of all six colors: red, blue, green, yellow, orange, and purple, grading the colors to white. Use the instructions for making color blends in Chapter 6 as a guide. You want the blends to run from one point of saturated color to pure white. The finished slab should be 1/8" (3 mm) thick.
5. Lay the full sized, diamond template on top of each blend and cut out the diamond shape as shown. It doesn't matter if all the blends do or don't match in their blend progression.
6. Mark the center of the 12" clay circle and lightly lay each diamond shape, colored point, out on the clay circle. The white point should be at the center point.
7. When all the diamonds are placed around the circle, lightly roll them in place. Because of the possibility that all the diamonds may not be the same size, you might have to compress the edges of the diamonds slightly to make each fit next to the other.

Template for blends and marble indents. Enlarged, this will be a 6" diamond.
Small circles indicate the marble placement. The dots inside the circles are where you mark marble positions in step 9.

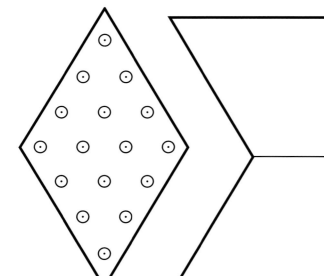

Chinese Checkers
Game Board Template
Enlarge 200 percent.

8. Optional: For playing pieces you can make a choice between making your own playing pieces or using glass marbles. If you choose to make your own, use the colored scrap clay from the diamond blends. Make 10 clay marbles about 1/2" diameter from each color. Bake them for 20-30 minutes at 265° F. Let them cool, then sand (400 and 600 grits).

9. Cut the star shape from the circular template and lay it on top of the clay. Pierce holes at each intersection according to the template.

10. Remove the template and lightly score a line through each set of pinholes. Use a dull straight edge rather than a knife and don't cut through the star. Refer to the finished piece.

11. Press one of your marbles into the intersection of each line. Make the impression as accurate as possible. Press the marble deep enough so it won't roll out, but not so deep that it distorts the board. Make all the impressions the same size. (You may want to put some cornstarch on the marble to prevent it from sticking to the clay.)

12. Roll out a black and white snake, 3/8" (9 mm) in diameter and long enough to encircle the game board and cover the black and scrap clay layers. Slightly flatten the snake against the game board to make sure it sticks.

13. Bake the board at 265° F for one hour. Let it cool (sand if desired) and you're ready to play!

Playing Chinese Checkers

Objective: The winner is the first player to move all her or his marbles to the point directly opposite their starting point.

Set-up: Chinese checkers can be played by two to six players. Each player covers his or her point of the star with 10 matching color marbles.

Rules: In one turn, a player may move only one marble. He or she may move one hole in any direction or jump over another marble, their own or their opponent's. He or she may also jump a series of marbles, one marble at a time, zigzagging in any direction so long as each jump is directly over a marble. Two marbles in a row always forms a block. No marbles are ever removed from the board after they are jumped.

Chapter 10

Home Decor

(Photo: Roger Schreiber)

"Refraction." This polymer clay tapestry by Grant Diffendaffer *was constructed with Fimo over WireForm mesh and small mirrors were inset into the clay. More detailed information about WireForm can be found in Chapter 7. 17" x 22".*

Polymer clay can be used all over our homes, inside and out, to wear (as jewelry and more), to use, and to play with even after it is cured. Some of it might be functional and some of it for show only. While I prefer objects to be useful and aesthetically pleasing, I also love objects made only for their beauty. As mentioned at the beginning of this book, polymer clay can be made to look like wood, glass, plastic, metal, enamel, ceramic, stone, precious metals, textiles, paper, and yes, even plastic!

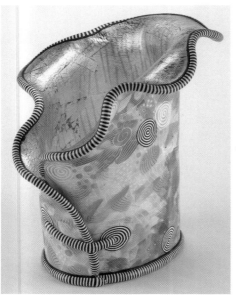

(Photo: Krause)

Donna Kato
This open vessel would accompany a bouquet of flowers or spray of greenery beautifully. It is made of Fimo Soft with an internal armature of WireForm mesh. The interior of the vessel has been gilded with metal leaf. 12".

In the Garden

Gardening is a popular hobby of both urban and suburban people and many things can be made from polymer clay for the garden. Consumer trends show a surge in garden accessories, including garden pottery, birdhouses, fountains, mobiles, wind chimes, and rocks with inspiring messages.

Bringing the garden inside is also a continuing trend as natural products and the "green" movement continue to grow in popularity.

(Photo: Jacqueline Gikow)

Slab-built vase using cardboard form and Premo clay in blue pearl and gold. 3-1/4" x 12". Artist: Jacqueline Gikow.

Birdhouses

Everyone needs a home, and birds are no exception. Just like people, different species of birds need houses constructed to suit their particular needs. Elaborate houses that aren't cozy for birds may actually harm them!

The functional houses illustrated are ideas for various birds and can be made with clay-covered wood. Illustration 2 shows the specifications for different types of birds' houses.

Songbirds are among nature's greatest indicators of a good environment. Where there are no songbirds, the elements are usually toxic in some way. Those who enjoy the companionship of birds, or just designing birdhouses, will find they are fun to build. A functional birdhouse should be durable, rainproof, and readily accessible for cleaning.

This birdhouse by Vicki Domansky is a network of polymer clay vines and sculpted flowers covering a papier-mâché base. The vines were made by rolling long, thin snakes of brown polymer clay. The branch is a dowel covered with polymer clay and textured to look like a piece of wood. The birdhouse is finished with a spray varnish. 7" x 4-1/2" x 6".

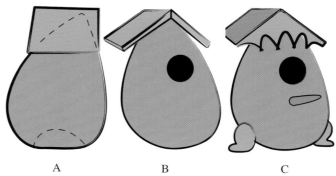

Birdhouse

A. Refer to Chapter 4 for a review on making closed pinch pots and make yours approximately the shape above. Also make two small slabs for the roof and mark where you want the hole to be. It's a good idea to indent the hole deeply as it's easier to do that now than to carve the hole out later. B. After firing, glue the roof together and sculpt the front facing. Also sculpt the two feet. One foot should be made slightly larger as you want to support the uneven bottom (see drawing A - the dotted line at the bottom shows the reverse raised side). C. Refire with everything glued in place. If you want to add a perch, drill a hole below the bird opening.

A decorative clay birdhouse can also add an attractive touch to the landscape or the living room. Nonfunctional birdhouses can be designed and made completely with clay, or by covering with a variety of materials from papier-mâché to wood. Think outside the box when you approach a design idea like a birdhouse. Even though most birdhouses are made with straight sides, if you aren't accommodating a bird, working with polymer clay allows you to express yourself any way you want.

A pinch pot is the starting point for this decorative birdhouse. Clean, contemporary color is the focus and I followed current color trends in my choices. 5". By Jacqueline Gikow.

Living a Crafted Life

A. This is an appealing style birdhouse and attracts a variety of species. It's easy to make and can be embellished with polymer clay by any method. Laminating sheets of fired polymer panels is well suited for this birdhouse. B. Chickadees, Titmice, and Nuthatches prefer rustic homes built to simulate natural abodes. Chickadees often nest within a few feet of the ground, but nuthatches and titmice prefer higher elevation.

More than likely, the art of handicraft and its objects won't regain the high position they held a hundred years ago. We no longer need to make our own spoons, but handicraft can be a prescription for peace of mind. And what better way than including it in the very structure and function of your space both outside and inside?

Knobs, handles, and switch plates are integral parts of a home as well. Although largely ignored as an element in a home, they can bring a stamp of individuality in a unique way. Knobs and handles can be made either by covering an existing form or by forming them yourself. For details on making switch plates from polymer clay, refer back to Chapter 5.

(Photo: Blaire Davis)

Cynthia Tinapple and Blare Davis
"Stairway with Inlay on Oak." *Blaire routed a channel in the oak cap board for Cynthia to work with. Cynthia made one 15-color striped, caned from a palette of favorite colors, which she then marbled, scored, and ran through the pasta machine at #7. The channel was primed with glue and inlaid with unbaked clay. Completing the 11' channel took 500+ tiles. The tiles were baked using a heat gun, first by heat setting the pieces and then returning to completely cure the clay. 11' x 1-1/2".*

(Photo: Julian Beveridge)

Krista Wells
"Gecko Door." *This door consists of polymer clay tiles and sculpted geckos with canework detail. The tiles were made with a pasta maker using custom colors and some color blends. Sanded, buffed, and finished with Flecto Varathane. Tile size: 3/4" to 1-1/2". Door size 30" x 77". By Krista Wells.*

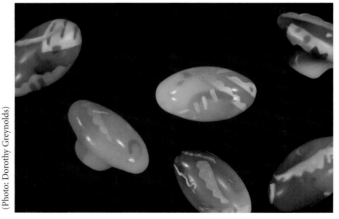

(Photo: Dorothy Greynolds)

"Door Knobs." *Oval shaped ceramic knobs were used as a base and covered with color blends. One blend was made with Fimo transparent color clays and another was combined with white pearl to create a pastel sheet. The ceramic knobs were coated with PVA and then covered with the clay. After curing, the knobs were sanded and buffed to a high shine. 2" x 1-1/4" x 1". By Dorothy Greynolds.*

"Door handles." *These unusually shaped handles* by Amy Zinman *are carved and sculpted in green, white, translucent, and black clay. Approximately 5" to 6" x 1" x 2".*

"Switchplates." *These elegant switchplates are covered with various colors, textures, and patterns of polymer clay, which is then carved and baked.* By Margi Laurin.

Tabletop

Tabletop refers to anything that is related to the kitchen or dining room including cutlery, dinnerware, serving platters, teapots and teacups, trays, wine glasses, etc. No matter whether their purpose is practical or decorative only, there are many ways to design tabletop wares with polymer clay.

"Goblet." *Believe it or not the stem on this goblet is made completely out of polymer clay. I removed the glass stem and replaced it with various shapes of polymer clay and inserted thin pieces of piano wire between the pieces of clay as I was constructing it. 3-1/2" x 6".* By Jacqueline Gikow.

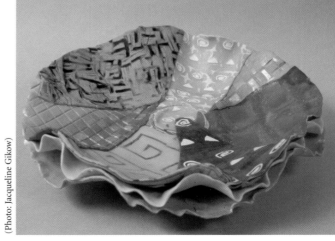

"Baklava Platter." *This lacy-looking platter is actually quite sturdy. It's built with three layers of clay slabs 1/8" thick. The platter's delicate look is due to the pinched edges of each layer of clay. The top layer is a collage of various clay pattern pieces. 11" x 2".* By Jacqueline Gikow.

"Spirit Feast," by Lynn D.T. Hershberger. *A full place setting of polymer clay on found objects such as glass, metal, and ceramic. Some of the items are useable and some not, but Lynn's objective was a reflection of her artistic philosophy.*

Teapots

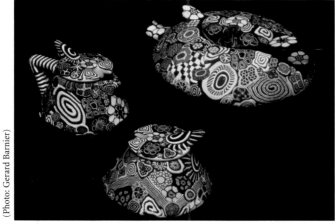

"Teapot, Sugar, and Creamer Set" by Christl Pelikan. *Each is black and white millefiori covering porcelain pieces, which allows them to be used. Teapot: 5-1/2" x 3".*

"Berry Explosion." *This is another functional teapot covered with hand-sculpted strawberries, blackberries, raspberries, and millefiori leaves in polymer clay. 5" x 9" x 6" By Lisa Pavelka.*

Karen Kozak

Karen's teapots are covered with polymer clay, which makes them functional. However, it's hard to think of them as merely covered teapots. Karen's method of making these beautiful works is to design them, throw the clay on a potter's wheel, and then make a mold of the pot. In the next step she casts a thin porcelain pot, adds a thin glaze, and fires it. Finally she is ready to complete the design using polymer clay.

The story of teapots began with their necessity. The development of tea and its regular consumption required an efficient, and later an aesthetically pleasing, vessel for brewing and drinking. The historical development of tea is virtually unknown and mostly the stuff of legends.

Teapots were not used immediately upon the discovery of tea. What we do know from the eighth century is that tea leaves were rolled by hand, dried, and ground into a powder. At first, this powder was mixed with salt and formed into cakes that would be dropped into bowls of hot water to form a thick mixture. Eventually the powder was left in its loose form, to be mixed in a bowl with boiling water and whipped into a froth. This method of tea-making was introduced into Japan in the early ninth century C.E. Tea was considered medicinal in both China and Japan for the next five hundred years.

The emergence and early evolution of teapots spanned several hundred years. Today teapots are some of the most popular items for craftspeople to make. Both functional and fanciful teapots are in demand by collectors and the everyday user. Many craft competitions use the teapot as a theme.

Teapots made from polymer clay won't be useful unless you cover an existing functional form, but you can add to the illusion of practicality by making the spout hollow. Here are a few ways you can do that:

Make a long, narrow, pinched cylinder to attach to the main vessel. See Chapter 4.

Cover a piece of tubing with clay, such as copper, and attach that to your vessel. See Chapter 5.

(Photo: Larry Sanders)

Rebecca Zimmerman
This teapot is representative of Rebecca's style. Built over a paper mold she creates a teapot that could also be an undersea creature or one out of Dr. Seuss. She first makes a base clay form and then the decorative layer is built on top. 12" x 12".

Roll a slab into a cylinder, or assemble it into a geometric shape and tape the spout towards the end. See Chapter 6.
Make a two-piece press-mold in the shape you want. See Chapter 7.

Frames for Pictures and Mirrors

(Photo: Jacqueline Gikow)

Cassie Doyon
"Frames" by Cassie Coyon. A wooden picture frame was covered with a tiled veneer of polymer clay. Creating the tiles involved making a collage of clay that was cut, pierced, textured, and then painted with metallic inks. Further information about covering wood can be found in Chapter 5. 5" x 7".

There is no limit as to what can be framed … wedding and graduation mementos, original artwork, needlework, sea shells, sports equipment, family photos;

(Photo: Lypowy Studio)

"Strawberry Sundae." This piece is constructed of two mirrors with gold leaf on polymer clay sheets run through a pasta machine to attain a crackled effect. Using a pointed tool, the clay is carved into on both mirrors, which exposes strips of mirror. The joined mirrors are baked and glazed with Flecto Varathane. 10-1/2" x 11-1/2". By Matt Hamblem.

it's just a question of selecting the proper materials, methods, and presentation for your personal treasures. With polymer clay you can start with a frame and cover it, or you can work directly in polymer clay to begin with. Depending on your intended use for the frame you might make a shadow box frame or add glass to protect your framed item.

Mirrors have a long history of use both as household objects and as objects of decoration. A framed mirror like Matt's doubles its appeal, and framing a mirror is easy to do with polymer clay. When you use polymer clay to make a mirror frame, it is akin to using glass with any application of polymer clay. So if you want the mirror to stick to the clay, be sure you apply the right adhesive or create a mechanical bond to hold the two materials together.

The typical mirror today is a sheet of glass that is coated on its back with aluminum or silver that produces images by reflection. The earliest mirrors were hand mirrors; those large enough to reflect the whole body did not appear until the first century A.D. The mirrors used in Greco-Roman antiquity and throughout the European Middle Ages were slightly convex disks of metal—bronze, tin, or silver—that reflected light off their highly polished surfaces.

Mirrors and picture frames are good for using up some of your scrap clay. If you work with vessels for awhile, however, you'll find you will never run out of scrap clay—scrap begets scrap. I love the way scrap clay patterns are never the same twice. Even the ugliest gray is different from one evolution to another (and thank goodness for metallic and pigmented powders).

"Grandfather Clock." *Polymer clay, acrylic paint, and gold leaf with quartz clock workings, metal hands. The faces are made by sculpting an original, making a mold from that, then casting the four faces for the clock. This piece uses many techniques including canework, ghosting through thin layers of ivory colored clays, tamping, carving, sculpting, molding, painting, sanding and buffing, and finishing. 14" x 15". By Krista Wells.*

The clock is one of the most influential discoveries in the history of Western science. At best, historians know that five thousand to six thousand years ago, great civilizations in the Middle East and North Africa started to examine forms of clock making instead of working with only a monthly and annual calendar.

Sundials

The sundial is an instrument for measuring time by means of locating a sun shadow cast by a marker. A sundial consists of two parts: a gnomon and a dial placen.

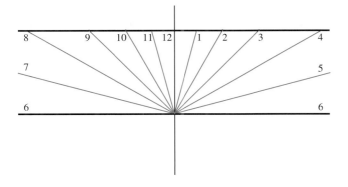

This is 12 hours, or half a day on a sundial. That's how long one position of a sundial works. For the other 12 hours you have to physically rotate the dial 180 degrees. This chart is oriented to 38° latitude, which will work for most of the continental United States.

The gnomon is the shadow-producing device. The principal of the sundial was discovered about 1500 B.C., and allowed early man to divide the day into hours. Chaldean astronomer Berossus described the first hemispherical sundial about the third century B.C. Sundials were used for determining the time until the eighteenth century, when clocks and watches became available.

A sundial is ideal for expressing creativity and function in artwork. A sundial consists of a horizontal or vertical dial plate marked out with hour lines, and a gnomon, the raised projection that casts a shadow. Other than requiring an easily acquired measurement specific to your location so you can figure out where the hour lines go, making a sundial is pure creativity. The inclined edge of the gnomon produces the working edge of the shadow that is used to tell the time. The angle is equal to the latitude of where you are. A sundial of this type can be constructed easily from polymer clay, and a latitude of thirty-eight degrees will work in most of the continental United States.

This is a simply designed sundial, but it contains all the necessary elements—a dial, hours calculated to my local latitude, and a gnomon. Set it on a surface outside, point it at true north at noon, and you will have a fairly accurate reflection of the current time. 6". By Jacqueline Gikow.

If you want the time indication to be accurate, you can make the angle of the gnomon equal to the local latitude, which will point it to the proper elevation. The time lines are also a function of local latitude, and are arrayed around the center of the dial differently in different places. The dial must be oriented so that the gnomon lies on a true north-south axis to ensure that it points to the North Pole of the sky. When these alignments are all correct, and the sun is at its zenith, the gnomon's shadow will fall on the line representing solar noon.

Positioning Your Sundial

If you live in the Northern hemisphere, finding true north is as easy as finding the North star and setting your dial to point at it. Do not use a compass to find north; A compass shows magnetic north, which is not the same as true north.

Another way to find true north is to watch the shadow of a vertical rod; when the shadow is at its shortest length, it is pointing true North/South. If you orient the dial on April 15, June 10, September 1, or December 20, any error will be negligible.

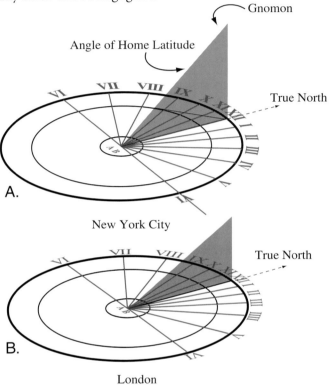

New York City

London

All that is left is to add the gnomon and set the dial in the sun. The gnomon is a right-angle triangular piece with one angle equal to the latitude of the location where the dial is to be used. Affix the gnomon at the center of the dial pointing towards 12 noon and take the dial outside and start to tell time. Orient your dial so that the 12:00 hour line and gnomon are pointing toward true north.

Modern Clocks

In the early to mid-fourteenth century mechanical clocks appeared, and for many centuries were the most accurate and perhaps the most common instruments for measuring time.

Mechanical clocks were largely replaced as the standard by quartz crystal clocks in the 1930s and 1940s. Quartz crystal clocks are an improvement because they have no gears or escapements to disturb their regular frequency. Quartz clocks continue to dominate the market because their performance is excellent, and they are inexpensive.

"Clock" by Varda LevRam-Ellison. *This clock was created by covering a CD disk with Premo gold polymer clay. The faces are from a mold made by Varda. A color blend using Premo polymer clay was made for the leaves and the shapes were cut using a leaf-shaped cutter. Seed beads are at the center of leaves at the top and bottom of the clock. The clock face is framed in an extruded clay shape. 5".*

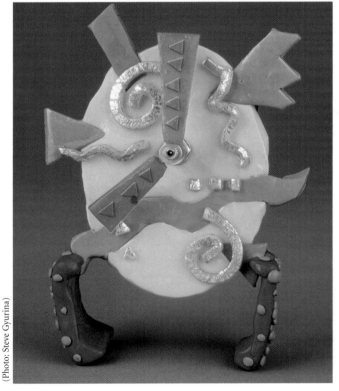

Cassie Doyon

"Funky Desk Clock." *The production method was sheets of polymer clay cut into geometric shapes and notched together like a jigsaw puzzle. More information about working with slabs of polymer clay can be found in Chapter 6. 5" x 5".*

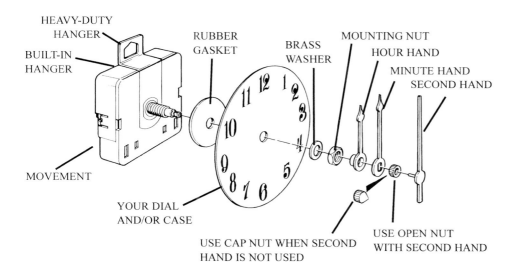

HEAVY-DUTY HANGER

BUILT-IN HANGER

MOVEMENT

RUBBER GASKET

YOUR DIAL AND/OR CASE

BRASS WASHER

MOUNTING NUT

HOUR HAND

MINUTE HAND

SECOND HAND

USE CAP NUT WHEN SECOND HAND IS NOT USED

USE OPEN NUT WITH SECOND HAND

Here is an exploded view of a quartz clock movement. When you buy a quartz clock movement it usually comes with the hour and minute hand, but second hands are optional. Notice that the labeling at left indicates two types of hangers. It doesn't matter which one you get. (Permission for illustration usage provided by Klockit.)

Quartz clock movements make clock making a snap. No clock building expertise is required so you can spend all your time creating. All you need is a battery-run movement from one of many craft suppliers, such as Klockit. The diagram above shows how a quartz movement is attached to the clock dial and hands. The instructions come with each quartz movement. Quartz movements are incredibly accurate and operate on a double-A battery that will run for at least a year. There are many options for making the clock face and embellishing it because the movements come with shafts that range from 1/8" to 3/4" in length. Quartz movements usually come with clock hands, but you can make your own if you are careful to balance them.

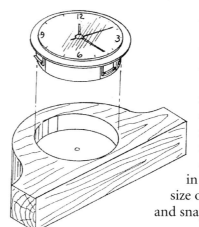

Another quartz movement available is an all-in-one clock insert. It has a snap-in mounting system so all you do is cut a hole in your polymer clay the size of the insert diameter and snap the insert in.

(Photo: Jacqueline Gikow)

"After Before Time." This clock harks back to ancient times in its imagery, but with the latest quartz clock movement makes it quite modern. This is a two-part construction. Each main piece, the gold disk and faux fragment, are fixed apparently and then LS is used to bond them together in a final firing. 7-1/2" x 8". By Jacqueline Gikow.

Light and Lighting

For the people who lived before the dawn of history, there was no such thing as a solar system. They saw their world as a small patch of land bounded by hills and by the blue line of the sea. Overhead was the sky, and across it rode the sun—a god who gave light and warmth. The moon was a lesser god, shining with a lesser light.

Prehistoric peoples used primitive lamps to illuminate their caves. These lamps, made from rocks, shells, horns and stones, were filled with grease and had a fiber wick. Lamps typically used animal or vegetable fats as fuel. Early man also realized that a crude reflector would help direct and intensify the light. Niches have been found carved into cave walls that are thought to have served this purpose.

Until the early 1800s, available light sources consisted of candles, oil lanterns, and gas lamps. Although he wasn't the first to experiment with incandescent lighting,

(Photo: Dixon Withers-Julian)

"Mid-Summer Night's Dream." *A lamp created from translucent and colored clays with a carved illustration. WireForm is used as a support layered between two slabs of clay. 8" x 5". By Diane Dunville.*

(Photo: Zelda)

Jacqueline Gikow
"Tea Lamp." *Tea candles are small and delicate and that always influences me to create romantic holders that complement them. 4".*

it is well known that Thomas Alva Edison invented the first reasonably practical incandescent lamp, using a carbon filament in a bulb containing a vacuum. Then, for the first time in history, it was possible to provide odorless and controlled lighting and, by the twentieth century, development of lighting fixtures flourished. The first electric lamps using tungsten filaments appeared in America in 1907.

The modern counterparts to these early lighting vessels using natural illuminators are candles and oil. If you look through the Internet you'll find oodles of polymer

clay candleholders. Refer to Chapter 5 for how to work with polymer clay and covered glass. Although it's easy to make candleholders as well, working with translucent clay either alone or over glass makes elegant lighting. And the profusion of candles these days makes it easy to find different ways to use polymer clay for making candleholders.

This quote from Oscar Wilde presents a wonderful commentary about light in the context of seeing: "No great artist ever sees things as they are. If (s)he did (s)he would cease to be an artist. Light is much more than something that allows us to see. It defines space, creates atmosphere, and sets the mood by which we live."

(Photo: Steve Meltzer)

"Sea Turtle." *On the unlit night-light you can see the intricate carving and combination of colors. This shade is mounted on a night-light base that plugs into any outlet. The lit lamp reveals the effect light has on the carved motif. 5" x 9" x 6". By Linda Goff*

(Photo: Steve Meltzer)

Today artificial lighting comprises everything from spotlights to the cozy light in a corner at home. It's easy to make a polymer clay lamp. There's (almost) no wiring needed these days. Remember that polymer clay softens around too much heat, so it's best to make lighting that is appropriate as "mood" lighting, rather than as a reading lamp.

Polymer Clay: Creating Functional and Decorative Objects

"Fluted Shell." *This lamp* by Diane Dunville *started out as two large circles of translucent clay sandwiching a WireForm armature. The embellishment was added after the circles were finished, but not fired. The fluting is achieved by setting the clay on a support and carefully pressing and bending the open edges inward. The wiring is done after firing. 11" x 9".*

Furniture

The purpose of furniture has not changed significantly since the first person quit his animal posture and pulled up a rock to sit upon. In the sense that branches, stumps, or rocks were functional, utilitarian, and used for comfort, they were similar to furniture. Use your imagination and experiment with combining polymer clay and furniture.

Polymer clay doesn't lend itself easily to large items such as furniture since most of the time the pieces won't fit into an oven. Additionally, it is structurally unsound and won't hold much weight by itself. However, there are decorative approaches to working with furniture, including embellishment and laminating. You could also use a heat gun to cure the polymer clay directly on a piece of furniture. This is a long, slow process, but often worth the effort, as can be seen in Chapter 10 with Cynthia Tinapple's and Blair Davis' stairway.

Trudy Schartz-Burrill
"Book Shelf." *Made of dozens of millefiore canes attached to a hand-made shelf unit.*

PROJECTS

PROJECT 1. JEST IN TIME

Intermediate

It takes the same amount of time to become a traditional clockmaker as an architect—seven years—but thanks to the tiny quartz clock movements that are so easily and inexpensively available today, you can make a clock much sooner than that. The shape of this clock is inspired by kings' jesters of medieval times and the colors are inspired by the circus. 5" x 5"

Materials and Supplies

Fimo Soft polymer clay
4 oz. sunflower yellow
2 oz. purple violet
2 oz. white
1 oz. Indian red
Small amounts of various colors and patterns
Mini quartz clock movement with a shaft length long enough to go through the clock
Implement to pierce a 1/4" hole
Sharp knife
Tissue blade
Pin or needle tool
Pasta machine or roller
Small brayer
Wall hanger
Clay gun (optional)

Preparation

1. Enlarge the template 200 percent. You might want to make two copies.
2. Condition and roll out the sunflower clay at the #1 setting on the pasta machine, the purple violet at #3, and the white at #5.
3. Roll out various colors and patterns at #5.

(Photo: Jacqueline Gikow)

Making the Clock

4. Lay the sunflower clay on top of the white and cut the outside perimeter of the clock. Separate the extra of the two colors of clay before they bond together. You will need this later. Roll the two layers of the clock shape lightly together so there are no air bubbles.
5. Cut the large bottom shape (B) and position it on the sunflower. I used the Purple Violet with a thin pattern in translucent clay on it.
6. Cut the hatband, decorate it with stripes, and position it on the sunflower clay.
7. Roll out a piece of sunflower clay at #5 and cut the largest star of the clock center (C). Then cut the rest of the pieces following the template. Assemble this shape and then position it as shown on the template.
8. Use solid and patterned clay on shapes E, F, G as shown in the finished sample.
9. Pierce a 1/4" hole in the center of the star (C) for the clock shaft.

10. Use one of the colors in the clock as a finishing border. Extrude a flat or round shape, 1/8" high, and press it onto the edges of the clock shape.
11. Fire at 265° F for 30 minutes.

Assembling the Clock

12. Follow the instructions on the back of the quartz clock movement to attach it to your clock face. Also refer back to the clock section in this chapter for more information.

13. Insert the battery and set the time.
13. Attach a wall hanger to the wall and slide the hanger opening on the clock movement onto it.

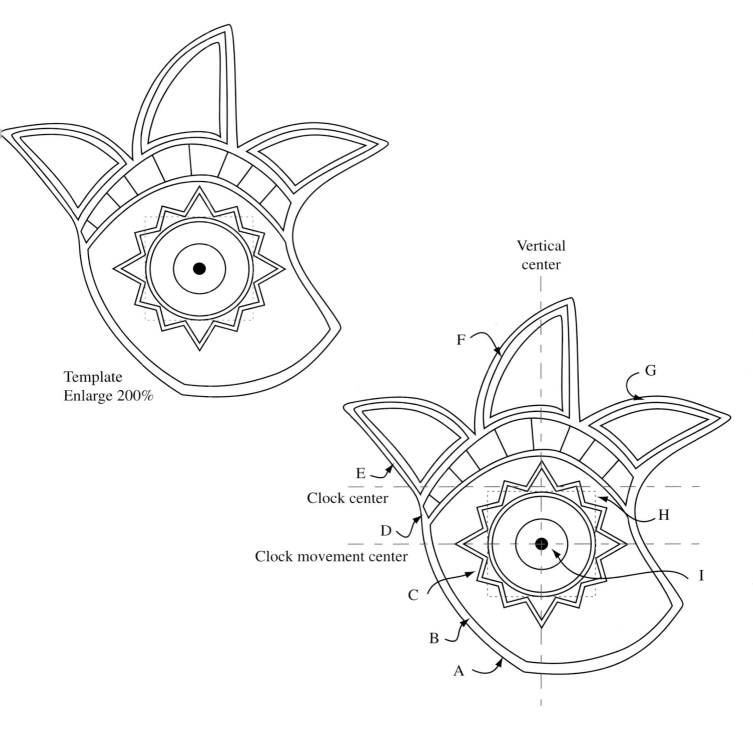

Template
Enlarge 200%

(Photo: Jacqueline Gikow)

Advanced
6" x 4" diameter

Materials and Supplies

Polyform Premo clay
10 oz. translucent
2 oz. white
6 oz. black
Translucent Liquid Sculpey (TLC)
WireForm aluminum diamond mesh
Round salt or oatmeal box covered with
    aluminum foil
Kemper clay gun
1/4" flat brush
Pasta machine
Beacon glue
Ruler
X-Acto knife and/or tissue blade

Elements for Lamp Wiring

Small light bulb socket (Approximately
    3/4" diameter)
7 to 15 watt bulb to fit socket
6 ' of electrical cord with plug
1 cord switch
1 piece of threaded pipe, 3/8" outer
    dimension
1 to 1-1/4" washer with 3/8" hole
2 nuts with 3/8" hole

The Shade

1. Condition the translucent and white clays. Roll out one slab of translucent clay at the second thickness of your pasta machine. The size should be 5-1/2" the length of the salt box.

2. Using the 3/16" flat die, extrude enough clay for 4 horizontal lengths of the translucent slab. Lay the strips on the slab and carefully roll the clays together being careful not to distort the stripes or widen them.

3. Trim the slab's top and bottom straight and wrap it around the salt box, white stripes out, trimming the ends and blending them together neatly where they meet. Fire in a 275° F oven for 20 minutes and then let cool.

4. Roll out a second slab of translucent clay 5-1/2" x the length of the salt box at the third thickness of your pasta machine.

5. Extrude enough white clay strips to make vertical stripes the same distance apart as the horizontal ones on the first layer of clay. Follow the instructions in Step 3 to combine them.

6. With the flat brush, spread a light coat of TLS on the white stripes of both the fired and raw clay. Wrap the raw clay slab, white stripes to the inside, around the fired one and trim neatly. Eliminate as many air bubbles as you can.

7. Apply Beacon glue to the top of the clay cylinder and let it tack up. Using a 1/4" diameter round die, extrude enough black clay to attach to the top and press it in place.

8. Extrude a second coil of clay using the 1/16" round die and wrap it around the cylinder butting it up against the 1/4" coil. Fire in a 275° F oven for 20 minutes and then let cool.

The Base

9. Roll out a slab of black clay at the thickest setting of your pasta machine and cut two 4" circles. Cut a 3/4" diameter hole in the center of the clay disks.

10. Cut a circle of WireForm 3-1/2" in diameter with a hole 1" in diameter in the center. Lay the WireForm circle on top of one circle of clay, roll it into the clay so it is flat, and spread a layer of TLS on top.

11. Spread PVA glue on the washer and center it on top of the hole. Lay the second clay circle on top and roll the sandwich together taking care not to distort the circle.

12. Roll 4-3/4" black beads and attach them to the clay circle. Fire for 20 minutes at 275° F.

13. Roll out a slab of black clay at the thickest setting of your pasta machine and as long as the circumference of the clay disk. Cut the slab in half lengthwise and lay one piece on the other and roll them together. Cut a 1/2" wide strip from the clay. Round the edges. Wrap the strip of clay around the clay disk edge and smooth the seam where the ends meet. Fire for 20 minutes at 275° F.

Wiring the Lamp

14. Split the electrical cord in half for about 1-1/2" from the unfinished edge. Cut about a half inch of the plastic or rubber away leaving the bare wire. Be careful not to cut the wire.

15. Thread the base elements on the cord as follows: Washer, base, washer, threaded pipe, and socket.

16. Loosen the screws on the socket, wind the wires around them, and tighten the screws. Thread the small pipe into the hole below the socket. Screw the nut tightly to the socket.

17. Fit the base closely to the first nut and screw the second nut tightly to the base.

18. At about 1 to 2 feet from the lamp base separate the cord by slicing between the halves. Be careful not to slice through to the wires. The cord is made up of two pieces of wire that run side by side through the length of the cord. Cut out a 3/8" section of one of the wires.

19. Open the switch. Don't lose the tiny nut that comes with it. Place the cut section of the cord so that it goes around the hole in the plastic where the screw goes through. The cord should run through the slots at the top and the bottom of the one side of the plastic switch. Fit the other side of the switch over this and replace the screw and the nut and tighten up.

20. Set the lampshade in the base. Plug in and let there be LIGHT! (If there isn't, check your connections.)

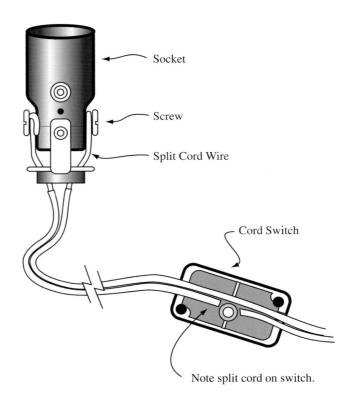

Socket

Screw

Split Cord Wire

Cord Switch

Note split cord on switch.

Appendix I - Bibliography

Polymer Clay

Ashcroft, Pierette Brown, et. al. 1998. *Artists at Work: Polymer Clay Comes of Age.* Flower Valley Press.

Burrill, Bob and Trudy E. 2000. *The Polymer Clay Week-by-Week Calendar* series. To Clay Or No To Clay. Approximately 100 polymer clay images. An international juried competition and exhibit of polymer clay artists available for sale in several countries.

Dean, Irene Semanchuk. 2000. *The Weekend Crafter: Polymer Clay.* Lark Books.

Dierks, Leslie. 1994. *Creative Clay Jewelry: Extraordinary Colorful Fun: Designs to Make from Polymer Clay.*

Heaser, Sue. 1999. *The Polymer Clay Techniques Book.* North Light Books.

Hilton, Syndee. 2000. *Polymer Clay for the First Time*, Syndee Sterling/Chapelle.

Holt, Richards, Kris. 1997. *New Ways With Polymer Clay: The Next Generation of Projects and Techniques.* Chilton.

Hughes, Tory. 1999. *Hinges in Polymer Clay* (video). Gameplan/ArtRanch.

Kato, Donna. 1997. *The Art of Polymer Clay: Designs and Techniques for Making Jewelry, Pottery and Decorative Artwork*, Watson-Guptill Crafts.

McGuire, Barbara E. 1999. *Foundations in Polymer Clay Design.* Krause Publications.

Roche, Nan. 1992. *The New Clay: Techniques and Approaches to Jewelry Making.* Rockville, Maryland: Flower Valley Press.

Bookbinding

Doggett, Sue. 1998. *Bookwork: Books, Memory and Photo Albums, Journals, and Diaries Made by Hand.* Watson-Guptill.

LaPlantz, Shereen. 1999.*Cover to Cover: Creative Techniques for Making Beautiful Books, Journals & Albums.* Lark Books.

Zeier, Franz. 1990. *Books, Boxes, and Portfolios: Binding, Construction, and Design, Step-By-Step.* Design Press.

Metal

Baskett, Mickey. 1999. *Wonderful Wire Works: An Easy Decorative Craft.* Sterling Publishing Co., Inc.

McCreight, Tim. 1999. *The Metalsmith's Book of Boxes & Lockets.* Hand Books Press.

Pottery

Berensohn, Paul S. 1997. *Finding One's Way With Clay: Pinched Pottery and Colored Clay.* Biscuit Books, Inc.

Birks, Tony. 1998. *The Complete Potter's Companion.* Bulfinch Press.

Music

Making Simple Musical Instruments, Bart Hopkins, Lark Books, 1995

General Design

Gikow, Jacqueline. 1992. *Graphic Illustration in Black and White.* Design Press.

Blue and Yellow Don't Make Green, Michael Wilcox, Northlight Books, 1994

Magazines

American Craft Magazine
http://www.craftcouncil.org/

Bead & Button
800-446-5489 (800-400-2482)
www.beadandbutton.com

Jewelry Crafts Magazine
512-479-7644
Subscription: jewelrycrafts@pcspublink.com
http://www.jewelrycrafts.com/

Ceramics Monthly
http://www.ceramicsmonthly.org/

The Craft Report
http://www.craftsreport.com/

GlassArt
http://www.artglassworld.com/mag/glassart/

Lapidary Journal: Jewelry and gem publication
800-676-4336
http://www.lapidaryjournal.com/

Metalsmith Magazine
http://www.sarantos.com/metalsmith.html

Ornament
Wearable art publication
800-888-8950
ornament@cts.com
http://www.ornamentmagazine.com/

Accordion: A length of paper folded in a zigzag. Also called a concertina.

Armature: A skeletal framework built as a support on which a clay, wax, or plaster figure is constructed. It supports the sculpture and reduces the amount of clay needed.

Bake: To heat polymer clay to the manufacturers' recommended temperatures for various lengths of time until the plastic becomes hard to the touch (see cure, fire).

Block: A two ounce package of polymer clay.

Brayer: A roller tool that has a handle for leverage and increased pressure. Acrylic brayers are suitable for work with polymer clay because an artist can see the surface while rolling.

Bone folder: A flat tool used to crease cardstock along a fold when making books or greeting cards.

Buffing Wheel: A machine-driven wheel that has a muslin or flannel disk used for buffing. Drill pads with muslin bonnets, which can also shine polymer surfaces, are also available.

Burnisher: A tool with a flat, blunt wand used to smooth or shine an area using friction.

Cane: A term borrowed from glass working referring to glass rods either plain or with a pattern through them, to be used as an addition to glass pieces. Canes were used to make millefiori beads. (see millefiori.)

Clasp: A fastening, used to hold a vessel and its lid together. Also a hasp.

Clay, traditional: A very fine suspension of aluminum silicate that is moldable when wet and can be fused by very high temperatures into a permanent form. Also refers to polymer clay.

Clay extruder: A hand-operated tool that presses clay through an opening to extrude the clay in a continuous shape. A small clay extruder, called a "clay gun," is used by polymer artists to create coils and decorative edgings.

Codex: Book structure with sewn-in signatures along the folded edge.

Coil: A cylindrical piece of polymer clay. Also a method for forming pots by winding cylindrically or spirally.

Color blend: A technique in which two or more slabs of colored clay are joined, folded and rolled into a smooth gradation of one color to another.

Condition: To prepare polymer clay before use. Polymer clay must be kneaded or run through a pasta machine to make it pliable before use. Conditioning aligns the molecules in the clay properly for creating vessels.

Cure: To heat polymer clay to the manufacturers' recommended temperatures for various lengths of time until the plastic becomes hard to the touch. Term is used interchangeably with "bake" or "fire" polymer clay.

Cyanoacrylate glue: A quick-setting glue such as Surehold or Zap-a-Gap. Used for quickly attaching various materials to polymer clay after the firing process is finished. Cyanoacrylate glues do not hold up well when exposed to heat over 150 F.

Faux effect: A technique used to create the illusion of a real material. Some materials that can be imitated with polymer clay include ivory, marble, and turquoise.

Fire or Firing: Term used interchangeably with "baking" or "curing" polymer clay to a hard plastic.

Findings: Components used in making jewelry; usually refers to the mechanical apparatus.

Flange: A protruding rim, edge, or collar on a vessel, used to hold the lid in place.

Food processor: A motorized chopper intended for food but can be used to condition polymer clay.

Glass: A hard, brittle, non-crystalline, transparent substance produced by fusion, at high temperatures, made of silicates containing soda and lime.

Glaze: A clear painted finish applied to the surface of an artwork. With polymer clay, a glaze must be a water-based finish rather than enamel. Many artists use a clear acrylic coating, such as Flecto Varathane Diamond finishes.

Grit: Coarseness of texture in sanding papers or powders.

Hinge: A jointed or flexible device that allows a vessel cover to open and close.

Hue: The color of an object, classified as red, blue, green, or yellow in reference to the spectrum. The actual color.

Inlay: A piece of polymer clay, of the same thickness as the main clay surface, but usually of a contrasting color, texture, or both, cut to a desired shape for placing into the clay from which a piece of the exact same size and shape has been removed. Inlaid decoration is often mistakenly described as "onlaid."

Inro: A small container worn exclusively by Japanese men suspended from the sash. Originally intended to hold the individual's seal and ink or to store a supply of medicines, the inro soon became an object of high fashion.

Intaglio: Refers to recessed carving as opposed to carving in relief.

Lacquer: A surface coating that dries as a protective finish; gloss or matte.

Lamination: A construct often of wood, made of layer upon layer.

Leaf: An extremely thin sheet of metal similar to a foil. Leafing comes in gold, silver, and variegated.

Loaf: A long square shape that will eventually be sliced. A block of clay having a complex pattern running throughout, usually square or rectangular in shape. It is available in imitation and real metallic composition.

Log: A thick roll of clay (used interchangeably with the word "cane").

Marble: To mix two or more colors of clay to produce a streaked or marbled effect resembling stone.

Marquetry: A woodworking technique that involves inlaying colored woods into a background.

Millefiori: An Italian glassworking process, meaning "Thousand Flowers," that Venetian glassworkers used to describe their copies of ancient mosaic glass. It refers to decorative glass rods or canes made by fusing multicolored elements together, cutting them crosswise, and melting them onto the surface of beads or other objects.

Mokume gane (pronounced Moe-koo-may Gah-nay): An ancient Japanese metalworking technique developed in feudal Japan. Translates as "wood grain metal," referring to one of the most popular patterns created with the laminated metals technique. It has been adapted by polymer artists with excellent results. A metal-smithing technique that is currently popular in polymer clay. Layers of clay (and leaf) are altered by pushing up or sinking objects or clay into the layers to create positive/negative special relations. When the layers are sliced horizontally, the "terrain" of the clay resembles rings or patterns as the artist altered the layered clay.

Mold: A hollow form used to give a particular shape to a soft or molten substance that is poured or pressed into it and allowed to harden.

Mold Release: An agent that, when applied to the mold, allows the cast element to come out of the mold when set.

Onlay: A method of decorating by means of thin, variously colored pieces of polymer clay, usually of a different color than the base form, which are attached with PVA to the surface of the object. The onlay technique is sometimes mistaken for "inlay."

Organic: As it pertains to chemistry, this term refers to compounds that are derived from plants or animals. Petroleum is the liquid remains of ancient forest and consists of complex mixtures of hydrocarbons.

Parchment paper: Oven baking paper that is used when baking polymer clay to eliminate "shiny spots" on pieces.

Pasta machine: A mechanical device intended to roll out handmade pasta, but used in the polymer clay industry to condition, blend color, texturize, and roll clay.

Pearlescent: Having shimmering quality; clay that includes a non-metallic filler that reflects microscopic bits of light and which sparkles softly.

Photocopy transfer: The transferring of an image printed on a photocopier and then applied to polymer clay in a technique that transfers the ink and subsequently the image to the clay.

Pinch pot: A vessel made by rolling a ball of clay, making an opening with your thumb, and forming the shape by pinching with your fingers.

Plastic: A generic term, referring to any group of synthetic or natural materials which may be shaped when soft and then hardened, including many types of resins (amber), polymers, cellulose derivatives, casein materials, and proteins.

Plasticizer: An organic compound used in modifying plastics, to incorporate flexibility and toughness.

Polymer clay: A man-made, oil-based alternative to natural clay. Polymer clay is made up of fine particles of polyvinyl chloride (PVC) suspended in plasticizer.

Poly-vinyl acetate: Commonly known as PVA, a polymerized vinyl chloride compound, thermoplastic resin. Used chiefly in the manufacture of floor coverings and as an insulator for metal pipes and wire.

Reduction: The term for shrinking a design pattern to a smaller scale. Usually refers to a cane that is created in a large scale and then reduced in proportion by various techniques.

Saturation: Vividness or intensity of a color.

Sheet: Thin slab of clay.

Shade: The degree of darkness of a color determined by the quantity of black added.

Signature: A cut and folded piece of paper used either alone or in multiples as a unit of a book.

Slab: A term for a rolled-out piece of clay. Used interchangeably with "sheet."

Snake: For polymer clay working, this term refers to a small log or roll of clay.

Stamping: A patterned tool is impressed or forcibly struck into a piece of metal or clay.

Tensile strength: The ability to be stretched, elongated, or extended.

Text block: Name for a completed set of book signatures.

Tint: Lightness of a color. Also the amount of white mixed with a hue.

Tissue blade: An extremely sharp, smooth blade borrowed from the medical industry that has the ability to slice thin, precise layers.

Translucent: Admitting and diffusing light so that objects beyond cannot be clearly distinguished. When referring to translucent polymer clays, it is similar to porcelain, having a soft depth, but not clear like glass.

Vessel: A hollow utensil, such as a cup, vase, or pitcher, used as a container.

Value: The degree of lightness or darkness in a color.

Wedge: Condition clay by kneading it. The process is similar to kneading dough, but the goal is to eliminate air bubbles, not to add them. Also similar to marble-mixing patterns in clay.

Appendix III - Resources

American Craft Council (ACC)
The ACC is a national educational membership organization dedicated to the advancement of the American craft movement. Membership is open to anyone with an interest in fine American craft.
http://www.craftcouncil.org/

Association of Crafts & Creative Industries (ACCI)
ACCI is dedicated to providing innovative opportunities for the exchange of ideas, goods and services to develop the crafts and creative industries.
http://www.accicrafts.org/

Hobby Industry Association (HIA)
HIA is a national, nonprofit organization focusing on craftspeople and other hobbyists involved in the production and sale of the types of craft products found in art, craft, hobby, sewing, and other leisure industry outlets.
E-mail: hia@ix.netcom.com
http://www.hobby.org/

National Polymer Clay Guild (NPCG)
National organization of people interested in polymer clay. There are also local guild chapters in many states.
http://www.npcg.org/home.htm

Society of Craft Designers (SCD)
The Society of Craft Designers (SCD) is a professional organization serving those who design for the consumer craft industry.
E-mail: scd@offinger.com
http://www.craftdesigners.org/

Appendix IV - Safety

Safety in Plastics, Tools, and the Studio

To be truly proficient in your artistic process, you need to respect your materials and tools and thoroughly understand the medium. This includes not only how to "work" with them to create a beautiful and durable product, but also a good understanding of any hazardous properties they may have. Polymer clay is a lot of fun to work with, and shouldn't be considered "dangerous," however, its properties should be understood.

General Safety

Polymer clay is certified to be nontoxic by OSHA, but it is not FDA approved, so you should take some common-sense precautions in your exposure to any chemical ingredients in this and other artists' materials; so, **don't**:
   accidentally eat bits of clay
   burn or scorch the clay during firing
   eat food in the polymer work area
   use kitchen tools used in your craft pasta machines, food processors, coffee grinders, rollers, or knives, for kitchen duty afterward.

And **do**:
   keep your hands away from your face, mouth and ears when using polymer

   use polymer in a well-ventilated area
   wash your hands before eating

Safety Guidelines for Baking Polymer Clay

Polymer clay normally gives off a slight odor when firing. This is neither a health hazard nor a sign that the clay is burning, although burning clay smells acrid and may cause your eyes or throat to sting. Whether you enjoy the smell or merely tolerate it, be sure to use good ventilation while baking. If you do burn a batch of clay, turn off the oven, open windows, and turn on fans, and leave the house for an hour or two to give the fumes time to clear.

The recommended temperature for baking polymer clays is around 265° F to 275° F for 20 minutes per 1/4" of thickness. The curing temperature for Premo and Super Sculpey is 275°F, while Fimo should be cured at 265°F.

Lighter colors and translucent clays may darken or scorch at those temperatures, and the manufacturers recommend using a lower temperature for pieces that incorporate or are made up totally of translucents. Use an oven thermometer to assure even and consistent baking. Note that if a piece is baked at a lower-than-recommended temperature, the clay will not completely cure and may be brittle. At the same time, baking polymer clay at the correct temperature for a longer period can increase its flexibility and strength without increasing the risk of burning.

To avoid burning the clay, don't let your oven temperature get too high. If the clay gets hotter than 300° F (polymer clay burns at 350° F to 375° F), it can burn, and burning PVC **does** give off toxic fumes. If you notice an acrid, burning smell that is different from the normal scent, turn off the oven, throw open the windows, and go somewhere else until the odor has dissipated.

It's not uncommon for home ovens to be 25°F off the temperature on the dial. Fire in a well-ventilated room, open your kitchen windows and, if you have a stovetop fan, turn it on during firing. For an extra margin of safety, some clay artists fire in a toaster oven or portable convection oven that is placed outside, on a deck or patio.

If you fire polymer clay art in a home oven, you should clean the residue by heating the oven to 450°F for 20 minutes with all windows and doors open and people and pets out of the house before using the oven for food.

What is this gunk on my hands?

Polymer clay is compounded with colorants, inert fillers, antioxidant(s), and plasticizer. Manufacturers take much care to remove vinyl chloride from the PVC before compounding polymer clay; however, plasticizer, that oily stuff that leaches out of the polymer clay when it rests on a porous surface, is present in about fifteen percent of uncured polymer clay. For cleaning your hands, a rough towel or wet wipes will remove the worst of the residue when you want to switch between colors of clay, but polymer clay sneers at soap and water.

Using a small pumice stone with soap will help remove the clay from your hands; so will some hand creams and facial scrubs. Another effective cleanup method is to rub a little oil (cooking or mineral oil) onto your hands, then wash it off with ordinary dish soap. I've experimented with different soaps and scrubs while writing this book and the best soaps I've found are Octagon Soap by Colgate-Palmolive and Winsor-Newton's hand soap that is based on their brush cleaner. Octagon Soap is a harsh lye soap intended primarily for laundry purposes, but cuts through the oil in polymer clay. The most satisfactory hand cream for me has been Vaseline Intensive Care.

With all the washing you do to keep your work clean, it's easy to develop dry, or chapped, hands. You can avoid chapped hands by washing them in cool water instead of warm or hot. My experience from working as a potter with my hands constantly in water led me to this solution. Cold water doesn't open your pores up, so you are less apt to retain the water in your skin. After drying your hands, use a barrier cream (such as Winsor-Newton's Artguard); it will help prevent additional external reactions you may have to your working materials. This is important both in winter, when the air is cooler and drier, as well as in hot weather.

Polymer Clay and Food-Serving Utensils

To be safe, don't use utensils for food again once you've used them with clay. (You may even want to label your clay utensils to make sure no one accidentally uses them in the kitchen.)

Residual plasticizer can remain in the clay after firing, and this plasticizer might leach out into food that touches even the fired clay, so it may not be safe to use polymer clay on surfaces that will be in contact with food. If you want to use polymer clay for a serving dish, consider sandwiching your clay design between two pieces of glass. That way it can be seen without touching the food on the dish.

Safety when Finishing Clay Work

The rules for safety while sanding or buffing clay are similar to the rules for sanding wood or other materials. If you're dry-sanding (instead of sanding under water) or drilling a clay piece, use a face mask to avoid inhaling the tiny clay particles coming off the sandpaper. You should also use a facemask when working with aluminum-based metallic powders since these fly everywhere and can cause damage if they're breathed into your lungs.

Always, without exception, use eye protection when using any power tool with the clay, whether for drilling, buffing, or sanding. It's very easy for a bead you're buffing to get loose and go flying, possibly into your face. Even the tiny clay particles can get into your eye and cause injury. You can buy plastic safety goggles at any hardware store.

Studio Safety

Toxicity of materials isn't the only issue in safety. Studio safety is also important to polymer artists, and it is worth being reminded of some main points. How you sit, stand, move, and work can affect you in the short- and long-term. Do some research. A lot of information about safety and ergonomics is available free from government agencies and sites on the Internet.

"Ergonomics," or human factors, refers to keeping your body safe while working so you don't cut short a creative career. All of us, whether artists or not, could significantly reduce our risk of injury if we could adhere to the following ergonomic principles:

Don't overreach your range of movement. This applies particularly to the head, trunk, and upper limbs.

Don't repeatedly lift heavy objects, especially when your posture is not in balance.

Don't stand or sit in one position or perform the same task for several hours without taking a break. Vary your tasks throughout the day.

Don't work in an awkward position.

Do work in an area with proper ventilation.

Ominous Cuts and Treacherous X-Acto Knives

When using sharp hand tools, such as an X-Acto knife or tissue blade, keep your eyes on the prize: Your fingertips. Keep a guard on your X-Acto knife when not in use, and keep the blade in your utility knife retracted. When cutting a material, always pull the blade toward you and keep your fingers out of the way. Wrap dull knife blades in tape and carefully dispose of them.

Always use sharp blades. Blunt blades are more dangerous than sharp ones, so change your blade regularly, and dispose of old blades carefully.

No matter how safe you are when working with knives, you will cut yourself while working. It's a Murphy's Law type of truism. Make up a first-aid kit—with Band-Aids in different sizes, and anti-infection medicines containing antibiotics—and keep it handy.

Lighting

Lighting is an important part of a workspace. I can't say enough about adequate lighting. Use good general lighting. Use task lighting. Adjust window shades or curtains throughout the day to minimize glare. There is nothing more tiring than working under poor lighting conditions, and it is not good for your eyesight.

The key to good light is in having it bright and without glare. Full-spectrum lighting isn't as important as enough light. Unless you know your work will always be seen in natural light, incandescent lights are just fine.

If you do want natural light, you can save yourself some big bucks through buying daylight-spectrum bulbs for your regular light fixtures. The secret is in the bulb, not the fixture. If you have a fluorescent desk lamp that uses a standard 13" fluorescent bulb, buy a full-spectrum replacement bulb. Some office supply stores have the 13-watt replacement Ott-lite bulbs. There are also full-spectrum incandescent bulbs that can be found at plant stores and home planning centers.

I use a 75-watt bulb in my swinging-arm drafting lamp. I keep the lamp really close to my work, below my vision, which gives me a bright light without a glare to either my eyes or the work. When I want to focus on a different part of my artwork, I swing the arm and light around to that area.

Seating and Table Heights

One of the themes that recurs in ergonomic analyses of factories is that a lot of damage can be avoided by using different working heights for different tasks. People often perform tasks at inappropriate heights. Some jobs should be done at waist level, while others should be done at higher or lower work levels. If you are doing the same job repeatedly all day, as occurs in a production situation, it can help dramatically to work at varying heights. This may mean different workstations, but also may mean easily adjustable chairs and tables. Studies have linked mostly standing or mostly sitting jobs with more lower-back pain problems than jobs where changes in posture occur.

Because it's easier to find adjustable chairs than adjustable tables, make sure you invest in a well-designed chair. Use a studio chair that allows you to adjust its height according to your individual needs. The seat should lower, raise, and tilt backward. The front edge of the seat should be curved for your comfort, and the base of the chair should have wheels (preferably five of them), allowing you to swivel around. The back of the chair should be high enough and wide enough to support your shoulders. And when seated, your feet should be on the floor. Adjust your chair back vertically to allow your forearms and thighs to be parallel to the floor when working.

A worktable should be no deeper than 30" because it's about as far as you can reach comfortably (less, when seated). If it's deeper, you'll just turn the rest into a rat's nest of inaccessible storage.

Avoiding Long-term Injury

The human body needs movement to keep blood circulation at its optimal rate—the oxygen in the blood relaxes tired muscles and tissues, etc. So, it's good to move around frequently, at least every twenty to thirty minutes or so. Changing position from sitting to standing while you work so that your movements can be whole-body is also recommended. Do this for about five minutes every half-hour or so; that way you don't have to stop working. If you forget to do it for a while, start again. Make it a habit.

Make sure your work surface is at a comfortable height, or that you have an alternate place to work. Sometimes I find that if I move from one table to another, it helps. I live and work in a tiny apartment and I have four "work stations," not including the floor. It sounds impossible, but it's true.

Of course, this one is something only you can do: Do not slouch. Good posture helps reduce fatigue and supports the lower back.

Safety Resources

Ergonomics Resources
http://www.ergoweb.com/

OSHA
http://www.osha-slc.gov/SLTC/ergonomics/

Carpal Tunnel Syndrome
http://www.sechrest.com/mmg/reflib/ctd/cts/cts.html

Discussion Groups

Google Groups
(rec.crafts.polymer-clay)
A Usenet newsgroup for polymer clay artists from beginner to professional.
http://groups.google.com/groups?oi=djq&as_ugroups=rec.crafts
or
http://www.mailgate.org/rec/index.html#rec.crafts.polymer-clay
Yahoo Groups
A moderated list of polymer clay enthusiasts.
http://groups.yahoo.com/group/PolymerClayPeople

Appendix V - Artists Appearing In This Book

Deborah Anderson
A Thousand Canes
265 N. 13th St.
San Jose, CA 95112-3445
Phone: (408) 279-0266
ames@aol.com

Linda Bernstein
Artique
Lbernstein@Artique.org
http://www.Artique.org/

Jody Bishel
548 Wakelee Ave.
Ansonia, CT 06401-1226
jbishel@earthlink.net

Diane Black
http://www.glassattic.com

Merrie Buchsbaum
Merrily Made
P.O. Box 265
Cromwell, CT 06416
Phone: (860) 635-1231
Fax: (860) 632-0162
merrily@connix.com

Elizabeth J. Campbell
Ft. Collins, CO
http://thepolyparrot.com

Jane Cook
Ornamental Originals
358 Cedar Run Road
Bonn Terre, MO 63628
Phone: (573) 431-0077
jcook@socket.net

Terry Lee Czechowski
TLC Creations
7 Sevilla Dr.
Cliften Park, NY 12065
Phone: (518) 383-3769
tlc@tlc-creation.com

Grant Diffendaffer
333 49th St. #A
Oakland, CA 94609
Phone: (510) 653-8412
grant@diffendaffer.com
http://www.diffendaffer.com/

Vicki Domansky
Clay'cetera Crafts
Vancouver, B.C., Canada
vicki.domansky@ubc.ca
http://crosswinds.net/~clecetera

Dayle Doroshow
Zingaro
P.O. Box 354
Ft. Bragg, CA 95437
Phone/Fax : (707) 962-9419

Cassie Doyon
Cassie Doyon Designs
3 Rainbow Dr.
Bradford, MD 01835
Phone: (978) 469-8188
cmdoyon@prodigy.net

Diane Dunville
Illuminart by Diane Dunville
15309 Moysonike Ct.
Lanexa, VA 23089
DMDUNVILLE@aol.com

Kathleen Dustin
469 Dustin Rd.
Coontoocook, NH 03229
Phone/Fax: (603) 746-2669
dustin@compuserve.com
http://www.kathleendustin.com

Patricia Echeagaray
PLM Enterprises and Designs
Germantown, MD
http://patticlay.freeservers.com/
plem@erols.com

Louise Fischer Cozzi
419 Sixth St.
Brooklyn, NY 11215
Phone: (718) 499-8728
Tempestal@aol.com

Emi Fukushima
ecreations@aol.com

Linda P. Geer
Puffinalia
Seattle, WA
caneguru@drizzle.com
http://www.drizzle.com/~caneguru

James Gilbert
Great Barrington, MA
jgilbert@bcn.net

Ilysa Ginsburg-Bierer and Edward Bierer
Heart in Hand Studio™
500 N.W. 96 Pl.
Branford, FL 32008
Phone/Fax (904) 935-0780
Ilysaart@alltet.com

Lori Glessner
239 Roxborough Ave.
Philadelphia, PA 19128
Phone: (215) 487-2224
lorigles@idt.net
http://home.earthlink.net/~lorigles

Linda Goff
Quirkworks
1024 South Fir
Olympia, WA 98507-0234
Phone: (360) 352-4701
Linda@lindagoff.com
http://www.lindagoff.com

Karen Goulet
Idaho Springs, CO
kgclay@earthlink.net
http://home.earthlink.net/~kgclay

Dorothy Greynolds
Claywear
5678 Eldridge Dr.
Waterford, MI 48327
claywear@yahoo.com
http://mdpag.org/greynold.htm

Matt Hamblen
Wallgems Art Mirrors by Matt Hamblen
MattorScott@aol.com
http://www.wallgems.com

Hershberger, Lynn
P.O. Box 26261
Lansing, MI 48909

Debora Jackson
Debbie's Adornments
1694 Niagra Road
Columbus, OH 43227
Phone: (614) 237-2406

Valerie Kanter
2909 W. Farwell Ave.
Chicago, IL 60645
Phone: (773) 973-7087
luv2clay4u@aol.com

Donna Kato
dkato@pcisys.net

Patricia Kimle
Patrica Kimle Designs
patti@kimledesigns.com
http://www.kimledesigns.com

Karyn Kozak
6363 N. Hermitage Ave.
Chicago, IL 60660-1129
kkozak@21stcentury.net
http://www.kkozakdesign.com

Kuskin, Judith
Seattle, WA
jkuskin@hotmail.com

Margi Laurin
Margi Laurin/Polymer Clay Art
52 High St.
Morrisburg, Ontario KOC 1X0
Canada
Phone: (613) 543-2835
mornet64@mor-net.on.ca

Varda Levram-Ellison
427 Oros Ave.
Solana Beach, CA 92075
varda@alex.uscd.edu
http://www.sdpcg.com

Barbara A. McGuire
Design Innovations
P.O. Box 472334
San Francisco, CA 94147
Phone: (415) 922-6366
barbara@claystamp.com
http://www.claystamp.com

Dotty McMillan
http://www.Kaleidoscopes4U.com

Laura Mehr
Designs by Laura
P.O. Box 803
Jensen Beach, FL 34958
Fax (561) 673-0467
designsbylaura@prodigy.net
http://www.designsbylauramehr.com

Bonnie Merchant
Fabulous Stuff
Box 1158
Lake Oswego, OR 97035
Phone/Fax: (503) 632-7012
bonnie@fabulousstuff.com
http://www.fabulousstuff.com

Petra
Zigzag Polymer Clay Supplies
8 Cherry Place, Casebrook
Christchurch 8005 New Zealand
petra@zigzag.co.nz
http://www.zigzag.co.nz

Cindy Pack
claycrazy1@yahoo.com
http://www.geocities.com/claycrazy1
claycrazy1@yahoo.com

Lisa Pavelka
Heart in Hand Studio™
9825 Tarzana Ln.
Las Vegas, NV 89117
Phone/Fax: (702) 243-6564
http://www.heartinhandstudio.com

Christl Pelikan
175-45 88th Ave.,#7-G
Jamaica Estates, NY 11432
Phone: (718) 739-1287
cporiginals@hotmail.com

Robyn Beth Priestley
Painted Turtle Design
St. Paul, MN
bpturtle@mtn.org
http://www.mtn.org/~bpturtle

Margaret Reid
2 Stone House
Howey
Llandrinod Wells
Powys LDI 5PL
United Kingdom
mfhreid@polyopol.kc3ltd.co.uk
mfreid@aol.com
http://members.aol.com/polyopoly

Nan Roche
The New Clay
4511 Amherst Rd.
College Park, MD 20740
Phone: (301) 864-1805
http://www.nanroche.com

Lucille Schacht

Killingworth, Connecticut
Lucille@cshore.com
http://creativeside.com/cache/eggersu/art-
works_by_lucille.htm

Rhea Schaefer
Oak Park, MI
rhea@coast.net

Trudy E. Schwartz-Burrill
To Clay Or Not To Clay
http://www.toclay.com
trudystoclay@mindspring.com

Hen Scott
Herefordshire, England
henscott@compuserve.com

Marie Segal
The Clay Factory
P.O. Box 460598
Escondido, CA 92046
Phone: (760) 741-3242
Fax: (760) 741-5436
Mureecgul@aol.com
http://www.clayfactory.com

Wanda Shum
wanda@escape.ca
http://albums.photopoint.com/j/AlbumList?u=6
27657

Jeanne Sturdevant
3600 Highmeadow Dr.
Greenville, TX 75402
Phone: (903) 450-0234
jeannest@airmail.net

Arlene Summers
9361 E. Laurel Circle.
Mesa, Arizona 85207
Phone: (480) 354-1918
Fax: (480) 354-5053

Liz Tamayo
2926 Holyrood Dr.
Oakland, CA 94611
lizzeet@aol.com

Laura Timmins
Madison, WI
Phone: (608) 277-0683
lmgtimm@aol.com

Cynthia Tinapple and Blair Davis
1 Hartford Ct.
Worthington, OH 43085
Phone (614) 885-7328
Cynthia@tinapple.com
http://www.tinapple.com

Will Truchon
Red Deer, Alberta, Canada

Tracy Van Buskirk
NovaClay
19 Poverty Hollow Rd.
Newton, CT 06470
kriksubnav@hotmail.com
Info on Bottles of Hope
bottlesofhope@hotmail.com

Diane Villano
Foxon River Design
1355 N. High St.
East Haven, CT 06512
Phone: (203) 467-7090
dianev_scpcg@yahoo.com

Krista Wells
ArtWare
General Delivery
Diligent River, Nova Scotia
Canada BOM 1H0
Phone: (902) 254-3788
flyingart@ns.sympatico.ca
http://www.artware.ns.ca

Robert Wiley
Sugarland, TX
rwiley@hic.net
http://www.crosswinds.net/~rwiley/

Carol Zilliacus
13303 Collingwood Terrace
Silver Spring, MD 20904
Phone: (301) 236-4395
Fax: (301)384-7394
carolz@concentric.net

Rebecca Zimmerman
Wauwatosa, WI
Phone: (414) 774-9949

Amy Zinman
114 Hauxhurst Ave.
Weehauken, NJ 07087-6836
Az@al-berg.com

Feel free contact me as well:
Jacqueline Gikow
New York, NY
Phone/Fax: (212) 439-9604
Jgikow@nyc.rr.com

Index

A

Adhesives and Glues
cyanoacrylates 22
polymer clay-related
bonding materials 23
pva (polyvinyl acetate) 22
silicon-type glues 23

B

Baking
oven temperature 25
oven thermometer 25

Books
accordion books 93
book binding 97
codex books 95
flexible hinges 95
polymer clay covers 96
polymer clay pages 97
signature 96

Buffing
by hand 29
by machine 29

C

Clay gun pusher
bellows clay gun pusher 19
caulking clay gun pusher 19

Conditioning
additives 24
hand 24
leaching clay 24
meat grinder 24
pasta machine 24
white clay 25

Color
mixing 13
personal color palette 16
theory 14
translucent clay 15

Constructed Objects
boxes 62
joining slabs 62
rolling guides 60
slabs 60

Covering Vessels
glues 48
non-porous vessels 49
ceramic 49
glass 49
metal 49
plastic 49
porous vessels 51
terra cotta 51
wood 51
preparing clay to cover
objects 47

D

Decorative techniques
faux ivory 107
faux jade 41
mokume gane 57

E

Equipment
baking 20
buffing wheel 21
food processor 21
heat gun 20
pasta machine motor 21
scrolling/jigsaw 22

F

Finishing
buffing 29
fingerprints 29
glazing 30
sanding 28
vessel feet 68
vessel rims 68

Free-Form Modeling
bubble vessels 38
coil vessels 38
pinched vessels 33
weaving vessels 40

G

Games
board games 108
game pieces 109
tanagram 109

H

Hasps
dimple catches 67
hook hasps 67

Hinges
rules 64
polymer clay hinges 64
piano hinge 64
tube and pin hinges 65
embedded hinges 66

Home Décor
birdhouses 122
teapots 126
frames 127
time pieces 128
lighting 130

M

Mold Making
core molds 73
found molds 74
mold releases 80
plaster molds 79
polymer clay molds 77
press molds 80
Super Elasticlay molds 79
undercuts 73

Music
flutes 112
rain stick 113
whistles 111

P

Polymer clay
brand characteristics 10
color 13
history 9
mixing 13
storage 12

Projects:
Bird Head Finger Puppet 43
Cane Appliqué Clock 53
Chinese Checkers 119
Concertina Book 105
Contemporary Lamp 134
Faux Raku Bowl 85
Hanging Vessel 89
Hinged Vessel 71
Jade Mouse Bottle 41
Jigsaw Puzzle Stool 54
Pinwheel 116
Postcard 103
Slab Box 69
Teapot 87

Wok Utensils 57
Woven Container 45

Project planning
calculate quantity of clay 26

S

Slabs, sheets
cutting 18
rolling 60
using pasta machine 20

Special Techniques
Liquid Sculpey (ls) 12
polymer clay on a lathe 84
polymer clay on a potter's
wheel 84

Supplies
adhesives and glues 22
mold releases 23

T

Tools
bellows clay pusher 19
caulking gun 19
extruder 18

Toys
kaleidoscopes 114
tops 115

W

Writing
ball-point pens 99
pencils 100

FOOTNOTES

[1] A glass vial containing mingled tears, symbolizing the joy and sorrow friends have shared (page 6).

[2] *Bead & Button*, June 2000, Issue #37.

[3]. *The Metalsmith's Book of Boxes & Lockets*, Tim McCreight, Hand Press Books, WI, 1999, pp. 46-48.